The Collapse of the
Democratic Presidential Majority

TRANSFORMING AMERICAN POLITICS
Lawrence C. Dodd, Series Editor

Dramatic changes in political institutions and behavior over the past three decades have underscored the dynamic nature of American politics, confronting political scientists with a new and pressing intellectual agenda. The pioneering work of early postwar scholars, while laying a firm empirical foundation for contemporary scholarship, failed to consider how American politics might change or to recognize the forces that would make fundamental change inevitable. In reassessing the static interpretations fostered by these classic studies, political scientists are now examining the underlying dynamics that generate transformational change.

Transforming American Politics brings together texts and monographs that address four closely related aspects of change. A first concern is documenting and explaining recent changes in American politics—in institutions, processes, behavior, and policymaking. A second is reinterpreting classic studies and theories to provide a more accurate perspective on postwar politics. The series looks at historical change to identify recurring patterns of political transformation within and across the distinctive eras of American politics. Last and perhaps most importantly, the series presents new theories and interpretations that explain the dynamic processes at work and thus clarify the direction of contemporary politics. All of the books focus on the central theme of transformation—transformation in both the conduct of American politics and in the way we study and understand its many aspects.

FORTHCOMING TITLES

Revolving Gridlock, David Brady and Craig Volden

Congress and the Administrative State, Second Edition, Lawrence C. Dodd and Richard L. Schott

Governing Partners: State-Local Relations in the United States, Russell L. Hanson

The Divided Democrats: Ideological Unity, Party Reform, and Presidential Elections, William G. Mayer

Seeing Red: How the Cold War Shaped American Politics, John Kenneth White

New Media in American Politics, Richard Davis and Diana Owen

Extraordinary Politics: How Protest and Dissent are Changing American Democracy, Charles C. Euchner

The Irony of Reform: Roots of American Political Disenchantment, G. Calvin Mackenzie

The Tragic Presidency, Robert L. Lineberry

The Collapse of the Democratic Presidential Majority

REALIGNMENT, DEALIGNMENT, AND ELECTORAL CHANGE FROM FRANKLIN ROOSEVELT TO BILL CLINTON

David G. Lawrence

WestviewPress

A Division of HarperCollinsPublishers

Transforming American Politics

Copyright © 1997 by Westview Press, A Division of HarperCollins Publishers, Inc.

Published in 1997 in the United States of America by Westview Press, 5500 Central Avenue, Boulder, Colorado 80301-2877, and in the United Kingdom by Westview Press, 12 Hid's Copse Road, Cumnor Hill, Oxford OX2 9JJ

A CIP catalog record for this book is available from the Library of Congress.
ISBN 0-8133-8984-4 (hc)—0-8133-9981-5 (pb)

The paper used in this publication meets the requirements of the American National Standard for Permanence of Paper for Printed Library Materials Z39.48-1984.

10   9   8   7   6   5   4   3   2   1

Contents

List of Tables and Figures

TABLES

FIGURES

Preface

I began graduate study at the University of Chicago in 1969, in the extraordinarily stimulating and supportive environment created by people like Norman Nie, Sidney Verba, Kenneth Prewitt, Paul Peterson, and J. David Greenstone, and in the golden age of realignment theory. It was an era in which the dynamics of system-level electoral change was being explained as a function of the tension between stable mass partisan loyalties and constantly changing underlying social and economic conditions. Realignment theory essentially argues that party loyalties are sufficiently powerful to prevent these changed circumstances from altering voting behavior for extended periods of time, allowing the stable patterns of electoral outcomes that have characterized periods like 1896–1930 and 1932–1966; but the accumulation of tensions over time caused by the inevitable emergence of new issues and accompanied by generational replacement of those whose party loyalties were forged in past realignment crises means that the natural life-span of such party systems was limited to approximately forty years. Sometime around the forty-year mark, some systemic crisis would cause the tension between long-standing partisan loyalties and new political circumstances to become unbearable, causing citizens to adjust their party loyalties to make them consistent with new highly-salient issues and causing the sudden sharp change knows as realignment. This new party/issue nexus, forged in systemic crisis, would provide the stable equilibrium of political attitudes that could underlie a new era of stable electoral outcomes likely to last for another forty years.

Around the time I arrived at Fordham, in 1973, the conventional wisdom was that the United States was on the verge of such a realignment: forty years after Franklin Roosevelt's election as president, the passing of the New Deal generation and emergence of new issues like race, crime, and Vietnam that would undermine Democratic domination and make the Republican Party the national majority. By the early 1980s, it was clear that such a classic realignment had not occurred: the Republicans had of course won most of the recent presidential elections, but it had failed to gain in sub-presidential elections or in the partisan loyalties of ordinary citizens that realignment theory predicted. A new and competing theory of dealignment was gaining adherents: dealignment essentially argued that weakening of parties and of party loyalties had created a world in which stable party systems could no longer exist and in which realignment could no longer occur.

In the mid-1980s, to some extent stimulated by discussion with colleagues at Fordham, I began to think about the ways in which neither realignment theory nor dealignment theory could account for contemporary patterns of electoral outcomes and mass vote choice. This book is the result of attempts to make sense of electoral politics in terms of the tensions between (and individual inadequacies of) realignment and dealignment.

⁓◦⁓

Projects like this one evolve over extended periods of time and result from the encouragement, support, and creative disagreement of many people. The conversations and arguments that stimulated thought and data analysis (presumably in that order) are too often forgotten by the time an end product is published.

Almost all the data I report are from the American National Election Studies, originally collected by the Center for Political Studies and made available for secondary analysis by the Inter-University Consortium for Political and Social Research at the University of Michigan. The producers of this magnificent resource are in no way responsible for the use I have made of it.

Much of this book was researched and written during sabbaticals made possible by Fordham, an institution whose concern with both research and teaching allows the two core activities of modern academic life to have their expected beneficial consequences for each other. Fordham also provided generous computer and technical support.

Two of my colleagues at Fordham have been particularly helpful in the discussion and argument that are the immediate basis for the manuscript. Richard Fleisher collaborated in the early conceptual piece that helped me initially articulate the puzzle of post-war electoral politics, and he was an invaluable source of combative feed-back on all intermediate stages that led to the finished product that resolves it. Paul Kantor constantly suggested how the perspective of the broader discipline could broaden the scope and accessibility of what could have been a narrower and more technical work. Three other colleagues, Bruce Berg, Stephen Thomas, and Dale Nelson, read and/or reacted to core arguments in ways that contributed to the whole. Walter Dean Burnham and Everett Carll Ladd made useful comments and provided useful encouragement on the co-authored piece with Fleisher that started the project. Assorted referees, for the book-length manuscript or for the articles that preceded it, have left their anonymous helpful marks on the final product.

Two other people deserve special recognition in any acknowledgement of the process that produced this work. Some of my earliest memories are of discussing politics with my mother, Sylvia Lawrence. This book represents indisputable evidence of how maternal concern with the not-necessarily related topics of politics and academics can get entirely out of hand. My wife, Cynthia, has been a constant source of encouragement and stability—intellectual and other—in an increasingly dealigned social universe. This book is dedicated to them both.

David G. Lawrence

1

Introduction

Bill Clinton's election as president in 1992 hardly signified a re-creation of the Democratic presidential majority that dominated American politics between 1932 and 1968. While the Democrats were undoubtedly pleased to win their second presidential election in the last seven, they won it with only 43 percent of the popular vote, a total not much different from the percentage they gained in losing a series of contests widely regarded as disasters for the party. When compared to the five consecutive elections won by Franklin Roosevelt and Harry Truman or even to the Democratic resurgence under John Kennedy and Lyndon Johnson, Clinton's achievement is modest. He may of course yet create a *new* Democratic presidential majority, but his election was hardly evidence that such a majority exists. Clinton's subsequent difficulties in implementing a legislative agenda and the dramatic defeat of his party in the 1994 congressional elections raise further doubts about the long-term significance of the 1992 presidential outcome.

To claim that the Democratic majority which dominated American presidential politics between 1932 and 1968 has collapsed is neither original nor very interesting. Even a casual observer will be aware that Republicans won five of the six post-1966 presidential elections, four of them by comfortable margins. The most recent Democratic victory before Clinton's was an extremely narrow win by a southern moderate who had re-united his party after a decade's division over race, running against an unelected incumbent widely perceived to be somewhat out of his depth who had become president in the immediate aftermath of Watergate. That Jimmy Carter was elected under such circumstances is hardly surprising; that he won so narrowly is a sign of the extent of Democratic problems in the mid-1970s.

The focus here is less the *fact* that the Democratic presidential majority has collapsed than the *process* by which the collapse occurred. Existing literature and popular wisdom suffer no lack of possible explanations: racial polarization at a time when the Democrats have become generally perceived as the party sympathetic to black political demands; a divisive and ultimately unsuccessful military involvement in southeast Asia initiated by a Democratic administration; belief that the Democrats were excessively permissive at a time of rising crime rates and other symptoms of social disintegration or "moral decay"; nomination of a series of weak candidates, ideologically out of touch with mainstream America and incapable of organizing a campaign, much less an administration; Democratic failure to master new techniques of fund-raising, candidate packaging and media control; a dramatic turn to the right in American public opinion in response to the excesses and failures of the liberal ideology that had dominated Democratic administrations; economic and foreign policy failures of the Democrat who had taken advantage of Watergate-centered problems of the Republicans in the mid-seventies; the personal attractiveness of Ronald Reagan, a candidate and president unparalleled in his ability to dominate a media age. All of these explanations have at least some superficial plausibility; some of them in fact play substantial roles in the Democratic collapse. But their interaction and the precise role that they play are far more complex than the simple check-list suggests.

When Dwight Eisenhower ended twenty years of Democratic control of the White House in 1952, it was widely seen as a straightforward case of what would later be called a *deviating* election: a short-term interruption of a continuing pattern, attributable in this case both to the extraordinary attractiveness of the popular general and to the very particular problems of the late Truman administration. The picture of Eisenhower as temporary interruption of a stable on-going pattern was reinforced by the Kennedy victory in the first post-Eisenhower election and, even more, by Lyndon Johnson's overwhelming landslide over Barry Goldwater in 1964. What is clear in retrospect is that Eisenhower was in fact the first sign of a more general Democratic decline, a decline of which Kennedy's very narrow victory might well have eventually been seen as a second symptom had not the 1964 landslide by the martyred president's successor (over the nominee of a badly divided Republican party) given so misleading a sign of the party's resurgence. The twenty years after 1952 in fact are as volatile a period of presidential election outcomes as any in our recent history, with Republican, Democratic, and Republican landslides following each other at eight year intervals; they show no evidence of any stability at all, much less of a stability in which one party is clearly dominant.

The volatility of American politics in the twenty years after 1952 stands in sharp contrast to the events of the twenty years preceding it. The five presidential elections beginning in 1932 constitute a clear-cut example of a stable political order: the Democrats were indisputably the majority party, winning all five contests; they dominated the House of Representatives and the Senate, as well as most governorships and state legislatures; a solid majority of the nation's voters *thought* of themselves of Democrats; domestic politics was dominated by a straightforward issue agenda focused on government management of the economy and social welfare on which the parties were accurately seen by the electorate as taking rather clear opposing positions and on which most voters thought the Democrats' offering superior; social class provided the primary basis of cleavage in the electorate, with both lower- and high-status voters identifying their economic interests with one of the two major parties and voting accordingly. The result is a classic picture of a stable party system: agenda and cleavages, party leaders and ordinary voters, all in balance for twenty years of clear-cut Democratic control.

Beginning in the late 1950s and increasingly in the 1960s, scholars began to develop an interpretation of the American party system that placed both the stability of the New Deal system and the early stages of its decline in the more general theoretical context of what came to be known as realignment. Realignment theory came in two varieties: one, generally referred to as secular realignment, directed attention to gradual shifts in the balance of party forces caused by changes in the social composition of the electorate; the other, often called critical realignment, is the more well-known and more significant variant, focusing on sudden, dramatic, large-scale, and lasting political change. It is what most scholars mean when the use the term realignment without a qualifying adjective, and it is the primary sense in which the term is used here.

Critical realignment theory provided a powerful account of how to read American electoral history at a time when symptoms of impending dramatic political change were becoming apparent. Developing the initial insights of V.O. Key, Jr. and Angus Campbell, theorists such as Walter Dean Burnham and James Sundquist developed a theory of electoral change that accounted for the initial stability of party systems, their gradual disaggregation over time, their sudden disappearance in a moment of systemic crisis, and their replacement by a new and stable system that begins the cycle all over again. The changes identified by critical realignment theory were attributed to the interplay of factors quite familiar to students of voting behavior: the staying power of partisan loyalties, the ability of strong partisan attachments to color a citizen's reaction to the issues and personalities of the day, the ways in which new issues and new generations inexorably infiltrate a party system whose origins are increasingly receding into ancient history. Realignment is the working out at the system level of these quite natural individual-level processes; it is more or less inevitable, with its life cycle linked to the life expectancy of a political generation of approximately forty years.

The specifics of the realignment process will be spelled out in considerable detail below, with particular attention to how the different parts were seen to fit together into the newly-perceived whole, but a brief overview is in order even at this early point. On the first day of a new party system, there is an equilibrium among the many elements in voters' political world: the issues they think most important, the party that can best handle the problems they care about, the party they identify with, their voting preferences across levels of government. Some cataclysmic event has focused voter attention on a set of issues which clearly assume a central position on the political agenda. There is general agreement on which issue should provide the focus for political debate, and the parties take clear opposing positions on it. Citizens see this issue as so important relative to those previously of concern that unusually large numbers of them adjust their party loyalties to bring them into line with their preferences on it. Many formerly uninterested citizens become politicized for the first time, developing party loyalties that provide a continuing link to a political process that was previously of little concern to them. The party favored on the cataclysmic event seizes control of government, becoming clearly dominant in all branches of the federal government as quickly as the electoral calendar allows and extending its dominance across the bulk of state and local governments as well.

For the first few years of the new party system, stability is maintained. The majority party uses its unified control of government to implement its policy agenda, and it continues to win support from voters it attracted during the realignment. New issues and new candidates of course emerge over time, but in the years immediately after realignment memories of the cataclysmic event and dominance of the issue that caused it are sufficiently powerful to keep most voters loyal to their new party; the party identification created or reinforced in the realignment provides a powerful lens or filter through which political reality is perceived, and that lens or filter guarantees that ambiguous political reality will be selectively perceived in ways that contribute to a consistent, self-reinforcing set of political attitudes.

Over time, however, a party system inevitably erodes. The crisis that caused the realignment recedes into history, while the number of new issues increases. Although the filter of partisan loyalty encourages citizens to adopt positions on new issues consistent with the interrelated bundle of old issues and party loyalty, some of these new issues inevitably cut against the old, putting at least some citizens in a position in which they have to choose between the new agenda items and their combination of party loyalty and issue concerns from the last realignment. Generational replacement continually reduces the numbers of citizens who themselves experienced the previous realignment and increases the numbers of those who came of political age in the post-realignment world for whom the past realignment is known through tales of parents and grandparents rather than experienced personally. Such inherited memories can have considerable impact, particularly when connected to a reinforcing party loyalty, but historic accounts necessarily have less impact than personal experience.

The result of these changes over time is, eventually, to undermine the party system. Increasingly, there are sufficient new voters and sufficient new cross-cutting issues for the process of unraveling to begin. The first symptoms are tensions *within* the parties. The minority party is constantly looking for electoral strategies that appeal to dissident members of the majority, i.e. new issues that have arisen since the last realignment on which the old majority is not united; the majority party is constantly forced to reinvigorate the majority it inherited from the last realignment or to replace defecting groups with newcomers who can be mobilized on new issues. Disagreement over how to respond to new issues combines with disagreement about electoral strategy to divide the leadership of both parties. Third parties emerge, symptoms of irreconcilable differences among former allies, often serving as intermediate stops for both politicians and voters *en route* from a traditional party home in which they no longer feel comfortable to the opposition.

The second half of the forty-year cycle will tend, therefore, to show signs of disaggregation—the falling apart of the previously stable system. In the absence of some precipitating event, a system crisis that produces a clear new focus for partisan conflict, the intra-party turmoil and electoral volatility may continue for an extended period of time. If, on the other hand, such a crisis does occur, the potential develops for a rapid new realignment. Minimally, the crisis can become a source of powerful one-sided retrospective evaluations that alter the balance of partisan forces. If the two parties adopt clearly differing responses to the crisis, it can become the point around which a stable new pattern of partisan/ideological debate is organized; it can both create a new set of highly salient issue concerns and act as the catalyst that causes citizens to bring party loyalty and issues into a new balance. In other words, the crisis creates exactly the equilibrium, balance, and stability that characterized the new party system with which we began several paragraphs above.

Much of this picture, most of it except the very end, can be applied to the New Deal party system that was created in 1929–1936. The centrality of economics in the thirties, the dominant position of the Democrats as the party believed better able to manage the economy and produce prosperity, the clear differences between Democrats and Republicans on the role the federal government should play in managing the economy, and Democratic control of the White House as well as of most sub-presidential offices are all signs of a classic new party system. By the late 1940s, the change in the country's world situation and the subsequent emergence of new and potentially cross-cutting foreign policy concerns, the similar emergence of race as a divisive issue within the Democratic majority, the decreasing attractiveness of New Deal economic appeals in a post-war world of increasing affluence, and the replacement of voters who remembered the depression and Franklin Roosevelt directly by those who knew both only through parental stories and history books had made the Democratic majority vulnerable. Internal divisions within the parties, culminating in the Goldwater insurgency and the Wallace third-party effort, constitute symptoms of impending change approximately thirty years into the old party system. What was needed to provide the spark for full-blown realignment was a systemic crisis that would crystallize the confused mass of issues, allowing one to dominate the others and to form the focal point for a new stable party-linked set of popular preferences.

It is now clear that a classic realignment did not happen. The Democrats certainly began losing presidential elections, producing a pattern of consistently low percentages of the popular vote as stable as the classic pattern that scholars had considered typical of a mature party system; after a 1968 election in which Wallace served as a way-station for disaffected Democrats who could not quite bring themselves to actually vote Republican, the Republicans actually began to win comfortable popular vote majorities. Only the extraordinary circumstances of 1976 produced a Democratic victory, and then by a very narrow margin. But none of the subsequent stages of a full-blown realignment occurred: the Democrats did not lose control of the Congress, with the temporary exception of the Senate in 1980 that lasted only until the class of 1980 came up for re-election in 1986; Republicans made no general gains in state and local government; party loyalties remained predominantly Democratic, with modest Republicans gains only very late in the period; countless efforts to find the increasing mass conservatism that could explain Republican electoral victories produced mixed or even negative results. Realignment remains the most powerful theoretical statement of electoral change, but its usefulness is increasingly a benchmark against which to observe the ways in which the current era fails to fit existing theory rather than an accurate picture of on-going developments.

The increasingly apparent failure of political developments to conform to the expectations of realignment theory led scholars to develop the competing hypothesis of *de*alignment. Dealignment theorists argue that political parties have weakened in the post-war world, to the extent that they can no longer play the central role they are assigned in realignment theory; the result is the substantially decreased stability of American electoral politics since World War II.

Dealignment rests to some extent on societal changes not directly related to politics: expansion of the media, particularly television, greatly increased the availability of political information to citizens at the same time that increased education levels made voters less dependent on the stability-inducing interpretative role that party identification had filled for the less sophisticated and knowledgeable electorate of the past. At the same time, party organizations declined as an increase in the number and impact of primary elections reduced their ability to control the presidential nomination process and as they were increasingly circumvented by independent campaign organizations and independent sources of campaign finance. The result is a weakening in mass psychological attachments to the political parties: although the number of true Independents has never exceeded a small minority of the population, the *strength* of identifiers' loyalties weakened substantially in the fifteen years after 1964, as did the impact of party identification on vote choice; citizens' images of the parties became increasingly empty, with the parties themselves increasingly seen as irrelevant.

With parties increasingly incapable of providing linkages among political institutions or continuity of electoral stimuli over time, claim dealignment theorists, ambitious candidates more frequently operate on their own: they compete with each other for the right to bear a party label, but the label is of less and less value in providing real information to voters about policy or ideology. Winning nominees are increasingly independent operators who confront the electorate *de novo* at four-, or at best eight-, year intervals. The result is a series of unconnected candidate-centered presidential campaigns, with considerable volatility in outcome and decreasing linkage to voting in sub-presidential contests.

Dealignment seemed an attractive argument in the years in which volatility of election outcomes over time and divided control of government raised questions about whether it made sense to speak of a stable party system at all. But despite the success of many elements of the dealignment argument, its theorists have much exaggerated the volatility of outcomes that lies at its very core: such volatility has largely been an artifact of one aberrant election in 1964 that obscured an otherwise fairly clear pattern of Democratic decline. What we in fact see once 1964 drops out of any sequence of elections under consideration is a remarkable stability in Republican dominance as great as that in any mature party system, as great as in the twenty years of calm before Eisenhower, but unaccompanied by the shifts in sub-presidential outcomes and in the partisan loyalties of ordinary citizens expected in a full-fledged realignment.

Investigation of these developments with the joint goals of understanding post-war electoral politics and developing/evaluating realignment/dealignment theory is the purpose of this book. The central thesis is that there have in fact been two mini-realignments since the end of World War II, voting shifts *at the presidential level alone* smaller than those found in the realignments of the past, but whose cumulative impact is to produce the current Republican presidential majority. Each of the mini-realignments improved Republican presidential election performance: the first began in the late 1940s and transformed a pattern of Democratic dominance into one in which the parties were quite evenly balanced; the second occurred in the late 1960s and transformed an essentially balanced system into one in which Republicans dominate. And despite the apparent gaps between the sequence of events and elements of *either* realignment and dealignment as a whole, the specifics of the two mini-realignments make considerable sense in terms of a transition from a stable party system of classic realignment theory to a dealigned electoral world.

The first mini-realignment begins with the increasing affluence of the post-war world, undermining the clarity of the economic issue agenda that had sustained the New Deal system and reducing the size of the Democrats' traditional blue-collar base. The weakened focus on economics allows new and cross-cutting issues to emerge. Foreign policy takes on an increasingly Republican coloration by the early 1950s as the full implications of the post-war tension with the Soviet Union and its allies develop and war breaks out in Korea. Even more importantly, racial polarization, a potentially divisive problem for the Democrats since Franklin Roosevelt united blacks and southern whites in the New Deal coalition, was finally activated in 1948 (and to a far greater extent in 1964) by Democratic civil rights activism; the Democrats as a result gained an overwhelming majority of the increasingly large black vote, but at the cost of the white votes that had long provided them a solid electoral college base in the south.

The second mini-realignment is driven by two very different processes. First, race combined with the rest of the Great Society domestic program, internal Democratic divisions on Vietnam, and reform of the Democrats' nomination procedures to push popular images of the Democrats in the late 1960s and 1970s well to the left, generating an image of the party as so ideologically extreme as to be out of touch with many of its traditional constituents; the result is a substantial increase in defection (in presidential elections) among centrist and moderately liberal Democrats that would normally constitute the party's ideological and partisan core. Second, the economic problems of the later Carter administration destroyed the Democrats' long-standing image of the party of good times, removing an area of remaining party strength that had been important since the 1930s.

Integrating the two mini-realignments into the debate about realignment and dealignment can best be left to the Conclusion, when all the strands of argument developed in the pages that follow can be brought together; but the task is less complex and less difficult than one might initially expect. The first mini-realignment is almost entirely consistent with classic realignment theory: war and economic recovery accelerate the process of change above and beyond what one might normally expect; the events of the late 1930s and 1940s are so dramatic as to make the shorter-than-anticipated lifespan of the classic New Deal system entirely plausible. The second mini-realignment begins as further and final deterioration of the New Deal system, deterioration quite consistent with the last stages of system decline in classic realignment theory. But the weakening of political parties that is central to dealignment theory prevents crises at the presidential level from producing the stable new system that realignment theory expects: they do not create the powerful new party loyalties which can impose order on the system as a whole. The crises therefore produce changes of shorter duration—two or three elections rather than eight or ten—and they do not penetrate sub-presidentially, creating neither the unified control of government nor the policy coherence (even when one party does, from time to time, control both presidency and congress) on which the new stable party system of classic realignment theory depends. The longevity of Republican dominance at the presidential level after 1968 is due to the fact that Republican domination is built on two very different processes, with the shift from one to the other taking place around 1980.

It is essential to stress how different the two sources of Republican strength after 1968 were from each other and how important the transition between them in 1980 was. The Reagan nomination, and particularly the first Reagan administration, pushed popular images of the Republicans sufficiently far to the right to remove the ideological disadvantage from which the Democrats had suffered for the previous fifteen years: the Democrats were no longer perceived to be particularly out of the mainstream. At the same time, however, the Democrats' loss of their long-standing image as the party of prosperity combined in Reagan's first term with the apparent success of Reaganomics to produce the powerful comparative retrospective evaluations that underlay the Republican victories of 1984 and 1988. Reagan continued a pattern of Republican dominance of presidential election outcome; but he substantially altered the basis of his party's dominance.

This Reagan trade-off represented a danger for the Republicans: retrospective economic evaluations would seem to be a far more fragile basis of electoral support than the advantage of relative ideological position than preceded it. The natural workings of the business cycle, even in the absence of any long-term or structural problems with Reaganomics, would make it likely that at some point the prosperity issue that supported the Republicans in 1980 would at some point turn against them. That is precisely what seems to have happened in 1992.

Bill Clinton's 1992 victory represents a continuation of trends that have dominated American presidential elections since retrospective economic evaluations replaced ideological extremity as a basis of Republican strength in 1980. Retrospective economic evaluations remained the prime factor driving the electorate in

1992; the only novelty is that such issues cut against the Republicans after three elections in which they had cut very powerfully against the Democrats. Whether the economic difficulties of the early 1990s were due to the natural workings of the capitalist business cycle or to the flawed economic policies of the Reagan/Bush administrations is of relatively little importance in understanding 1992, even if it is critical to an understanding of the prospects for Clinton's presidency. Deprived after 1980 of the ideological advantages that had served it so well for the previous fifteen years and still a minority in terms of party identification (despite its gains in the mid-1980s), the Republicans were extremely vulnerable to economic downturn. Bill Clinton's ability to create a new era of Democratic presidential success is likely to depend to some considerable degree on his ability to build on perceived Republican economic failure in order to restore his party's image as the party of good times.

———— ~ꝺꝏ~ ————

    The chapters that follow make the case that this sequence of events explains the pattern of recent Democratic presidential failures. Chapter Two argues that there is a pattern to explain: although developments since World War II clearly do not constitute a classic realignment, presidential election outcomes since 1946 are quite consistent with the pattern that first attracted the attention of realignment theorists. At two points, 1946–1950 and 1966–1970, there are changes in the nature of presidential outcomes smaller in magnitude but quite similar in form to those of the classic realignments. Their cumulative effect is to transform a Democratic presidential majority into a Republican presidential majority.

    Chapters Three and Four deal with the processes underlying the first mini-realignment that deprived the Democrats of their presidential majority and created a system of partisan balance. Chapter Three argues that there is a rise in overall levels of affluence in the immediate post-war years that decreases the size of the class base that had sustained the Democrats through the New Deal period; the result is a lessened impact of traditionally successful Democratic class-based appeals just as foreign policy is emerging as a newly salient basis of Republican strength. Increased affluence coincides with a decrease in the class depolarization in vote choice that actually helps the Democrats offset somewhat the changed composition of the electorate. Chapter Four argues that race plays an important role in both of the mini-realignments: the Dixiecrat revolt in 1948 is a symptom of increasing white southern opposition to civil rights activism in the post-Roosevelt Democratic Party that accelerates considerably in the 1960s with emergence of clear inter-party differences on racial questions that had moved to the center of the political agenda. The magnitude of Johnson's landslide initially obscures somewhat the impact of this change, but race produced considerable immediate changes in the coalitional basis of the parties and served as a precursor of the more general changes in images of the Democrats that were to occur shortly thereafter.

Chapters Five and Six deal with the second mini-realignment that produces a Republican presidential majority. Chapter Five demonstrates the ideological basis of Democratic failure in 1968–1980, arguing that the party's perceived lurch to the left around 1966 created a gap between even centrist Democrats and their party that underlies that party's ability to activate effectively its nominal partisan majority. Chapter Six argues that the 1980s were dominated by Republican capture of economics and the ability to produce prosperity, using Carter's domestic failure and Reagan's domestic success to overcome the simultaneous loss of ideological advantages caused by Reagan's pushing public images of the Republicans to the right. The 1980 election marks the transition between the two phases of the second mini-realignment: Carter's failures set up the subsequent comparison of performance that so greatly helped the Republicans after 1980, even as the Reagan campaign and administration were destroying the ideological advantages they had enjoyed since the similar surge of governmental activism pushed images of the Democrats to the left in the mid-1960s.

Chapter Seven applies the basic logic of the analysis to 1992. The decline of a Republican ideological advantage around 1980 left the Republicans increasingly and precariously dependent on public perceptions dating back to the Carter-Reagan contest that they were the party of good times, perceptions which the economic difficulties of the later Bush years substantially undermined. The 1992 election outcome in fact makes most sense as a simple continuation of post-Carter processes: a balance in ideological placement of the parties that allows the election to be determined by retrospective economic evaluations; the sole novelty in 1992 is that such evaluations for the first time in many years worked against the Republicans. The conditions of 1992 give the Democrats *opportunity*: incumbents have an opportunity to mold the political process that challengers lack. But the complexity both of the problems Clinton faced and of the underlying state of public opinion raises obvious questions about his ability to translate his 1992 victory into long-term gains for his party.

Finally, the Conclusion allows a return to the central themes of realignment and dealignment with which we began as a means of developing the significance and implications of the two mini-realignments and of the more general changes in American electoral politics since World War II.

2

The Collapse of the
Democratic Presidential Majority[*]

Few concepts in the social science literature have aroused as much interest and controversy in recent years as electoral realignment. The term conjures up images of dramatic change in the nature of political conflict: upsurge in mass political involvement and participation, large-scale and lasting shifts in the balance of party forces, sharp alteration in content of the political agenda and in the nature of political outputs. Realignment attracted attention because it was thought to be highly topical as well: Walter Dean Burnham's elegant argument (1970) about its periodicity suggested that the United States was "due" for realignment in the 1960s, precisely at a time at which many of its warning signs were becoming obvious.

Symptoms of impending realignment of the New Deal party system in the mid-1960s were in fact quite numerous: the national issue agenda clearly changed, with emergence of new issues of race, social order, and foreign affairs that altered the clear issue landscape of class-based economic conflict that had dominated the previous forty years; increased intra-party conflict demonstrated the inability of the existing cleavage system to successfully contain a newly invigorated ideological debate; party coalitions shifted in response to the new issues, with intra-party debate often spilling over into third-parties movements that could constitute the classic way-stations of voters *en route* from one major party loyalty to another. Most importantly, the party that had dominated presidential elections from 1932 through 1964 clearly became the minority party at the presidential level, winning only one of the next six contests and only once exceeding 46.5% of the popular vote.

At the same time, there are substantial aspects of the realignment package that have not fallen into their expected places. The increased levels of mass political involvement thought characteristic of realigning eras never occurred: voter turnout fell consistently between 1960 and 1988, the period in which the most important of these changes took place. Two more important problems are the failure of Republican dominance at the presidential level to be translated into gains in sub-presidential politics and the failure of the Republicans to make progress in party identification. Republican capture of the Senate in 1980 proved to be temporary, lasting only as long as it took for the class of 1980 to come up for re-election, rather than part of some majestically unfolding process of creating a new Republican majority; party loyalties were the centerpiece of realignment theory, explaining both the initial sharp change in the pattern of presidential election results and the trickle-down effect on party-based sub-presidential voting, producing the unified control of government that allowed enactment of a coherent legislative agenda.[1] The Republicans won the 1968, 1972, and 1980 presidential elections while clearly remaining the minority party in party identification; and the improvement in their relative position in 1984 was still insufficient to provide them with a party identification majority.

The failure of the package as a whole to hold is troubling. One of the things that initially made realignment theory so attractive was that its various elements were tightly linked to each other in a developmental structure: they did not simply occur in a certain sequence; they were causally linked, natural causes and consequences of each other, and it was the extraordinary complexity of their interaction that gave the theory as a whole much of its intellectual power. As early as the mid-1970s, failure to find evidence of changed party loyalties or of sub-presidential Republican gains led to debate about the relevance and usefulness of the notion of realignment itself, a process of conceptual revisionism that led to development of the competing notion of dealignment and culminated in the early 1990s with the claim that the whole realignment literature has largely been a waste of time and energy.

On a more empirical level, failure to find evidence of the full realignment package has caused scholars to fail to recognize or to fully appreciate very real changes that have occurred in American electoral politics. For lost in the widespread observation that the last quarter-century has not seen a realignment of the classic sort is realization that at the presidential level, at least, the pattern of election outcome of the past forty years constitute almost exactly the kind of change that realignment theory would predict. The deviation from the classic pattern here is quite modest: instead of one dramatic change in the balance of party forces after forty years, there have been two smaller changes at twenty-year intervals. These two "mini-realignments" have cumulatively produced the same change in both magnitude and direction that one would expect from a single, larger, realignment, but neither of them has been accompanied by changes in sub-presidential voting or in mass partisanship that classic realignment theory would have led us to expect. The failure of the rest of the package to fall into place makes the changes at the presidential level more intriguing, not less.

REALIGNMENT: CORE COMPONENTS

The term realignment has in fact been used in two somewhat different ways since the 1950s, with V.O. Key, Jr. playing a major role in each of them. In 1959, Key introduced the notion of *secular* realignment, a gradual shift in the relative fortunes of the political parties due for the most part to slow but steady change in the composition of the electorate. In 1955, Key, although using a rather different terminology, had begun what was to become the more common and more influential strand of realignment theory, a variant at times referred to as *critical* realignment, which deals with a far more dramatic and sudden pattern of change and which is the primary focus here.

Two fundamental aspects of critical realignment were identified in the early literature. First, Key himself (1955) argued that there had been a small number of elections in which the composition of party coalitions changed in a way that persisted over time. Second, Angus Campbell (1966a) argued that there had been a small number of elections in which sharp and persisting changes in the overall balance of party forces in presidential voting had occurred. Walter Dean Burnham (1970) linked the two elements to each other, demonstrated that they represented two aspects of a single process of electoral change, and produced a comprehensive and elegant explanation in which the increase over time in incongruity between citizens' partisan loyalties and the political system's underlying social and economic realities made realignment a natural, inevitable, and regular aspect of American political life.

Key had used the term "critical elections" to identify elections in which:

> voters are ... unusually deeply concerned, in which the extent of electoral involvement is relatively high, and in which the decisive results of the voting reveal a sharp alteration of the pre-existing cleavage within the electorate.
>
> Moreover, and perhaps this is the truly differentiating characteristic of this sort of election, the realignment made manifest in the voting in such elections seems to persist for several succeeding elections (1955: 4).

The change in political cleavages that Key refers to consists of differing patterns of change in voting behavior among different social groups: some segment of the population moves towards one of the two major parties, while other groups either move in the opposite direction or maintain a pre-existing pattern. Clubb, Flanigan, and Zingale (1980: 78) refer to such outcomes as "differential" or "interactive" change. Key explicitly excludes from his concept of critical elections a situation in which all segments of society change their behavior in the same way, what Clubb et al. call "across-the-board" change or a "surge." For example, an election in which all groups move towards the Republicans (like 1896 in Massachusetts) is not a critical election, whereas an election in which some groups become more Democratic while others become more Republican or do not change at all (like 1928) clearly is.

Although the initial quotation from Key suggests that there are three characteristics of a critical election (voter concern, electoral involvement, and alteration of cleavage patterns), the second refers to alteration of cleavage patterns alone: voter concern and electoral involvement may well occur in the critical election itself, but it is the change in cleavage patterns alone that persists over time; his later discussion of New England in the late 1920s clearly deals only with cleavage patterns. Key's substantive focus is on how the pattern of partisan cleavage in Massachusetts and other New England states changed in 1928: the years before 1920 had produced roughly similar levels of Democratic support throughout the state, with urban and rural areas, industrial and farm areas, and Catholic and Protestant areas differing little in the degree to which they supported the Democrats. During the 1920s, however, and peaking in 1928, these social characteristics seem to have taken on a new political significance: urban, industrial, Catholic towns moved to the Democrats, while rural and Protestant areas moved towards the Republicans. The result is a clear difference in the degree of Democratic support in the two kinds of areas that persists at a fairly stable level through 1952. What is striking is Key's demonstration that what later came to be thought of as a distinctively New Deal pattern of electoral cleavage emerged well before the Depression and well before even the Democratic presidential nomination of the Catholic Al Smith in 1928.

Angus Campbell's "Classification of the Presidential Elections," (1966a) an expansion of the ideas first advanced in the last chapter of *The American Voter* (1960), introduces the term "realignment" in the "critical realignment" sense that is now most often used. In a realigning election, "popular feeling associated with politics is sufficiently intense that the basic partisan commitments of a portion of the electorate change, and a new party balance is created" (Campbell 1966a: 74). Realigning elections are to be distinguished from maintaining elections, in which the absence of powerful one-sided short-term forces allows the majority party to win. They also differ from deviating elections, in which powerful one-sided short-term forces produce outcomes different from the underlying balance of party forces but which represent only temporary disruptions of the previous stable pattern that later reasserts itself. In a realigning election, short-term forces actually change the underlying party loyalties of at least some citizens, producing the basis for continuation of the new pattern in later electoral contests.

Examples that Campbell cited give a good idea of the nature of realigning change. His two clear cases of realignment are 1896 and 1932. In both years, a fairly stable existing pattern of election outcomes was transformed into a new, equally stable, but quite different pattern. In 1896, an extended period of very competitive presidential elections was transformed into one of clear-cut Republican dominance: the economic collapse of 1893 (occurring with a Democrat in the White House) damaged and divided the Democrats, leading to capture of the party by its populist faction; the combination of economic failure, intra-party conflict, and perceived radicalism produced electoral disaster.[2] The Republicans proceeded to win presidential elections for the next 32 years, losing only the two-election sequence that began with Wilson's winning with a minority of the vote in a year in which Taft and Roosevelt split the Republicans. In 1932, an even greater economic collapse during a Republican administration transformed an era of clear-cut Republican domination into one in which the Democrats won every presidential election for a generation. The sole exception to the pattern of Democratic victory for 36 years after 1932 is a classic example of a deviating election: Dwight Eisenhower's victories are attributable to the extraordinary personal popularity of the victorious general rather than to any long-term gains for the Republican party: the temporary and personal nature of his victory is shown by the Democrats' return to power as soon as Eisenhower himself left the political scene.

The genius of the "Classification" piece is that it explicitly links the powerful new micro-theories of individual vote choice developed in *The American Voter* to the macro-level phenomenon of party-system change, introducing party identification as the psychological mechanism that underlies realignment. Realigning elections differ from deviating elections in that short-term factors that cause partisans to temporarily defect from the party they identify with in a deviating election are powerful enough to cause the citizen to change party loyalties in a realigning election. Deviating elections involve defection; realigning elections involve conversion. And it is the newly converted who provide the basis for the stable new pattern of electoral outcomes: their new partisanship continues to influence their voting behavior long after the specific events which generated it have faded.

Yet, for an article that had tremendous impact on the subsequent literature on party systems, the "Classification" piece is surprisingly lacking in detail on the *process* of realignment: the nature of the disruptive short-term forces, the factors determining whether the crisis has long-term rather than merely temporary effects, the process by which underlying party loyalties change, and the internal dynamics of the old party systems that fail or of the new ones that replace them are discussed very briefly if at all. The lack of attention to the mechanics of electoral change is particularly striking given the much more developed analysis of the link between micro- and macro-concerns in Campbell's and his co-authors' articles on the concepts of a "normal vote" (Converse, 1966) and "surge and decline" (Campbell, 1966b).

Walter Dean Burnham's (1970) two substantial contributions to the realignment literature make his *Critical Elections and the Mainsprings of American Politics* the capstone of the classical realignment literature. First, Burnham develops in great detail the causal process that underlies realignment, linking together the individual and systemic factors which interact to produce periodic, large-scale, enduring shifts in the pattern of election outcomes; second, he develops a powerful yet straightforward empirical device for determining when realignments have occurred.

It makes sense to focus on Burnham's empirical test for realignment first, if only because it produces the evidence of periodicity that stimulates investigation of realignment's causal structure. And the test Burnham develops is extremely simple. Although his initial discussion, like Key's, refers to a broad range of factors such as increased intensity of political discussion, high levels of intra-party and inter-party ideological conflict, and changes in the coalitional bases of the parties (Burnham, 1970: 6–10), all of which had been referred to in earlier studies and all of which prove important in his later explanation of the process underlying realignment, such considerations are irrelevant to Burnham's measurement.[3] Burnham's means of determining when realignments have occurred is extremely simple, a formalization of Campbell's initial observation that some elections mark the replacement of one stable pattern of electoral outcomes by another such stable pattern during a brief period of sharp change.

Burnham charts the Democratic percentage of the popular vote for president over time for each election since the re-emergence of two-party competition in 1824. He then takes the first ten elections, divides the forty-year period into two twenty-year segments (with a midpoint between elections five and six), and determines the significance of the difference in mean Democratic percentage of the popular vote for president in the two parts of the period. The resulting statistic (t) is low if the two means are very close to each other or if the difference in means is small compared to the standard deviation of percentage voting Democratic *within* each five-election segment; the statistic is large when the two periods are internally consistent but differ markedly from each other. Burnham then drops the first election, adds an eleventh, and repeats the calculation with a new midpoint between elections six and seven.[4] The procedure is repeated for each set of ten elections up to the ten most recent.

In examining the magnitude of the test statistics for the full range of possible midpoints, Burnham finds a striking and unambiguous pattern: the value of t is rather low for most years, suggesting that most midpoints divide two periods that pretty much resemble each other. A small number of midpoints, however, produce values of t that are distinctively large: these years divide two relatively homogenous periods within which levels of Democratic support are similar to each other but which differ substantially from each other, representing the sharp, clear transition from one pattern of electoral outcome to another that marks realignment. Two of the peaks occur in the years that Campbell had already identified as realignments: 1896 and 1932. A third peak occurred in the period immediately before the Civil War, the era in which the new Republican Party was replacing the Whigs. The regularity with which these realignments seem to occur is striking: forty years appears to be the natural life-span of a party system.[5]

Burnham's second contribution is even more important: an extensive development of the causal process underlying realignment that makes clear its periodic character and its central role in allowing/causing system evolution and change. The critical role of partisanship in producing realignment is made explicit in Burnham: it is the key to the pre-realignment period of stability, the post-realignment period of stability, *and* the transition between them. Burnham accepts the argument by Campbell et al. (1960) that party identification, once established, is extremely resistant to change. Citizens who have developed a party loyalty are in fact likely to maintain it even as social and economic circumstances change, creating tension between their current political interests and their party identification. This is the individual-level manifestation of what Burnham elsewhere (1991: 118) calls "the persistent relationship between dynamic socio-economic development and a static political order."

The inevitability of social and economic change in a context of stable party loyalties is the underlying cause of realignment. When the gap between the two becomes too large, i.e. when the number of new issues unrelated to those underlying the existing party system increases, the tension is resolved by a sudden wrenching change in party loyalty, voting behavior, and election outcome. When "abnormal stress in the socioeconomic system" reveals the "incapacity of 'politics as usual' to integrate, much less aggregate, emergent political demand" (Burnham, 1970: 10), the result is realignment: the policy agendas of the political parties shift to focus on the newly dominant issues, large numbers of citizens resolve their existing tensions by bringing their party identification into line with the emergent issues of the new political order, and the existing party coalitions are transformed as political groupings choose up new sides on the basis of the new patterns of issue cleavage. Such a resolution may be delayed by the considerable power of party identification to structure and interpret political perceptions and by the continued vitality of whatever issues might have underlaid the old political order. The stability of party loyalties allows the tension between old and new issues to reach the magnitude that requires the massive and sudden changes of realignment for their resolution. "One is led to suspect that the truly 'normal' structure of American electoral politics at the mass base is precisely this dynamic, even dialectic polarization between long-term inertia and concentrated bursts of change …" (Burnham, 1970: 27). Once the change is completed, issue concerns and party loyalty are again in balance. The new party identification provides the basis for a new extended period of political stability, even as the emergence of newer and potentially disruptive cross-cutting issues begin inexorably to emerge.

The first signs of incipient tensions of a kind capable of destabilizing an existing party system is intra-party ideological ferment at the elite level. Burnham (1970: 27) discusses third parties as proto-realignment phenomena: indicators that the existing political order can no longer contain new, emergent, cross-cutting issues. Third parties may originate in the defection of disaffected components of a major party sensitive to these new issues or in the mobilization of entirely new political groupings. They generally provide an indication of the types of issues that will likely dominate the new order. These third parties act as a way-station for partisans not yet able to actually vote for the party they have traditionally opposed while allowing them to express their rejection of the party they have traditionally supported. The later stages of the realignment consists of the completion of the journey to a new partisan home in which a re-created party identification is in balance with positions on the newly identified issues of the day.

REALIGNMENT:
APPLICATIONS AND MODIFICATIONS

The years following publication of Burnham's book saw a virtual explosion in scholarly interest in realignment. The new literature is generally organized around two interrelated themes: further development of the conceptual/theoretical understanding of realignment and application of the general logic of the theory to the political events of the late 1960s and after. The purely scholarly concern with elaborating the theory of realignment was encouraged to a considerable extent by a widespread perception that the theory might help make sense of the dramatic changes which American politics seemed to be undergoing in the years after 1966.

Paul Allen Beck (1974, 1984) made a major contribution to explaining the periodicity of realignment by analyzing the implications of generational replacement for electoral change. Time creates incongruence between party and socio-economic reality even for those whose partisanship was formulated in the immediate aftermath of the previous realignment: the ability of party to act as a guide to understanding and interpreting evolving social and economic reality decreases over time, setting up the tension central to Burnham's argument. But for young partisans, whose experience of the previous realignment was obtained indirectly through the socialization process rather than experienced first-hand, the likelihood that short-term events will be sufficient to overpower party identification is even greater (Carmines, McIver, and Stimson, 1987). One of the things that happens during the normal forty-year life expectancy of a party system is that the number of people who remember the previous realignment era and whose partisanship was forged in the intense political events of the time decreases; those who know the previous realignment only indirectly are more likely to be affected by the short-term increase. It is not accidental that the forty-year life-span of a party system is approximately the amount of time necessary for those who themselves experienced the previous realignment to be vastly outnumbered by those whose memory of it is second-hand. It is the combination of new issues and new voters that drives periodicity.

If Beck's analysis of generational replacement helps explain the maximum expected life-span of a party system, others theorists have greatly expanded our understanding of the internal dynamics that underlie its initial power and stability. Clubb, Flanigan, and Zingale (1980) examine how the party leaders who assume political office in the earliest stages of a new party system produce an institutional and policy coherence that is a powerful source of its early stability (see also Brady, 1985).[6] Clubb et al. argue that this stability is due to the unified control of government (the presidency and both houses of Congress) by a single party that flows from the earliest realigning elections; this unified control of government produces a consistency and clarity in governmental policies, focused on the defining issue of the new era, far greater than that found in later stages of a party system (after the intrusion of new and cross-cutting issues) or in periods of divided government. The result is a clarity in elite politics—a clarity of issue positions of the parties and a clarity of party responsibility for policy outputs—that institutionalizes the new electoral order. Clubb et al. view realignment as a package of changes at both mass and elite levels: mass electoral behavior creates the unified control of government, which in turn produces the clear institutional referents which encourage the strong combination of partisan loyalties and issue concerns, which in turn continues the pattern of election outcomes.

Clubb et al. argue that this period of post-realignment coherence lasts but a short time: realigning eras tend to show weakness significantly before the subsequent realignment. Each of the three consensually-defined realignments (1856, 1896, 1932) in fact degenerated into blurred patterns of electoral outcomes, divided control of government, and an end to clear-cut policy agendas within approximately twelve years. The remaining years of a party system produce closer electoral outcomes, divided control of government, and policy stalemate. Clubb et al. identify 1946 as the year in which the New Deal realignment ended and the later stages of the declining New Deal party system began (see also Silbey, 1991).

The most comprehensive pursuit of both the theoretical elaboration of the concept of realignment and its application to the contemporary party system is by James L. Sundquist (1983). Sundquist draws on Schattschneider's (1960) discussion of the scope of conflict to greatly develop how old and new issues interact with each other to create the potential for large-scale electoral change, with particular emphasis on the response to the new issue played by the political parties. The process that can lead to realignment is set in motion when a powerful new issue arises that cuts across the issue(s) that dominated the old system: late in the life-span of an existing party system, such an issue can split the pre-existing electoral coalitions, putting pressure on at least some voters to choose between older issues linked to their long-standing party loyalty and a new issue that pushes them toward defection. Each existing party coalition is threatened by the potential loss of those cross-pressured between old and new; if one of the parties is more seriously divided than the other, the potential exists for a substantial shift in their relative strength.

What is required for the issue to provide a basis for a new electoral order is that the parties take clear and opposing positions on the new issue. The new issue may of course cause considerable short-term hardship for the party it disadvantages. But if the party disadvantaged on the new issue adopts new policies or new leaders that disassociate it from the failures of the past, the impact of the new issue is likely to be temporary. Sundquist argues for similar reasons (1966: 303) that valence issues have rather little ability to generate realignment: simple association of one party with some disastrous (or universally acclaimed) outcome rapidly becomes diluted over time if not reinforced by the parties' continued disagreement over relevant policy questions.[7] The Depression alone would have been insufficient to create the New Deal party system, claims Sundquist: on its own it would have been a powerful but temporary anti-Republican force, certain to fade in importance as the emergence of new substantive issues and the simple passage of time made Hoover's problems less politically relevant. What created the stable New Deal party system was the continued disagreement of Democrats and Republicans on questions about the role of the government in managing the economy in the years after the Depression; continued policy debate over issues made salient by the Depression guaranteed its continued relevance for at least the life-span of the political generation which had experienced it.

If the effort to develop realignment theory generally succeeded in producing a complex and subtle picture of the nature of electoral change, the attempt to apply the theory to the politics of the 1960s, 1970s, and 1980s has generally been seen as a failure. To put it more accurately, most authors who tried to use realignment theory to account for contemporary events concluded that there has not been and there is unlikely to be a realignment of the traditional kind. By 1968 there was in fact good reason to believe that the New Deal party system, created in the aftermath of the 1929 Depression, was coming to an end. The system had survived its forty years, and even those who had read Burnham superficially could not fail to be struck by the symptoms of its imminent collapse: proto-realignment phenomena such as new issues like race and Vietnam that cut across the New Deal's economic issue, intra-party ideological tensions that culminated in the Goldwater insurgency within the Republicans in 1964, and the split among Democrats that produced Wallace's third-party effort in 1968 all divided existing party coalitions and provided clear signs that realignment was due. Nixon's victory in 1968, the continued ideological polarization of the Democrats in 1972, and the Nixon re-election landslide seemed to suggest to many that the expected realignment might in fact be on the verge of taking place. And yet the subsequent event hardly corresponded to what the now rather impressive theoretical literature on realignment might have led one to expect.

Sundquist argues that application of such an analysis in 1983 to the period since the New Deal produces little reason to see realignment as having occurred or as imminent. Since the mid-1960s there has certainly been an increase in political volatility and in the frequency of the kinds of proto-realignment phenomena identified by Burnham. In particular, Vietnam and what Scammon and Wattenberg (1971) call the Social Issue (a sense of disruptive social change caused by perceived increase in crime, drug use, sexual permissiveness, and general social disintegration) produced sharp short-term anti-Democratic sentiments that contributed to the 1968 and 1972 presidential election results. But Sundquist sees in these developments no evidence of the kind of substantial change in the balance of party strength that occurs in realignment. Republican assumption of responsibility for pursuing the war after 1968 reduced the long-term damage to the Democrats on the valence issue of Vietnam, and the inter-party debate of 1969–1972 transformed the conflict over Vietnam into one over details of disengagement rather than a more fundamental question over the merits of the war itself; movement of Democratic party leadership to the right on the Social Issue after 1972 (see also Gold, 1992) allowed them to neutralize a potentially damaging issue on which the McGovern campaign had made them vulnerable at the same time that four years of Republican rule had diluted Democratic responsibility for continuing problems. In neither case were the Republicans able to establish the clear differences on position issues that would produce long-term advantages necessary for realignment.

The bulk of the political change that has occurred since the 1930s is in fact attributed by Sundquist to the spread of the class-based New Deal cleavage system.

In particular, gradual penetration of class-based politics into the white South and the subsequent disappearance of monolithic racially-based Democratic dominance in that region are simply delayed aftershocks of the New Deal realignment. The effect has of course been to damage Democratic electoral performance at the presidential level, but that was the result of the *extension* of the New Deal cleavage system rather than a sign of the system's demise.

One of the changes in the late 1960s and 1970s that is almost universally acknowledged is the decline in the public's overall strength of party loyalty. The emergence of genuinely cross-cutting new issues and the successive failures of administrations of both parties to deal satisfactorily with the problems they faced produced an indisputable general weakening of citizens' identification with the political parties and a rise in the number of Independents, particularly among the young (Beck, 1984). Nie, Verba, and Petrocik (1979) note the decline of partisanship as one of the most important ways in which the American electorate had changed since publication of *The American Voter* in 1960. The result of the decline is a certain amount of *de*alignment, a general weakening in the stability of the political order as the partisan glue that holds it together softens.[8]

Burnham (1965) had earlier argued that the entire twentieth century constitutes a period of dealignment from the high levels of party-organized electoral politics of the late nineteenth century, with introduction of the Australian ballot, the direct primary, and other reforms designed to weaken the power of party elites reinforcing the effects of a general decline in party competition (see also Rusk, 1970). The New Deal had temporarily and partially disrupted this process by increasing the relevance of parties at a time of national crisis, but by 1970 Burnham (1970: 91) could write of "the onward march of party decomposition."

An even stronger statement of the case for contemporary de- rather than realignment is made by Everett Carll Ladd, both alone (1982) and in his work with Charles D. Hadley (1978). Ladd reviews the cross-cutting issues and policy failures that decreased the attractiveness of parties in the years after 1964. In addition, he argues that two more general societal factors have produced a secular decline in the role political parties have traditionally served in providing stability and order to a political system: the modern mass media has greatly increased the amount of political information available to ordinary citizens; at the same time, increased mass education levels make voters more able to deal with political complexity without requiring the parties to provide interpretation and guidance (see also Shively, 1992). Both changes have added impact with entry into the electorate in 1968 of the first members of the Baby Boom generation—an extremely large group of young people, born after World War II, raised in an increasingly dealigned world, and likely to accelerate the pace of change by magnifying the effects of generational replacement (Delli Carpini, 1986).

Wattenberg's (1991: 34) extensive review of survey questions about voters' images of parties reinforces the portrait of their declining importance: party identification and party voting, he claims, have weakened over time because the parties have become largely *irrelevant*, with citizens increasingly having nothing—positive or negative—to say about them.[9] The result, for Wattenberg as for Ladd and Hadley, is a weakening in the electorate's dependence on and psychological attachment to a party, weakened impact of surviving party loyalty on vote choice, increased levels of split-ticket voting, and divided control of government (see also Jacobson, 1991; Cox and Kernell, 1991; Norpoth and Rusk, 1982).[10]

The decline of the parties as institutions was encouraged by reform of presidential nomination procedures in the late 1960s and 1970s (Ladd, 1982: ch. 3; Ranney, 1975; Polsby, 1983; Wattenberg, 1984). The increase in the number and significance of primaries took control of nominations out of the hands of party leadership, opening the way for individual candidates only loosely linked to parties to construct personal election-specific coalitions around the issues of the day; whereas John F. Kennedy as recently as 1960 had to win a very small number of primaries in order to convince party leaders who controlled the nomination process that his potential liabilities were not fatal, party reforms after 1968 made it possible to win nominations through primary campaigns alone. Individual campaign organizations and fund-raising activities allow candidates to appeal to small, unrepresentative self-selected primary electorates with little interest in party organization *per se* who are unwilling to sacrifice current issue-concerns to create stable long-term electoral coalitions. Party conventions increasingly became public relations events, media-focused coronations of a candidate whose nomination had been assured weeks or months previously rather than places where serious deliberation and negotiation takes place. The increase in independent campaign organization and finance have similarly increased the autonomy of a party's members of Congress or of office-holders in state and local government (see also Sorauf, 1988). The result is a decline in the parties as institutions capable of providing linkage and integration across levels of government.

On the national level, the result of this process is a collapse of the continuity that parties have traditionally provided to the electoral order. A party label is of course still necessary for a candidate to get on the ballot nationally and still has significance for (the shrinking number of) party-oriented voters. But it is increasingly superficial as an indicator of a ideology or policy or as a link to a party's tradition/history. Individual candidate-entrepreneurs seize and run with the party label, but there is little continuity of party appeal in the campaign or of party performance in office. At the governmental level, the result is the increased lack of coordination among the various components and levels of government: split-ticket voting produces increased likelihood of divided control of government; and even when the Presidency, House, and Senate are nominally in the hands of the same party, the party whose label they nominally share does not necessarily bind them together in a way that implies either real agreement on policy or a shared political fate.[11] At the mass level, the result is a succession of discontinuous election outcomes in which neither party is able to construct a stable basis for long-term electoral dominance. The sequence of landslides, Democratic and then Republican, within eight years between 1964 and 1972, followed by the defeat of a Republican and then a Democratic incumbent in 1976 and 1980 suggest the extent to which election outcomes reflect very short-term developments; dealignment argues that the stability required even to conceive of a party system has itself come to an end.[12]

THE STABILITY OF REPUBLICAN
DOMINANCE OF PRESIDENTIAL ELECTIONS

The change in the pattern of outcomes in American presidential elections since the New Deal is striking and overwhelming. The Democrats have lost five of the last seven presidential elections, two of them (1972 and 1984) by considerable margins. The only exceptions to the rule of Democratic failure since 1964 are 1976, when Jimmy Carter, running in the immediate aftermath of Watergate against an unelected incumbent, managed to win 51 percent of the popular vote; and 1992, when Bill Clinton, during a period of extended economic difficulty, won with 43 percent of the popular vote in a three-way race. No Democratic candidate except Carter in 1976 has exceeded 45.6 percent of the popular vote in a quarter century.

Yet one would be mistaken to assume that this failure was solely a post-Vietnam phenomenon. In the five presidential elections preceding 1968, the party's record is only marginally better. From 1948 through 1964, the Democrats received a popular majority only once—in 1964. Their two losses to Dwight Eisenhower were by sizable margins, and their victories in 1948 and 1960 were obtained with less than 50 percent of the popular vote. The Eisenhower triumphs looked like aberrations at the time, highly personal victories by a charismatic Republican after twenty years of solid Democratic control; but placed in historical perspective, they might well be seen as indicators of an pattern of ongoing Democratic decline. Johnson's landslide was of course impressive, but it was the only time the Democrats' have managed to win more than 51 percent of the popular vote since the death of Franklin D. Roosevelt.

The data are even more interesting if we group elections since the Depression as five-election sequences. In the presidential elections of 1932–1948—the Roosevelt years plus the first post-war election—the Democrats averaged 55.2% of the popular vote for president; for 1952–1968 the percentage fell to 48.0%; for 1972–1988 it fell further to 43.0%. Furthermore, although the Eisenhower, Johnson, and Nixon landslides of 1956–1972 do produce considerable volatility in election outcome in the middle of the period, the latter part of the period shows a consistency of poor Democratic outcomes as great as the stability of their good performances in the Roosevelt years: the standard deviation of Democratic percentage of the popular vote falls from 7.93 in 1952–1968 to a 4.93 in 1972–1988 that is barely larger than the 4.23 of 1932–1948. Petrocik maintains that election outcomes are too volatile and too idiosyncratic for vote totals to be useful indicators of realignment (1981: 25); Wattenberg argues that volatility has become "the new catchword of American politics" (1984: 131). But the data above impressively show volatility at relatively low levels despite the inevitable idiosyncrasies of individual elections at a time when Democratic percentage of the vote also remains low.

FIGURE 2.1

Percentage and Standard Deviation Democratic Five-Election Sequences

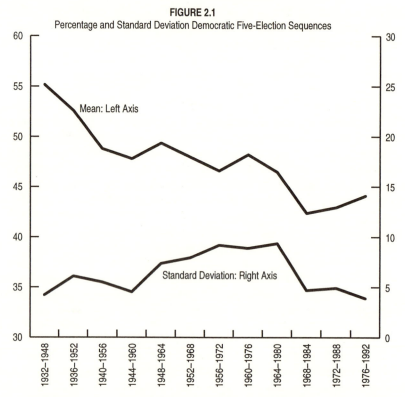

Note: Entries are mean and standard deviation of Democratic popular vote for president for five-election sequences.

Figure 2.1 presents these data in a somewhat more systematic form, graphing the mean and standard deviation of Democratic share of the total popular vote for each five-election sequence since 1932–1948. The top line shows the decline in mean Democratic vote from 55.2% to 42.4% in the 1972–1988 period that includes both Nixon's and Reagan's re-election campaigns. The changes in stability over time are quite different and even more striking. The Johnson re-election landslide, midway between two Republican re-election landslides, is what pushes standard deviations up in the middle of the period, to 9.21 in 1956–1972 and 9.38 and 1964–1980: the period after 1964 in which the Democrats do particularly poorly is also one of exceptionally stable election outcomes: the standard deviation of Democratic popular vote never exceeds 5.00, a level as low as that of the Roosevelt years. Clinton's 1992 victory barely alters these results: Clinton's winning percentage is so slightly larger than McGovern's losing percentage in 1972 that substituting 1992 for 1972 raises the mean Democratic percentage only from 43.0% to 44.1%, while its standard deviation actually decreases from 4.93 to 3.90! This is neither the weakening of a party system identified by Clubb et al. nor the alternation in power of candidate-based coalitions; it is a reversal of the pattern of Democratic electoral dominance at the presidential level (see also Shafer, 1991b).

A clearer image of the kind of change that has occurred since the end of World War II can be gained by updating Burnham's t-test analysis of presidential outcomes. Figure 2.2 reports a simple replication of Burnham's analysis for data through the 1992 presidential election. As explained earlier, high values of t indicate the kind of discontinuity between periods suggestive of realignment, whereas values approaching zero indicate that the periods on either side of the mid-point are essentially the same, either because the mean values are quite similar or because the difference in mean values is modest compared to the internal variation within each five-election sequence. Figure 2.2 shows clear peaks in the value of t in 1894 and 1930, exactly where Burnham found them and where Campbell led us to expect tem. Each of these peaks is followed by a considerable decline in the value of t.

FIGURE 2.2

Replicating Burnham: Five-Election Sequences: Democratic Percentage of Popular Vote

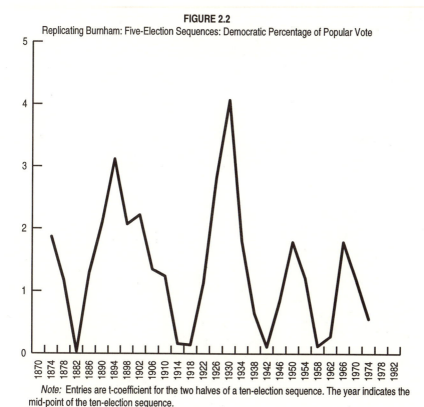

Note: Entries are t-coefficient for the two halves of a ten-election sequence. The year indicates the mid-point of the ten-election sequence.

If one looks at the recent pattern in the data, however, one finds an interesting and somewhat unexpected result. From a low of .11 for the 1942 mid-point, t in-creases to 1.79 in 1950 before falling off to .12 in 1958. This peak is clearly lower than in the two clear-cut realignments of the past, but it nonetheless marks a real spike in the curve considerably higher than any other mid-cycle figure. The 1950 election, of course, marks the midpoint between the four Roosevelt elections and Truman on the one hand, and the Eisenhower election through Nixon's first vic-tory on the other, and it corresponds to Burnham's (1970: 67) finding of a "subrealignment" in Pennsylvania around 1951. Here is evidence that the pattern of presidential outcomes changed considerably, if not quite as dramatically as in a conventionally-accepted full-blown realignment, shortly after the death of Roosevelt. Those pursuing the fate of the Democratic-dominated New Deal party system in the late 1960s are clearly missing some interesting signs of its partial demise as early as 1952 (see also Clubb et al., 1980: 104, 165).

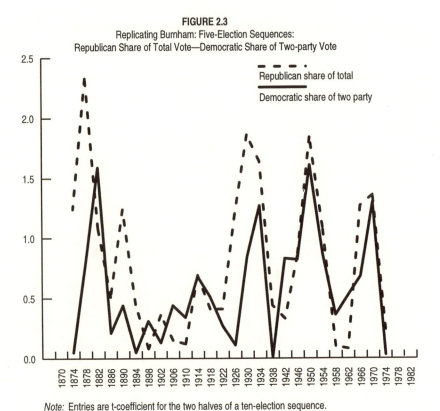

FIGURE 2.3
Replicating Burnham: Five-Election Sequences:
Republican Share of Total Vote—Democratic Share of Two-party Vote

Note: Entries are t-coefficient for the two halves of a ten-election sequence.

Furthermore, t rebounds from its low point of .12 in 1958 to another clear peak of 1.79 in 1966 before decreasing again to 1.20 in 1970 and .56 in 1974. The 1966 election, of course, separates the Truman through Johnson elections, which already marked a weakening of Democratic performance from the immediately preceding period, from the Nixon through Reagan period. The value of t is the same in 1966 as it was in 1950: it is not as large as for 1894 or 1930, but both spikes suggest a change in election outcome of the type, if not quite of the magnitude, of the earlier years that are rather consensually regarded as realignments.

But if neither 1950 not 1966 alone produces quite the *magnitude* of change of 1894 or 1930, it should also be clear that their partisan impact is cumulative: each marks a decrease in Democratic performance, and together they reduce the Democrats' share of the vote almost as much as the 1930 realignment increased it; mean Democratic percentage of the popular vote falls 12.8% between 1932–1948 and 1968–1984, a decrease nearly as large as the 16.2% increase that 1932–1948 registered compared to 1912–1928 and considerably larger in magnitude than the 5.5% loss the Democrats suffered in 1894.[13]

These results cannot be seen as an artifact of the way the data analysis in Figure 2.2 is set up. Figure 2.3 reproduces Figure 2.2 for two different ways of handling the election results: Democratic share of the two-party (as opposed to the total) popular vote and Republican share of the total vote. Figure 2.3 is a guard against the possibility that the third parties which have played a role in four of the post-war elections (1948, 1968, 1980, 1992) might have distorted results based on Democratic share of the total vote and, thereby, caused mistaken conclusions about the two shifts of 1950 and 1966.

A comparison of the curves in Figure 2.3 and between them and Figure 2.2 clearly shows some differences, but the differences are quite modest: Figure 2.3 clearly shows the two periods of abrupt post-war change. If anything, the changed focus of analysis alters conclusions about the consensually-agreed realignment of 1930: both curves show a considerably lower (if still clear) peak for 1930 than emerged from the Democratic percentage of total vote in Figure 2.2; the two post-war peaks in t are only very slightly reduced in Figure 2.3, making them much closer in magnitude to the classic realignment of 1930. The only other twentieth-century change in Figure 2.3 is that the second of the post-war shifts now appears to be centered more in 1970 than in 1966: the curve for Republican percentage of total vote shows this clearly, whereas the curve for Democratic share of the two-party vote hits two more-or-less similar peaks in 1966 and 1970.

Figure 2.4 replicates the preceding Figures using eight-election rather than ten-election sequences, relaxing Burnham's requirements somewhat, as Clubb et al. (1980) and Brady and Hurley (1985) did, to let sixteen years be sufficient to establish a baseline for electoral change. The changed procedures again generate some modest changes in results: the first of the post-war peaks increases considerably in magnitude, rivaling 1930, is centered more in 1946 than 1950;[14] it now greatly exceeds the (surviving) 1966–1970 peak in scale. But these are minor matters: the

FIGURE 2.4
Replicating Burnham: Four-Election Sequences

Note: Entries are t-coefficient for the two halves of an eight-election sequence: the year indicates the mid-point of the eight-election sequence.

differences across Figures 2.2, 2.3, and 2.4 are far less important than what all three of them show. Whether the mid-points are 1946 and 1966 or 1950 and 1970, whether the magnitude of the changes is as great as the classic realignments of the past; there is clearly a realignment-like shift in presidential election outcomes in both 1946–1950 and 1966–1970 that requires some serious scholarly attention.

It might be useful to use the term mini-realignment to convey the two factors that distinguish the two substantial pro-Republican shifts since World War II from the classic realignments of the literature reviewed above. First, the magnitude of changes in the pattern of outcomes is smaller than in 1896 or 1932: the clear peaks of Burnham's t-test analysis emerge for the two mini-realignments, but neither peak is as dramatic as those to which he referred. Second, the term mini-realignment refers to a pattern of presidential election outcomes alone rather than to the full package of changes associated with the classic realignments of the past; dealignment theorists are quite convincing about the lack of accompanying changes in sub-presidential voting or party loyalty and about the failure of Republicans to establish united control of government.[15] But the data make clear that there has nonetheless been a systematic reduction in the Democratic proportion of the popular vote.

The first of these mini-realignments occurred around 1946 or 1950 and transformed a clear Democratic presidential majority into a quite competitive system in which either party could (and did) win elections on the basis of short-term factors; the second occurred around 1966 or 1970 and transformed the balanced system of 1952–1968 into one in which the Republicans were clearly dominant. Each of these mid-points has already been identified as a point at which dealignment of the electoral system began (Silbey, 1991; Burnham, 1991); Figures 2.2 through 2.4 make clear that each of them also replaced one stable balance of party forces with another that lasted about twenty years. The mini-realignments occurred earlier in the life-span of the existing party system than the forty years that conventional realignment predicted; they produced changes smaller in magnitude that conventional realignment theory predicted; and they of course were not associated with the assorted side effects that over time had come to be seen as part of the realignment package such as surges in mass participation, changes in party identification, and shifts in the pattern of sub-presidential election outcomes. At the level of presidential outcomes, however, each took the *form* of a realignment, and their cumulative impact was clearly to transform a Democratic presidential majority into a Republican presidential majority.

THE PUZZLE OF POST-1968
PRESIDENTIAL ELECTION OUTCOMES

We seem to have here an intellectual puzzle of considerable interest. The pattern of outcomes at the presidential level is pretty much what generated the development of realignment theory nearly forty years ago: one stable pattern of outcomes separated from another stable pattern of outcomes by a relatively brief period of dramatic change. The two post-war mini-realignments began prematurely and were perhaps smaller in magnitude that a classic realignment should be, but they are nonetheless clear examples of the kind of sharp discontinuous change that Key and Campbell and Burnham observed, and their cumulative effect has certainly been equal to a classic realignment in magnitude as well.

And yet, timing is not the only problem with applying classic realignment theory to the post-1968 world: these changes in outcomes have occurred without any of the accompanying side processes that mature realignment theory would have had us expect. The discontinuity between the pattern of presidential outcomes and the continued Democratic domination of sub-presidential elections is the most obvious system-level anomaly: classic realignment theory would have allowed sub-presidential outcomes to lag the presidential pattern somewhat, but forty years between the first mini-realignment and Republican resurgence in congressional elections or at the state and local level seems excessive. Only Republican capture of the Senate in 1980 provides contrary evidence, and the capture lasted only as long as it took the 1980 class of new senators to complete their first terms; the Republicans' 1994 congressional gains occurred, ironically, only after the Democrats recaptured the presidency.

At the individual level, as well, there is again little evidence of the side processes that should combine with the pattern of presidential outcomes to produce a classic realignment package. Until 1984, there was no evidence of Republican gains in party identification of the kind that might underlie continued Republican presidential success: the Democrats had maintained their advantage over the Republicans between 1968 and 1976 even as the overall strength of partisanship in the electorate declined (Wattenberg, 1984; Beck, 1984). The Republicans did make gains in party identification in 1984, but at their height the gains left the party behind the Democrats at a time when the decline in strength of identification itself had halted.[16] New issues have emerged to crosscut the economic cleavages that defined the New Deal system, but there is evidence of neither a Republican majority on new issues (social or racial) nor of a move to the right sufficient to produce a conservative and Republican majority on the old ones (Smith, 1990; Robinson and Fleishman, 1988; Kelley, 1983; Sundquist, 1983). Social groups have lost their traditional issue-based partisan allegiances, but no current set of issues seems capable of producing clear-cut new ones (see Petrocik, 1981).

These cross-level and individual-level developments are of course what stimulated the dealignment thesis, the argument that the stable New Deal system has fallen apart without the emergence of any new stable pattern to replace it. But dealignment seems entirely incapable of explaining the pattern of presidential outcomes: the sequence of presidential election results looks almost exactly like the classic pattern of realignment that caught Campbell's attention and that Burnham so simply yet elegantly measured. It may be the case that we are seeing a series of short-term candidate-based coalitions or that election outcomes represent a series of retrospective judgments on incumbent administrations (Schneider, 1985: 205). But dealignment theorists cannot quite deal convincingly with the consistency with which the successful candidate-based coalitions have generally, since 1952, been Republican. Ladd and Hadley (1978: 377) write that recent political developments "surely [have] not, and will not produce a new Republican majority," but that does in fact seem to be the pattern of recent presidential election outcomes: there is hardly the random alteration of the parties in power or the volatility of election outcomes that dealignment theorists expect (see also Ladd, 1982: 108; Wattenberg, 1984: 131). It is precisely the sustained incongruence between what is happening in terms of presidential outcomes and what is happening sub-presidentially or in terms of individual attitudes that makes the era between 1952 and 1992 so distinctive. A full-blown traditional realignment has certainly not occurred; but the disaggregation that dealignment theorists point to in individual attitudes has clearly not produced the instability in presidential election outcomes that they expected.[17] And yet it is difficult to understand the stability of recent outcomes if all of the processes that realignment theory suggests should accompany and reinforce a stable pattern of outcomes are lacking.

The failure of the realignment model to account for the Democratic presidential majority is in a very real sense unfortunate: the argument of a new cleavage pattern, firmly anchored in party identification, that produces unified control of government and leads to effective implementation of a coherent policy agenda is an extremely powerful one, a tightly structured argument that accounts for developments at multiple levels of the political system. What is clear after some forty years of waiting for the other pieces to fall into place is that the theory, however attractive, simply does not describe the electoral system's current operation (Shafer et al., 1991a). If one accepts that there is a clear pattern to the presidential outcomes of the post-war world, as the figures above force us to do, and if one is reluctant to accept the *ad hoc* election-specific explanations of dealignment theorists that could, however unlikely, produce this (or any other) set of outcomes, one has to start with somewhat different kinds of explanations.

NOTES

* A much earlier version of this chapter (co-authored with Richard Fleisher) appeared in the spring 1987 *Political Science Quarterly*. Walter Dean Burnham and Carll Everett Ladd provided helpful commentary on earlier drafts of the article.

1. As Andersen (1979) points out, changes in the overall distribution of party loyalties can of course be due to mobilization of the previously uninvolved as well as to conversion from one party loyalty to another. She argues that mobilization was the primary source of Democratic gains around 1932; Erickson and Tedin (1981) disagree.

2. The across-the-board shift to the Republicans in 1896 causes Key (1955) to argue that 1896 was not a critical election in Massachusetts. The reinforced regional cleavages of course, make 1896 a critical election nationally, and it was certainly a realigning election in Campbell's sense even in Massachusetts.

3. Interestingly, Burnham argues that the transformation of competitive areas into areas of one-party dominance may in fact depress turnout, as occurred during and after the realignment of 1896.

4. The technique will always detect surges, but interactive change of the type that originally interested Key will be missed to the extent that the interactions offset each other and produce no overall change in the distribution of the popular vote.

5. Burnham also finds a peak in t at 1874, mid-way through the 1854–1894 party system. This premature change might be seen as damaging to the argument that realignment occurs at roughly forty-year intervals; Burnham (1970: 17) offers the more satisfying explanation that the 1874 peak is at least in part a result of institutional rather than behavioral change, a response to the readmission of the white south to full citizenship and to the subsequent surge in Democratic strength.

6. Clubb et al. make exclusive use of aggregate voting statistics—returns for states and counties—to analyze both interactive and surge aspects of realignment. Survey data, when available, is clearly superior for such arguments, but the nature of the data they use is not directly relevant to the use we make of their work here.

7. Stokes (1966) introduces the very useful distinction between position and valence issues. Position issues involve disagreement about courses of action: opposing sides differ

over what policy to follow. Valence issues involve generally valued or generally opposed states of affairs, with opposing sides differing over who can achieve the desired (or avoid the unpleasant) goal.

8. Sundquist believes that the familiar class-based New Deal system is nonetheless likely to continue: the decline of parties is limited in scope, even among the young, making full-blown dealignment unlikely; and there is no evidence of highly salient new issues on which the parties take clear and opposing positions of the kind that could create an issue-basis for a new party system either.

9. Wattenberg (1984) sets his discussion of the irrelevance of parties as a disagreement with the Nie, Verba, Petrocik (1979) conclusion that parties have become unpopular.

10. Wattenberg (1984: 91) adds that media coverage of campaigns increasingly focuses on candidates rather than parties, further weakening the public's use of party-based cues in vote choice.

11. The point holds, I think, despite there having been but one pre-Clinton period of unified control of government since the era of dealignment began; on the Carter experience, see Polsby (1983: ch. 3). Clinton's first half-term experience would seem to broadly confirm the generalization.

12. Keith et al. (1992) have made a powerful argument that dealignment theorists exaggerate the extent to which parties have declined. It is certainly true that the number of partisans remains high, a fact obscured by failure of some polling groups to ask the question the NES uses to identify leaning Democrats and leaning Republicans, groups Keith et al. argue share numerous characteristics with their less reticent partisan colleagues. And partisanship does remain the most powerful single predictor of individual vote choice. But dealignment theorists are undoubtedly correct in pointing to a relative decline in both the magnitude of mass partisanship and in its impact on vote choice.

13. Standard deviations were considerably smaller on both sides of the 1894 mid-point: for 1896–1912 it was 3.55, while for 1876–1892 it was an even smaller 1.74.

14. Silbey (1991: 16) sees 1948–1952 as the transition from the New Deal party system to what he calls a "postalignment" era characterized by sufficient dealignment to make the idea of a stable party system impossible. He echoes Clubb et al. (1980) on 1948's marking the end of the mature New Deal system.

15. Ladd (1995: 3) makes the useful point that parts of the full realignment package may be of interest (and significance) even in the absence of a full-blown realignment.

16. The 1988 NES survey had 13 percent fewer Republicans than Democrats if all identifiers are included and 21 percent fewer if the weakest, leaning partisans are omitted. The generally noted decline in strength of mass partisanship ends in 1976 and is partially reversed thereafter; for an extended argument that the extent and significance of the decline was greatly exaggerated by those who failed to realize that leaning identifiers (whose ranks increased most over time) act much as partisans do, see Keith et al. (1992).

17. We are not even in Clubb et al.'s second stage of a party system: divided control of government was not due to occasional capture of one of the agencies of government by a minority party recovering from years in the political wilderness, but by a former minority party that fairly consistently and fairly comfortably won presidential elections. Ronald Reagan became the first Republican since Eisenhower in 1952 to have a Republican majority in even one house of Congress. Shafer (1991b) recognizes the pattern of Republican victory, but presents only fragmentary evidence to support the rather complex explanation that he discusses.

3

The Decline of New Deal Economic Cleavage: Social Class and Issue Salience

The two mini-realignments that transformed a solid Democratic presidential majority in the 1940s into a solid Republican presidential majority in the 1980s were very different in character. Investigation of the first of them is limited by the fact that the golden age of academic survey research begins only after the 1946–1950 period when change occurred. But it is nonetheless possible to use more fragmentary pre-1946 materials to establish the broad outlines of the early post-war era and to then chart the continuation of trends and their consequences into the 1950s and early 1960s.

Class and the economics of class had been the single greatest building blocks for Democratic dominance of presidential elections since the Depression. The Democrats profited from such concerns in two distinct ways: first, as the party believed best able to produce prosperity in general; second, as the defender of the particular economic interests of the disadvantaged majority. Increasing prosperity in the immediate post-war years clearly threatened both appeals: rising affluence and the simple passage of time since 1929–1932 diluted the relevance of Republican economic failure in the Hoover years at the same time as it reduced the ranks of those who constituted the Democratic blue-collar base. Increasing affluence combined with increasing distance to the Depression to gradually but inexorably deprive the Democrats of the social basis of the Roosevelt coalition.

SOCIAL CLASS AND THE BASIS OF THE NEW DEAL COALITION

The realignment of 1896 is usually seen as introducing an era in which Democratic and Republican voters were little differentiated by social class. The Depression of 1893 occurred under a Democratic president: the result was catastrophic for the Democrats in general and for the conservative, eastern, hard-money faction of the party which Cleveland represented in particular. The nomination in 1896 of William Jennings Bryan, prairie radical and advocate of free silver, and the *de facto* union of Democrats and Populists were based on a strategy of uniting farmers losing out to the new industrial order with the emerging working class within the newly industrialized northeast and midwest. It was an unsuccessful strategy: Bryan failed to win over the industrial workers, while McKinley swept the country outside the south, mountain states, and parts of the great plains. Within the industrialized regions of the country, McKinley's victory was based on support from all social strata, as regional interests and identity replaced class as a basis for political loyalty. The election of 1896 ushered in the Fourth Party System, in which most of the country became non-competitive, with one party dominant and relatively low rates of mass political participation (Burnham, 1970: 84).[1]

The proto-realignment phenomena of the late Fourth Party System were various Progressive movements which dealt to at least some extent with issues of concentration of economic power and uneven economic distribution that one might expect would stimulate class-based politics at the mass level. But Progressivism was a movement within each of the major parties rather than a weapon of one against the other, and even if one accepts Sarasohn's (1989) argument that the Democrats were consistently more Progressive after 1896 than the Republicans (or than their own general image among historians), such concern did not lead to a strong class basis of vote choice at the individual level. Not until 1928, with the nomination of Al Smith—a northeastern reformer whose strength may well have been due more to ethnic/religious factors and his position on prohibition than to a more general reformist appeal—did the Democrats made gains among the urban, blue-collar, and Catholic voters who were later to become core components of the New Deal coalition and break the pattern of minimal class polarization that had characterized the Fourth Party System (Key, 1955; Lubell, 1965: 48 ff.; Burnham, 1970: 24; Sundquist, 1983: 193).

These changes may well have continued and come to dominate the divisions between Democrats and Republicans even without the onset of the Depression. But the greatest economic catastrophe in American history, with unemployment reaching 25 percent, accelerated and magnified the process that the 1928 campaign began. The Depression became a powerful pro-Democratic valence issue based on popular images of the Republicans as the party of hard times. As Sundquist (1983) convincingly argues, the fact that Democrats and Republicans took clear and different positions on government responses to the Depression, with the Democrats increasingly the party of governmental economic and social welfare activism that the Republicans opposed, allowed citizens to link opposing solutions to the central issues of the day to the parties even after simple retrospective judgments of Hoover might be expected to fade. Even a partial economic recovery under the Democrats in the mid-1930s created a powerful two-barreled economic appeal that provided the main underlying basis for the Roosevelt majority.[2]

The 1932 election was an across-the-board repudiation of the failed Hoover administration, with Roosevelt drawing electoral support from a broad range of social groupings. By 1936, however, simple retrospective considerations had receded somewhat, and Roosevelt's appeal was much more concentrated among the groups who were thereafter to form the basis of the new Democratic presidential majority: the Democrats became the party of blue-collar workers, the cities, immigrants, Catholics, and blacks; the Republicans made gains among rural, Protestant, and middle-class elements who had been temporarily swept up in the 1932 retrospective rejection of Hoover (Sundquist, 1983: 215). Several authors (Sundquist, 1983: 218; Abramson, 1975: 7–8; Burnham, 1970: 56) have linked the emergence of this class polarization to the failure of the 1936 *Literary Digest* poll to correctly predict Roosevelt's re-election landslide: the poll had successfully predicted Roosevelt's 1932 victory, but the new class polarization in voting patterns in 1936 made the *socially* unrepresentative upper-SES sample that had traditionally been used *politically* unrepresentative for the first time.

There is general agreement in the literature that social class became the core basis of partisan differentiation in the mature New Deal party system. Lubell (1965: 63) cited rent levels as a powerful predictor of the Roosevelt vote in 1936. Ladd and Hadley (1978: 69) report American Institute for Public Opinion polls indicating a 29 percentage point difference in Democratic between high and low socio-economic status citizens voting in 1936, increasing to 31 percent in 1940; 39 percent of the college educated voted for Roosevelt in 1940, compared to 67 percent among those with less than a high school education.[3] Sundquist (1983: 225) attributes the partial Republican recovery in 1938 both to the continued receding of simple negative retrospective evaluations of Hoover and the Republicans into the past and to defection by conservative Democrats dissatisfied with the new Democratic commitment to social and economic activism to a Republican party decreasingly tainted by its failures of the previous decade. But Democratic dominance based on economics and on class appeals for the most part remained strong. By 1940, Lazarsfeld et al.'s pioneering study of vote choice found considerable differences in preferences of lower and upper status respondents, with social class one of three social background characteristics so powerfully related to vote choice as to justify a conclusion that "social characteristics determine political preference" (1968: 27). Economics and social welfare became the central defining issues of the Roosevelt era, and on both the majority of the American electorate saw the Democrats as the party of choice. By the beginning of the age of widespread survey research in the post-war era, the vast majority of Americans had come to think of themselves as Democrats, and the economics/social welfare issues that had forged that identity in the 1930s continued to reinforce it.

By the end of World War II, however, two interrelated developments were changing the class basis of Democratic electoral strength: changes in the composition of the electorate and changes in the degree of electoral polarization on the basis of social class. A combination of economic reforms set in motion by the New Deal and recovery stimulated by the war itself had helped shift the numerical balance between those receiving and those paying for social welfare benefits in a way that undermined the electoral appeal of the party of the underdog. Increasingly in the

post-war world, voters were no longer dependent on government programs designed to off-set economic hardships: unemployment rates fell, real per capita income rose, educational opportunity expanded. The changed composition reversed
the economic and electoral logic of the New Deal, "taxing the many on behalf of
the few" rather than "taxing the few for the benefit of the many" (Phillips 1970: 37;
see also Edsall and Edsall, 1991: 12; Gopoian, 1993: 159). The argument is quite
consistent with Sundquist's (1983) claim that the basic cleavage structure of the
New Deal system remained intact in the 1950s: what had changed was that fewer
voters fell on the Democratic side of the class divide, making the party less likely to
win elections fought on such terms than they had been twenty years earlier.[4]

The second change is decreased class polarization of the electorate. Sundquist
(1983) is undoubtedly right in claiming that such polarization continues into the
post-war world, but there is considerable evidence that its magnitude is decreased.
Campbell et al. (1960: 347ff) report that the degree of class polarization in vote
choice declines between 1948 and 1956, a finding Ladd and Hadley (1978: 73) confirm for non-southern whites; Pomper (1975: 57) finds modest and slightly declining association between occupation (a simple dichotomy of manual and non-
manual occupations) and vote choice between 1960 and 1972 (see also Huckfeldt
and Kohfeld, 1989: 3; Abramson, 1975: 14). Individual elections in which economic
issues assumed particular prominence could of course lead to temporary surges in
the relevance of class to vote choice: Ladd and Hadley (1978: 102) and Pomper
(1975: 48) argue that 1964 was such an election. But the overall pattern since 1952
is for there to be a rather modest association between class and vote choice, and the
pattern of change since the high point of the New Deal system is certainly one of
decline.

Three bases exist for this decreased polarization. First, upward economic mo-
bility of a large number of previously Democratic voters did not necessarily translate into Republican votes. Party loyalties forged during the Depression were not
automatically abandoned with the first hint of post-war prosperity. A generation
scarred during their formative years by the Depression developed a powerful link
to the Democrats that they carried with them into adult life. The new middle class
created in the years of post-war economic growth was more professional and mana-
gerial (Ladd and Hadley, 1978: 107) and, therefore, more Democratic than the
traditionally Republican entrepreneurial middle class (Lubell 1965: 69), creating
the weakened Republican advantage among upper-SES voters and a reduced difference in the vote choice of higher and lower SES groups.[5]

Second, the simple passage of time diluted the impact of class on vote choice by
allowing the new issues and new voters that have long been seen as fundamental
sources of electoral change to emerge (Schattschneider, 1960; Sundquist, 1983).
One would expect that issues unanticipated in 1932–1936 would not necessarily
coincide with and reinforce the class-based concerns that shaped the New Deal
party system. All voters would be affected by these new issues, but their impact
would be most powerfully felt by younger voters who knew the 1930s second-hand

rather than through immediate personal experience. Research from the 1950s had already demonstrated that attitudes on economic issues were at best weakly associated with attitudes on race, civil liberties, and international affairs (see Berelson et al., 1954: 197; Key, 1961: chapter 7), with upper-SES groups relatively liberal on all three of the latter.[6] The increasing salience of race and of Scammon and Wattenberg's (1971) Social Issue in the early and mid-1960s, combined with emergence of Miller and Levitin's (1976) New Politics issues focusing on the environment, life style, and abortion on which the same pattern existed, further strained the class to vote link.[7] The result is a new issue basis for vote choice that cuts against and therefore weakens links between social class and vote choice.

Third, both parties altered the basis of their electoral appeal in the post-war years in ways that both respond to and reinforce the weakening of class appeals. The post-war Republicans avoided advocating a roll-back of the New Deal (Key, 1961: 124; Ladd and Hadley, 1978: 73), maintaining a decision to accept the bulk of Roosevelt's reforms initially made in the nomination of Wilkie in 1940 in choosing Eisenhower over Taft for the 1952 presidential nomination. Eisenhower's administration pursued moderate economic and social welfare policies designed to avoid antagonizing those supportive of or benefiting from Roosevelt's policies (Abramson, 1975: 38). Democrats had an interest in maintaining their appeal to those who were by tradition Democratic but whose economic and social status had changed since the depths of the Depression. Stevenson, initially drawn to politics through an interest in foreign affairs (Martin, 1976: 637), ran a campaign in which class-based appeals were subdued,[8] drawing criticism from those who saw his nomination and campaign as a retreat from the social and economic populism that was capable of mobilizing a left-wing majority (Newfield and Greenfield, 1972).[9]

Depolarization need not, of course, adversely affect the Democrats. Several authors (Ladd and Hadley, 1978: 102; Pomper, 1975: 48) have observed that class polarization seemed to increase somewhat in years like 1960 or 1964 in which the Democrats won (see also Ferguson and Rogers, 1986: 36 and Kusnet, 1992: 68). But changes in group voting patterns could in principle help either party or be entirely neutral in their effects: a decline in the Democratic character of blue-collar workers would of course have adverse consequences for the Democrats if white-collar workers were to retain their degree of Republicanism; but it is also possible that losses in blue-collar loyalty could be compensated for by comparable gains among traditionally hostile white-collar voters or that the same factors that push some blue-collar workers to the Republicans could push some white-collar workers in that direction as well, maintaining the gap between the groups and advantaging the Republicans generally. The partisan consequences of polarization or depolarization constitute an inherently empirical question.

COMPOSITION AND POLARIZATION SINCE 1952

Table 3.1 illustrates the decreasing size of the Democrats' class-based constituency over time. The fact that the American National Election Studies begin in 1952 force us to use other data sources to demonstrate the extent of the economic transformation that occurred between the height of the Depression and even the early years of post-war recovery.

Table 3.1 shows the conventional portrait of economic collapse and recovery in the period surrounding the Depression. Unemployment reaches a peak in 1933 at 25.2% of the workforce; disposable personal income falls over 30% between 1929 and 1933, while real mean weekly earnings for the employed fall 14.4% by 1932. Gradual improvement on all these indicators during the 1930s is interrupted in 1938: unemployment rises and earnings fall. But the subsequent recovery, accelerating with the approach of World War II, sees unemployment almost disappear by

TABLE 3.1

Class Related Characteristics of the Electorate Over Time:
Comparison of Pre- and Post-War Periods

Year	Unemployment[a]	Real Mean Weekly Earnings[b]	Disposable Personal Income[c]	Median Years of Education[d]
1929	3.2	43.0	1,286	
1930	8.9	41.1		
1931	16.3	40.5		
1932	24.1	36.8		
1933	25.2	38.2	893	
1934	22.0	40.5		
1935	20.3	43.3		
1936	17.0	46.4		
1937	14.3	49.4		
1938	19.1	46.7		
1939	17.2	50.6		
1940	14.6	53.1	1,259	8.6
1941	9.9	59.3		
1942	4.7	66.3		
1943	1.9	73.5		
1944	1.2	77.3		
1945	1.9	72.8	1,642	
1946	3.9			
1947	3.9	66.0		
1948	3.8			
1949	5.9			
1950	5.3	72.8	1,646	9.3
1955	4.4	84.3	1,795	
1960	5.6	89.5	1,883	10.6

Notes: a. Unemployment data are from Lebergott (1964: 512).
   b. Real mean weekly earnings are for workers in manufacturing and are expressed as a percentage of the level for 1967. Source is Robertson and Walton (1979: 482–483).
   c. Disposable personal income is in 1958 dollars. Source is U.S. Bureau of the Census (1969: 317).
   d. Median level of education is from U.S. Bureau of the Census (1969: 109).

1943 while earnings and income both increase. The difficult transition to a peace-time economy shows up in entries for 1945 and 1946, but by 1950 both earnings variables show considerable improvement. The dramatic fall in unemployment and the rise in various measures of real income make clear the extent of an economic recovery which cannot but reduce the ranks of the economically disadvantaged who had rallied behind Franklin Roosevelt and the New Deal.

Table 3.2 shifts attention from composition of the electorate to polarization, illustrating the rather consistently low levels of association (Somer's D asymmetric) between these measures of socio-economic status and vote choice over time.

Education, income, and occupation all[10] show relationships with vote choice after 1952 that could be characterized as modest at best. For education the D never exceeds .15 and is below .10 in five of the ten elections. The D for income is under .10 for the first six elections in the series, and although it moves somewhat higher thereafter it never exceeds the rather modest level of .15. The D for occupation is at its highest in 1952 at .24, but it exceeds .18 only one other time. These associations do not demonstrate the irrelevance of social class for vote choice since 1952, but they do indicate a pattern of association consistently modest in magnitude. Lazarsfeld et al. (1968: 27) concluded on the basis of their 1940 Erie County study that "social characteristics determine political preference," with social class one of the two core social characteristics they studied; one would find no reason to conclude the same from Table 3.2.

Alternate operationalizations of the variables used in Table 3.2 produce no particular changes in the results: separating those with college degrees from those without, use of the original NES income categories rather than the equal sixths, or placing non-voters in a category intermediate between Democratic and Republican

TABLE 3.2
Vote Choice and Socio-economic Status

	1952	1956	1960	1964	1968	1972	1976	1980	1984	1988
Education[a]	.15	.08	.09	.12	.15	.03	.14	.13	.09	.07
Income[b]	.08	.07	.00	.07	.08	.09	.15	.15	.15	.11
Occupation[c]	.24	.11	.15	.18	.18	.03	.21	.14	.07	.06
Subjective Class[d]	.27	.17	.15	.00	.18	.07	.21	.18	.11	.16
Union Membership	.21	.17	.24	.21	.10	.08	.19	.13	.17	.15

Entries are Somer's D asymmetric with the dependent variable in each case a vote intention with three categories: intended Democratic vote, planning to vote but uncertain for whom, intended Republican vote.

Notes: a. Education is a five-category variable in which the categories are grade school, some high school, high school graduate, some college, college graduate.

     b. Income is pre-tax family income, using the original NES income categories, which vary in number over time.

     c. Occupation is a simple dichotomy between manual and non-manual occupation of head of household, including all those currently working or temporarily laid off.

     d. Subjective class is the respondent's self-identification as working or middle class.

voters rather than excluding them all produce the same depressingly small values for D; separating out groups known to be insensitive to the effects of social class (blacks and southern whites) produces only modest changes for the remaining non-southern whites. Subjective class works no better than the objective measures, and even union membership has minimum impact on vote choice.[11] Social class may well have been the primary social cleavage of the mature New Deal electoral system, but its importance was already quite modest by the beginning of the NES studies in 1952 and has for the most part declined somewhat since.

Several authors thought in the mid-1970s that they saw initial signs of a new relationship between class and vote choice in which the most Democratic segments of the population would be found at the top and bottom of the status hierarchy. Ronald Inglehart (1977) argues that satisfaction of fundamental subsistence needs has allowed a new generation of affluent Americans (and others in wealthy western nations) to concern themselves with more abstract, higher-order values of self-realization and self-expression that might predispose them to vote for left-wing parties. Ladd and Hadley (1978: 213ff) argue that, among whites at least, high social status is associated with liberal positions on race and on other social/cultural issues included in Miller and Levitin's (1976) New Politics. This provides a basis for those at the top of the status hierarchy to cast a Democratic vote that cuts against both their most narrowly conceived economic interests and their traditional voting pattern. Pomper (1975: 53ff) agrees, finding that both education and occupation in 1972 show evidence of the top-bottom alliance against the middle: the most Democratic portion of the electorate consists of those with the highest and lowest levels of education, of professionals and unskilled blue-collar workers.

Ladd and Hadley (1978: 288) themselves concede that evidence for their class inversion weakens somewhat in 1976. Data analysis of the type reported in Table 3.2 makes clear that whatever tendencies of this type existed in 1972 remain at best extremely modest in size thereafter. For income, there is no evidence of the curvilinear pattern at all: the wealthiest sixth of the population is consistently the most Republican. For education, the rather weak link to vote choice in both 1976 and 1980 is entirely monotonic: each step up in level of education shows lower levels of Democratic voting and higher levels of Republican voting. For 1984 and 1988, the college-educated are clearly more Republican than any less educated group: strong monotonicity does break down if one separates out those who completed college degrees, but even there the reversal of the pattern is extremely small in 1988.

If one looks at the behavior of the groups defined by the variables in Table 3.2, one gets more evidence that these characteristics have simply not been of very great importance since the first of the mini-realignments that transformed the clear pattern of Democratic dominance in 1932–1948 into the competitive world of 1952–1968. The low Ds in Table 3.2 are due to considerable disagreements *among* the high and the low in SES: neither social group is overwhelmingly partisan in its vote in a way that sets up dramatic differences between the groups.

In 1960, for example, blue-collar workers intending to vote preferred Kennedy to Nixon by 48.5% to 38.7%, while white-collar workers preferred Nixon by 51.5% to 35.5%. This is a real difference, but substantial minorities of both groups defy Lazarsfeld et al.'s expectations, and the D of .15 reflects the modest nature of the overall relationship. In 1964, one does find the kind of solidarity among blue-collar workers that might have been more characteristic of the mature New Deal system, with 75.3% intending to vote for Johnson. But this is hardly a sign of class polarization: the short-term events of 1964 cause 58.6% of white-collar workers to vote Democratic as well. The D of .18 between occupational status and vote choice illustrates the rather modest degree of polarization on the basis of class.

Table 3.3 shows more systematically how divided all of the class-related groupings have been in recent elections. The Table shows the percentage of those who intend to vote for one of the major party candidates who vote consistently with what one would think would be their group norms. Given that non-voters and the undecided are omitted, a figure of fifty percent means only that the group as a whole divides evenly between the two candidates. An entry between fifty percent and two-thirds means that group's members follow the presumed norm by a margin of less than two to one, hardly an indication that the norm is effective.

Under those conditions, the entries in Table 3.3 are clearly indicative of weak or non-existent group norms. For occupation, for example, only two of the twenty entries exceed the two-thirds level that might even loosely be characterized as group agreement. In 1964, 82.8% of blue-collar workers voted Democratic, while in 1972, 70.8% of white-collar workers voted Republican. But neither figure is a sign of

TABLE 3.3
Percentage of Group Members Following Expected Group Norms

	1952	1956	1960	1964	1968	1972	1976	1980	1984	1988
Blue-collar workers	57.5	46.6	55.6	82.8	55.3	31.2	60.6	57.8	41.0	49.4
White-collar workers	66.0	63.7	59.3	36.3	62.9	70.8	60.2	56.9	64.7	56.4
No high school diploma	53.8	47.6	50.5	80.6	56.0	34.9	64.4	65.5	57.3	50.9
At least some college	72.5	67.9	67.7	40.2	68.3	69.0	59.2	57.3	63.2	56.4
Richest sixth	72.6	65.7	64.1	38.4	68.5	83.3	68.2	63.1	70.8	69.0
Poorest sixth	50.3	46.1	43.1	75.5	55.6	39.1	65.0	68.4	63.0	60.8
Union family	59.6	55.0	63.4	86.6	53.3	37.4	64.3	60.6	54.8	60.4
Non-union family	61.3	62.0	60.9	32.9	57.1	70.6	53.9	52.8	62.6	55.2
Subjectively working	56.2	50.1	50.1	73.0	54.4	34.4	61.0	59.4	46.3	56.6
Subjectively middle	70.8	66.4	64.6	26.9	63.7	71.6	60.3	58.6	64.0	59.7

Entries are percentage of those intending to vote for one of the two major party candidates. Excluded are those who did not intend to vote, who did not know for whom they would vote, or who intended to vote for a third-party candidate.

polarization of the electorate by occupation: the same factors which pushed blue-collar workers to the Democrats in 1964 pushed white-collar workers there as well; only 36.3% of white-collar workers voted Republican in 1964. Similarly, both blue-collar and white-collar workers responded in 1972 to the powerful pro-Republican short-term forces at work in that election: the 70.8% of white-collar workers voting Republican is not matched by such class solidarity among blue-collar workers; only 31.2% of blue-collar workers voted Democratic! In *no* case do the two opposing groups both vote consistently with their group norms; in half of the ten elections, both groups give a majority of their votes to the same party!

The same kind of pattern holds for education. In 1952, the college-educated *do* give 72.5% of their vote to the Republicans; but those with less than a high school education are at the same time pushed towards the Republicans as well, giving only 53.8% of their vote to the Democratic party that would seem to be their natural home. Again, what one finds is a pattern of both low and high SES groups' being pushed simultaneously by short term forces that reinforce the supposed group norm for one while undermining it for the other: there is no year in which more than two-thirds of the two education groups both vote consistently with their presumed groups norms. The same overall pattern holds for the extreme categories of incomes and for both union membership and subjective class identification.

The generally low levels of class-related polarization emerge quite clearly from these post-1950 data. It might be misleading, however, to suggest that this constitutes a dramatic decrease in polarization since the New Deal years. The unanimity with which the accounts of the New Deal party system cited earlier characterized the electorate polarized over class is impressive, but the prose used to describe such relationships often exaggerated the actual differences that even the original authors found. Lazarsfeld et al., for example, rather considerably overstated the strength of the relationships they found in their 1940 data: a calculation of the association between social class and vote choice for their Chart 3 (1968: 19) produces a D of only .16, a coefficient reasonably low in absolute terms and essentially the same as the .15 reported for 1952 in Table 3.2; one would probably be reluctant to write a sentence claiming that "social characteristics determine political behavior" on the basis of such a finding. Comparison of occupation categories over time produces much the same picture. Gallup reports a break-down of vote choice by occupation categories in 1944 (1972: 4 September 1944) that shows professionals ten percent and businessmen twelve percent less Democratic than the population as a whole; in 1952, the comparable figures are 17.1% and 8.8%. Gallup reports that union members were thirteen percent more Democratic than the electorate as a whole in 1940 (1972: 3 September 1940) and sixteen percent more Democratic in 1948 (1972: 9 October 1948); the NES survey difference in 1952 is 14.2% and is between thirteen and sixteen percent in 1952, 1960, 1964, and 1976. Such comparisons should allay fears that the NES studies are somehow tainted by having begun immediately after some substantial reduction in polarization of the electorate by class in the immediate post-war or post-Roosevelt years: such polarization is lower than much of the prose written about the earlier period might suggest, but there is reason to think that the prose was over-written rather than that the change in actual levels of polarization was extremely large.[12]

The Figures below are attempts to disentangle the two interrelated processes of composition and polarization to determine the extent to which they might have hurt Democratic electoral prospects.[13] First, they chart the actual percentage of the two-party vote that the Democrats received in the NES survey in each year. They then chart the percentage the Democrats would be expected to receive under two sets of hypothetical conditions: if composition of the electorate were frozen as it had been in 1952, but voting patterns of different social groups varied as they in fact did thereafter; second, if group voting patterns were frozen as they were in 1952 but real changes in composition were allowed to take place. Comparison of the three lines over time allow one to estimate the direction and impact of composition changes and polarization changes over time.

Figure 3.1 reports an analysis of these changes using data on occupation, here operationalized as a crude distinction between white-collar and blue-collar occupations of heads of households. The Figure takes 1952 as a starting point, using information from the 1952 NES study about the numbers of blue- and white-collar workers in the electorate and the percentage Democratic of each group to compute

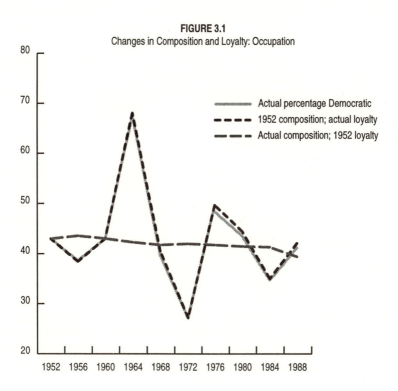

FIGURE 3.1
Changes in Composition and Loyalty: Occupation

Actual percentage Democratic
1952 composition; actual loyalty
Actual composition; 1952 loyalty

an expected Democratic vote in 1952 of 43.0%.[14] For the years after 1952, three data points are charted. The solid line is the actual vote produced in each year using the composition and loyalty data for that year. The two broken lines manipulate composition and loyalty in order to show the impact changing levels of each contribute to election outcome.

One broken line makes use of the 1952 composition data but takes the real loyalty data from each year's study: it reports the extent to which each year's change in loyalty would alter the percentage of the popular vote the Democrats would receive if the share of blue- and white-collar voters in the electorate remained constant. This is the broken line that very closely parallels the actual vote line: in each year, although loyalty of blue- and white-collar voters varies considerably in response to the short-term factors at work in the campaign, the factors affecting the two groups are more or less the same: Democrats may do better among their blue-collar base in some years, but the factors that cause them to do so produce an improved performance among white-collar workers as well. The net result is the generalized surge to or against the Democrats that closely parallels actual election outcome. Changes in polarization over time have only the most minor impact on election outcome. If anything, changed polarization produces a very small pro-Democratic effect after 1960: this is greatest in 1976, when the actual Democratic share of the vote was 48.2%; combining actual 1976 loyalty rates to the composition figures from 1952 produces a slightly higher expected Democratic performance of 49.5%. The difference is the largest for any of the nine post-1952 elections, and it is certainly small in absolute magnitude.[15]

The second broken line makes exactly the opposite assumption. It makes consistent use of loyalty data from 1952, assuming that blue- and white-collar workers divide their votes between Democrats and Republicans thereafter as they had done in the first Eisenhower-Stevenson contest, but it lets composition reflect the actual distribution of blue- and white-collar workers in each year. This second line clearly differs from the other two, showing no sign of varying with actual Democratic percentage of the vote. Rather, the line shows a steady but modest decline over the ten-election sequence, from the 43.0% of 1952 to 41.7% in 1968 to 39.4% in 1988 that mirrors the steady but modest deterioration of the Democrats' social base: the percentage of blue- and white-collar workers in the population has shifted in a way that over time reduces the number of votes that the Democrats can expect, even if polarization and its attendant loyalty rates do not change over time at all.[16] Figure 3.1 as a whole makes clear that changes in polarization over time have, if anything, a tiny pro-Democratic impact on election outcomes. The changing composition of the electorate, on the other hand, has had a clear negative impact on Democratic electoral fortunes.

Figure 3.2 shows even more dramatic examples of these trends, making use of data for education and income.[17] One can see in Figure 3.2a that changed composition effects of education after 1952 actually work to the advantage of the Democrats: their gains among the better educated more than offset whatever losses they suffer among the less educated. These gains do not occur suddenly after 1952 in a way that suggests that all that is at work here is atypical loyalty rates for 1952; rather, the changes occur gradually over the period as a whole, producing a small overestimate for the 1960s and somewhat larger ones beginning in 1976.

The line that traces the effects of changed composition is again distinctive in Figure 3.2a, and it again leads to the conclusion that changes in the educational composition of the electorate has hurt the Democrats. The deterioration is small in any one election but considerable in terms of the cumulative impact of small changes over time: combining actual composition with 1952 loyalty rates produces a decline in expected Democratic vote from 41.5% in 1952 to 38.4% in 1964 to 35.8% in 1976 to 33.8% in 1988. These changes are somewhat larger than for occupation. Again, the Democrats gain slightly from changed levels of polarization over time; they compensate for whatever losses they suffer in their core social groupings by gains in those previously disinclined to vote for them. But the decline in the size of their traditional social groupings constitutes a formidable accumulating source of electoral difficulty.[18]

Figure 3.2b looks remarkably like Figure 3.2a, increasing the likelihood that composition effects are real rather than some artifact of our operationalizations of the social structure variables. Changes in polarization work modestly to the advantage

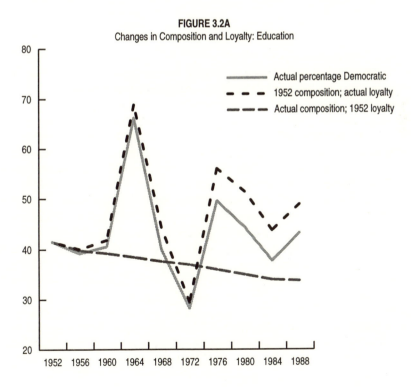

FIGURE 3.2A
Changes in Composition and Loyalty: Education

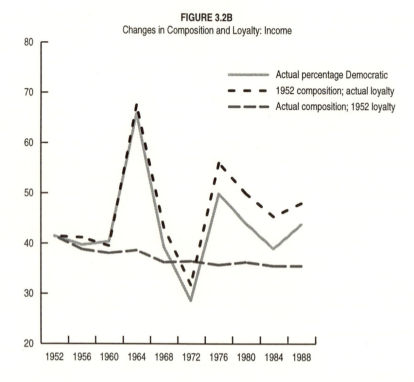

FIGURE 3.2B
Changes in Composition and Loyalty: Income

of the Democrats: if incomes had increased over time only to keep pace with inflation, the changed behavior of the income groupings over time would have produced a Democratic percentage of the popular vote in 1968 3.9% higher than they
actually received; in 1984, they would have done 6.5% better than they actually
did. The changed composition of the electorate, however, again shows pressures
working against the Democrats: because incomes increased faster than the rate of
inflation, the Democrats would have lost votes over time even if the loyalty rates of
1952 could have been maintained. As one would expect from the end of the rise in
per capita income after 1973, the bulk of this effect is apparent by 1972: composition effects reduce the Democratic share of the popular vote by 4.8% between 1952
and 1972; they drop only one more percentage point between 1972 and 1988.

Figures 3.1 and 3.2 produce a fairly clear picture of the impact traditional indicators of social class have on Democratic electoral performance. None of the three
indicators is entirely trustworthy, but the way in which they reinforce each other is
impressive. In all three instances, decreased polarization has actually helped the
Democrats. The magnitude of the impact is not great, but for education and income it is in the area of about five percent by the end of the period: decreased
polarization has changed the social basis of Democratic electoral support, but the

Democrats have gained somewhat more from upper-SES groupings than they lost from their traditional lower-SES constituency. But as the number of blue-collar workers has fallen, education levels have risen, and income growth has exceeded the rate of inflation, the ranks of those from whom the Democrats drew electoral strength have decreased in size. Changed composition has cost the Democrats between 3.6% and 7.7% of the popular vote, depending on which of the social class variables we look at; and these changes are since 1952, when much of the post-Depression change in composition of the electorate has already occurred. Scammon and Wattenberg pointed out to the Democrats in 1971 that the electorate was unyoung, unpoor, and unblack (1971: 45); Figures 3.1 and 3.2 make a powerful case for the shrinking of the Democrats' traditional social base and of the consequences such shrinkage could be expected to have for electoral performance.[19]

FOREIGN POLICY AS AN EMERGENT AREA
OF REPUBLICAN STRENGTH

The changed social composition of the electorate in the aftermath of the Depression provides a considerable problem for the Democrats: the number of citizens attracted by their program of help for the economically disadvantaged decreases as the state of the economy improves. But such changes are not the sole factor that troubles Democratic fortunes in the immediate post-war world. The war has many dramatic effects on American society: it is a major source of the economic growth that helps erase the remnants of Depression-based hard times; it sets in motion some of the social mobilization that helps propel race to the center of the nation's political agenda; and it has obvious major consequences for America's role in the new world order and for the significance of foreign policy questions in American electoral politics.

Foreign policy is usually assumed to have been of relatively little importance in the early 1930s. The United States had turned its back on international involvements in the aftermath of World War I, refusing to ratify the Treaty of Versailles or to join the League of Nations. And the centrality of economic concerns in the wake of the Depression itself would help crowd foreign affairs off the electoral agenda as well. But the changed circumstances of America's world position after World War II—one of the two super-powers, leader of one of the world's two armed camps, suddenly vulnerable to military attack by new weapons systems that make the traditional defenses of wide ocean boundaries and a strong navy insufficient—could be expected to give foreign policy new prominence on the electoral agenda after 1945.[20]

Gallup data make clear that foreign policy concerns are of importance to Americans even at the height of the New Deal, even if they take the form of citizens' merely wanting to avoid involvement in international affairs. Gallup asks respondents what they think are the most important national problems as early as November 1935, when they find that neutrality ranks third of over twenty different problems listed; two years later it advances to second place (Gallup, 1972).[21] In April 1939, when the approach of war in Europe is already clear, the 37 percent of the population who mention keeping out of war make it nation's single most important national problem (1972: 154). The immediate post-war period shows a relatively low salience of foreign policy questions. But by early 1947 the mention of foreign policy increases again: such problems either are mentioned by more than a third of the electorate (March 1948: Gallup, 1972: 726; March 1950: Gallup, 1972: 507) or are among the most frequently mentioned of a large number of problems (January 1947: Gallup, 1972: 623; July 1947: Gallup, 1972: 666; November 1949: Gallup, 1972: 867) cited in response to the most important national problem question.[22]

What is striking in the Gallup data, however, is that the rather infrequent questions about which party can best handle these foreign policy problems tend throughout the late 1940s to show an advantage for the Democrats. In September 1945, immediately after the end of the war in the Pacific, the electorate thought the Democrats more likely to work out a lasting peace by a margin of 45 percent to 14 percent (Gallup, 1972: 531). A question asked in October 1947 about which party could best handle foreign affairs shows the Democrats with a 33 percent to 28 percent advantage that is almost identical to their 35 percent to 29 percent advantage on domestic affairs (Gallup, 1972: 687). A July 1948 question on which party is best for dealing with Russia and other foreign countries produces a 30 percent to 24 percent Democratic advantage (Gallup, 1972: 836).

By the beginning of the 1950s, however, after the beginning of the Korean War, the Democratic advantage on foreign affairs is gone. Gallup shows the Republicans perceived to be best able to keep peace in August 1951 by a margin of 28 percent to 21 percent (Gallup, 1972: 1007), and the beginning of the NES surveys in 1952 show a pattern of Republican advantage on a highly salient set of foreign policy questions as well.

Table 3.4 shows the salience of foreign policy issues and the pattern of preferences on foreign policy for the first three NES presidential election studies. The data provide a fairly grim picture for the Democrats. Foreign policy is a highly salient area of popular concern: 45.9% of all respondents mention some foreign

TABLE 3.4
Salience of Foreign Policy Issues

	1952	1956	1960
Total	45.9	42.3	48.8
Party	29.0	23.8	25.2
Candidate	28.2	31.0	37.4

Entries are percentage of all respondents mentioning foreign policy as a basis for liking or disliking either party or candidate in response to open-ended questions.

TABLE 3.5

Preferences on Foreign Policy

	1952	1956	1960
Percentage preferring Democrats[a]	9.1	6.6	12.2
Percentage preferring Republicans[a]	34.7	34.0	32.8
Overall net preference[b]	−.441	−.507	−.375
Net preference: parties[b]	−.245	−.190	−.092
Net preference: candidates[b]	−.196	−.317	−.283
Net evaluation of Democrats[c]	−.146	−.136	−.046
Net evaluation of Republicans[c]	.296	.371	.329

Notes: All means are based on number of likes and dislikes of each party and candidate on the basis of foreign policy.

  a. Percentage of the total population with a net Democratic preference and a net Republican preference.
  b. Entries for total, party, and candidate are mean overall preference. Positive scores indicate a net Democratic preference; negative scores indicate a net Republican preference.
  c. Entries for Democrats and Republicans are net evaluation of each party/candidate separately. Positive scores indicate net approval; negative scores indicate disapproval.

policy concern as a basis for liking or disliking the parties and candidates in 1952, a figure that is essentially repeated in both 1956 and 1960. The salience of foreign policy cannot be attributed to the presence on the Republican ticket of Dwight Eisenhower, a military man with clear foreign policy experience: candidates are no more likely than parties to be evaluated in terms of such concerns in 1952, and both the relative and absolute frequency of comments about candidates increase in 1956 and 1960.

There is a pronounced partisan tilt to perceptions of the parties and candidates on foreign policy in all three of these elections. In 1952, for example, only 9.1% of the population have an overall preference for the Democrats, while 34.7% favor the Republicans. If one computes a simple net preference score by subtracting the sum of pro-Republican and anti-Democratic comments on foreign policy from the sum of pro-Democratic and anti-Republican comments, the mean score for the population as a whole is a large −.441. The consistency to which the issue favors the Republicans is striking: the public consistently favors the Republican Party over the Democratic Party; it favors Eisenhower over Stevenson twice and Nixon over Kennedy in 1960; it has a consistently negative net evaluation of the Democrats and a consistently positive net evaluation of the Republicans.[23] Even Democratic identifiers, as Table 3.6 shows, have an overall preference for the Republicans on foreign policy in all three years, by a comfortable margin of 25.5% to 13.9% in

TABLE 3.6
Cross-pressures Involving Foreign Policy

Party Identification				
Party Identification	Foreign Policy	1952	1956	1960
Democrats	Republicans	25.5	21.6	18.0
Democrats	Democrats	13.9	10.4	18.7
Republicans	Democrats	3.5	3.0	3.9
Republicans	Republicans	53.4	52.4	59.7
Preference on Economic Issues				
Economic Policy	Foreign Policy	1952	1956	1960
Democrats	Republicans	26.2	28.3	21.8
Democrats	Democrats	14.3	10.8	21.0
Republicans	Democrats	4.4	4.8	4.9
Republicans	Republicans	59.5	56.3	63.2

Note: Entries are percentage Democratic or Republican on party identification and on economic preferences with cross-cutting and consistent preferences on foreign policy.

1952; Republicans prefer their own party/candidate by the overwhelming margin of 53.4% to 3.5%.

Finally, there is clear indication that cross-pressures between foreign policy preferences and other attitudes extend beyond party identification to other kinds of issues as well. Economics was of course seen as a source of considerable Democratic strength during the New Deal period, and Chapter Six will show the continuing impact such issues have into the 1950s and 1960s. But the Democratic advantage on economics in 1952 is undercut by the fact that many voters favoring the Democrats on economics at the same time favor the Republicans on foreign policy. Table 3.6 also shows that more than a quarter of those with a Democratic net preference on economics in 1952 prefer the Republicans on foreign policy, with only 14.3% of them preferring their own party on the second set of issues. Among Republican identifiers, the two issue areas reinforce each other to a far greater extent: 59.5% of those Republican on economics are also Republican on foreign affairs, while the percentage of Republicans on economics who prefer the Democrats on foreign affairs is only 4.4%.

Estimating the impact that different types of issues have on distribution of the vote is taken up in far greater detail in Chapters Six and Seven, and a full explanation of the basis for the estimates must wait until then. But a brief jump ahead to Table 6.6 shows that even when the effects of other issues, party identification, and candidate orientation are taken into consideration, foreign policy questions added a rather sizable 5.7% of the vote to the Republicans in 1952, a figure that decreases only to 4.8% four years later. Only candidate orientation makes anywhere near so great a net contribution to Republican electoral fortunes.

The Democrats did make some gains on foreign policy in 1960. Net evaluation of Kennedy and his party is less negative (–.046) that it had been in the two previous elections, and the net Republican preference of .329 is slightly lower than in 1956 as well. The Democrats do somewhat better in holding their partisans (18.7% loyal to only 18.0% favoring the Republicans) and those who have Democratic references on economics (21.0% to 21.8%) than they had previously done as well. But even in 1960, foreign policy is an area of clear Republican dominance.

THE FIRST MINI-REALIGNMENT:
SECULAR AND CRITICAL CHANGE

The literature is sufficient to enable us to develop a fairly convincing picture of the period before World War II: economics and social welfare are the dominant issues, class is the primary line of cleavage, and the Democrats dominate on the basis of a majority composed of the less well off, blue-collar workers, and urban residents; economics remains both a powerfully Democratic valence issue with roots in remembered contrasts between Hoover and Roosevelt and a powerful position issue in which active government intervention in managing the economy is supported by those for whom the Depression remains a symbol of the potential downside of a free enterprise economic system.

Realignment theorists initially saw the 1950s as a temporary break in an extended period of Democratic domination, attributable to the short-term problems of the late Truman administration and to the extraordinary personal appeal of Dwight Eisenhower: Campbell's (1966a) original typology of presidential elections, for example, characterizes 1952 and 1956 as straightforward deviating elections, temporary interruptions in a pattern of Democratic success that reasserts itself with Kennedy's victory as soon as Eisenhower leaves the electoral scene. The 1950s produced no change in the partisan attachments of the electorate that could provide the basis for sustained Republican gains.

The Democrats in fact suffer from multiple fundamental problems in the postwar years that undermine the clear pattern of domination they had enjoyed during the earliest years of the New Deal party system, all of them linked at least indirectly to the wrenching changes caused by World War II. Eisenhower himself may provide the added appeal needed to actually win elections, but he does so against a backdrop of increased inter-party competitiveness that has more general causes. Changed composition of the electorate has had slow but steady anti-Democratic consequences: there is no sudden, dramatic fall-off in the number of people predisposed to vote Democratic, but reduction in economic hardship clearly reduces the number of citizens for whom the traditional motivations for a Democratic vote are relevant. The result is a secular decline of the Democrats' class base that is only partially offset by their gains from class depolarization.

A second change has to do with the altered international position of the United States in the aftermath of World War II. Changed world position and responsibilities could be expected to make foreign policy an area of some importance on the post-war electoral agenda, and the late 1940s do in fact see emergence of foreign policy as a major area of mass concern. And although the Democrats enjoy an initial modest advantage in perceived ability to produce peace, by the early 1950s, in the midst of the Korean war, the public has begun to develop a clearly Republican preference on such issues.

The third factor that plays a role in the first mini-realignment is race. Race had been a potential problem for the Democrats ever since Franklin Roosevelt first united white southerners and blacks in his Democratic majority after 1932. To the extent that the social mobilization of blacks stimulated demands for racial equality in the post-war world, race would emerge on the political agenda in a way likely to prevent the two party components opposed on racial policy from remaining part of the same electoral alliance. The role that race plays in Democratic decline in the post-war years, beginning in 1948 and culminating in 1964, deserves a chapter of its own.

NOTES

1. The decline in participation can be attributed to various forces. Non-competitive elections of course reduce the incentive to vote by making voters see no possible impact of their ballot on the outcome. Formal limits on voting in the south such as the poll tax and literacy tests were not necessarily limited to blacks alone, having the additional intent of disenfranchising the populists and others who had produced the Bryan phenomenon. See Burnham (1970).

2. There is some disagreement in the literature over the relative importance of mobilization and conversion in producing Democratic majority of the New Deal party system. The classic and ingenious statement of the mobilization hypothesis is Andersen (1979); for a skeptical view, see Erickson and Tedin, (1981).

3. Although Ladd and Hadley (1978: 86) point out that class alone may have contributed less to the Democrats than is commonly thought: the Democrats never commanded a majority among white Protestant blue-collar workers.

4. This is a specific example of a far more general strategic problem facing left-wing parties. Przeworski and Sprague (1986: 43) speak of socialist parties in Europe realizing by the middle 1920s that their traditional proletarian base would never be sufficient to produce electoral majorities.

5. Campbell et al. (1960: 357) argue that class polarization in the post-war years was greatest among those who came of political age at the height of the Depression and New Deal, those born between 1897 to 1906 who were 23 to 32 in 1929; Abramson (1975: 39ff) reports that class voting is particularly low within the 1924–31 birth cohort, children during the Depression who came of political age after World War II, with the bulk of the change due to rising levels of Democratic voting among younger members of the (expanding) middle class.

6. Foreign policy is dealt with later in this chapter. Race is the subject of Chapter Four.

7. Inglehart's (1977) discussion of post-materialist ideology, a concern with self-realization among the financially secure in affluent western nations, particularly young people born into a world of post-war physical and economic security, is a second attempt to argue that a substantial number of upper-status citizens maintain a non-economic basis for left-wing voting.

8. Stevenson's early political exposure came through his involvement with the Chicago Council on Foreign Relations, and his first Washington job was with the Agricultural Adjustment Administration in the early days of the New Deal. In the early 1950s, he opposed repeal of the Taft-Hartley Act and was opposed to Truman's national health proposals. Martin (1976: 631) cites Arthur Schlesinger's concern that Stevenson was inadequately devoted in general to New Deal and Fair Deal issues. See Martin (1976, especially 642–3) and Newfield and Greenfield (1972, esp. 25).

9. Almost all observers agreed that depolarization of electoral appeals along lines of social class occurred in the 1950s, but there was the disagreement over whether such moderation was a natural and inevitable response to changed underlying social conditions or a short-sighted political strategy. Ferguson and Rogers (1986: 36) argue for potential Democratic gains through polarization for an election as late as 1984, seeing Mondale as insufficiently attentive to the possibility of mobilizing a populist coalition with class-based economic appeals at its heart; Kusnet argues (1992: 68) that "trailing Democrats have staged remarkable recoveries in the polls when they've adopted populism," and wonders "how far we could go if we ran as populists from the start of the race." Przeworski and Sprague (1986) make a more general argument that socialist parties cannot move to the center in a appeal for middle-class votes without in the process losing even larger numbers of their working-class base and, at the same time, diluting their substantive policy agenda.

10. Education is a four category variable: categories are grade school educated, some high school, high school graduate, and some college. Occupation is a simple dichotomy into white-collar and blue-collar using the codes described in Appendix 1. The original income categories have been recoded into six categories, as equal in size as the raw data allows. As made clear in the text, alternate operationalizations produce essentially similar results.

11. See Sousa (1993) for a somewhat similar analysis of the relative impacts of composition and polarization effects for union membership from 1960 to 1988.

12. Alford (1963) points out that 1948 produced distinctively high levels of class polarization. On the other hand, even the levels he reports for 1948 fall short of the kind of absolute polarization that some of the earlier literature suggested.

13. Robert Axelrod (1972, 1984) regularly reports the composition of the Democratic and Republican coalitions as a function of the size, turnout, and partisan loyalty of different social groups. A similar logic is pursued for very different purposes here.

14. The figures are from the NES study and do not correspond exactly with the actual election outcome. Only those respondents who can be classified as blue-collar or white-collar are included.

15. 1952 is used as a starting point out of necessity: it was the first of the NES studies. The close approximation of the line charting 1952 composition to the actual vote nonetheless is an indication that 1952 can be taken to be a fairly representative starting point for the series. Were 1952 highly atypical, we would expect to see subsequent years showing a substantially different impact when their own loyalty rates are substituted for the 1952 starting point.

16. Note that the starting point for marking these changes is 1952, a point at which composition of the electorate has already been changing for some extended period of time.

17. Education is a far easier variable to work with than occupation: there are less missing data, fewer conceptual problems concerning head of household or employment status, and fewer questions of classification. Analysis of income is complicated by the fact that NES in each year grouped data rather than reported actual income level and by the need to adjust dollar levels for inflation.

18. The same general pattern holds for income, union membership, and subjective class. Income data are of course controlled for inflation.

19. Those arguing that class polarization is a fruitful course for the Democrats need, therefore, to modify the relevant coalition: Huckfeldt and Kohfeld (1989: 190) expand their notion of lower class to include the lower middle class.

20. For recent evidence that foreign policy attitudes can affect attitudes towards the president or vote choice, see Wilcox and Allsop (1991) and Aldrich, Sullivan, Borgida (1989).

21. These first two reports give a rank order of most important problems without indicating the actual percentage mentioning each type of issue. The nature of the question also limits our ability to determine what people mean when they mention neutrality: do they want to preserve it, see it as undesirable, believe it will be unsuccessful, etc.

22. The question is asked in a variety of formats: some questions refer to the most important problem facing the American people; others refer to the most important problem government should solve; others refer to the most important problem facing the country. The prevention of war is mentioned by 38 percent of all respondents in the March 1948 survey, making it the single most important problem cited. The July 1947 survey finds 22 percent mentioning foreign policy in general and 21 percent mentioning prevention of war, the second and third most frequent responses.

23. The fact that the Republican advantage in 1952 is not due to Eisenhower alone is shown by the fact that Eisenhower's advantage over Stevenson (–.196) is smaller than the Republican Party's advantage (–.245) over the Democratic Party.

4

Decreasingly Latent Cleavages: Race and the Roosevelt Coalition from 1948 to 1972

Race plays a substantial role in each of the mini-realignments. The Democratic majority had been vulnerable to the divisive power of race ever since northern blacks joined southern whites as core constituencies of the Democratic coalition in the aftermath of the Depression, but the relative unimportance of race as a topic of national political debate allowed the two groups to co-exist more or less peacefully within the party during the Roosevelt years. Anything that moved race to the fore-front of the political agenda, however, would threaten Democratic unity. Twice since World War II race did become a major issue, and each time it had detrimental effects on the Democrats: in 1948, the consequence was a substantial weakening of the Democratic white south that had existed since the Civil War; in 1964, the con-sequence was the disappearance of the Democratic white south, with the region becoming the most Republican part of the country.

The Democratic convention's acceptance in 1948 of a liberal civil rights plank was the first event to illustrate the disruptive potential of race: Strom Thurmond's Dixiecrats bolted the party, costing it deep south electoral votes that it had won for a century. The Democrats managed to keep the salience of race relatively low for some time after 1948, and the south remained the most Democratic part of the white electorate throughout the 1950s. But the level of white southern support for Stevenson never returned to levels common for Democrats before World War II. And although decreased salience of race allows party unity to more or less reassert itself in the 1950s, its disruptive potential is realized with far greater impact once the parties take clear and opposing positions on the new civil rights agenda of the 1960s.

The eventual commitment of the Kennedy and Johnson administrations to the cause of civil rights produces a second and far more severe split in Roosevelt's Demo-cratic coalition: blacks become all but unanimous in supporting Democratic presi-dential candidates, while southern whites become the most Republican part of the white electorate. The resulting shift in the coalitional basis of the parties is the most clear-cut of the post-war era, and it produces clear electoral costs for the Demo-crats.

But explicit mass concern with race recedes rapidly after 1968, with fewer and fewer respondents mentioning racial concerns *per se* as a basis for candidate evaluation. The differences in vote choice that persist are increasingly based on a broader set of issue concerns on which blacks and whites, southern whites and non-southern whites differ. Race plays a role in establishing the image of the activist Democrats as ideologically extreme in the mid-1960s: but explicit racial concerns play only a secondary role once the more general image of the Democrats as excessively far to the left is established.

REALIGNMENT (LARGELY) AVERTED:
1948 AND THE POLITICS OF RACE IN THE 1950s

The solidly Democratic south was of course the legacy of the Civil War. The role of the new Republican Party in setting off the conflict and in overseeing Reconstruction at its end produced a powerful association with the Democrats among white southerners that lasted for almost a century. With the re-enfranchisement of white southerners in 1876, the south became the most reliably Democratic region of the country. When Bryan's Democratic/Populist challenge to the emerging capitalist order failed to attract support among industrial workers of the northeast and midwest in 1896, the Republicans became the dominant party nationally, and region became the primary line of national electoral cleavage. Within the south, the conservative Democratic establishment recaptured the regionally dominant party from the defeated Populists, while dis-enfranchisement of black southerners deprived the party of Lincoln of its little remaining southern strength (Black and Black, 1992; Woodward, 1966). At the center of the link to the Democrats were the intertwined issues of regional autonomy and race: as Black and Black write, "Of all the ties that bound the South to the Democratic party in the first half of the twentieth century, by far the most compelling and sacrosanct was the shared understanding that the Democratic party was the party of white supremacy" (1992: 141); or, as V.O. Key wrote in his classic *Southern Politics*, "[t]he politics of the south revolves around the position of the Negro" (1949: 5). The south was solidly Democratic, the regional bastion of the national minority party, with a high level of voter loyalty in all sectors of the white population and race as the key issue anchoring voter loyalty.

The solidly Democratic south was threatened only once in the first part of the twentieth century. Nomination of the Catholic Al Smith in 1928 saw Herbert Hoover break the overwhelmingly Protestant Solid South by carrying five outer southern states.[1] But the Depression pushed the entire region back into the Democratic camp for an additional generation. The traditional partisan loyalty of the region was now reinforced by the same kind of valence economic concerns that affected the rest of the country as well: Roosevelt carried more than seventy percent of the popular vote of the old Confederacy in his first three races (Ladd and Hadley, 1978: 42), with more than 92 percent of the vote in the deep south in 1932 (Phillips, 1970: 212).

Roosevelt's support in the south after 1932 was more than a simple response to the valence issues of the Depression or a residue of the Civil War and its aftermath. Sarasohn (1989: 17) observes that the south had long favored reform elements within the party on issues other than race. Ladd and Hadley (1978: 130) argue that southern support for economic aspects of the New Deal was higher than that of any other region of the country, reviewing a large number of AIPO polls on assorted New Deal initiatives in the 1930s and early 1940s to show that the new economic appeals that the party used elsewhere with such success in the aftermath of the Depression were attractive to southerners as well. They and Sundquist (1983: 226) both cite evidence that Roosevelt's programs received high levels of support from southern Democratic leadership in Congress. Economic backwardness and remnants of southern populist hostility to "business nationalism" (Ladd and Hadley, 1978: 131) or to "northern corporate capitalism" (Sarasohn, 1989: 21) provided southern support for most economic aspects of the New Deal (see also Katznelson, Geiger, Kryder, 1993; Key, 1961: 101).

Blacks became a part of this coalition after the Depression, abandoning the party of Lincoln to vote Democratic in 1936. Their motivation was due more to New Deal measures designed to help the less-well-off generally than to any particularly racial calculation; although there were several visible figures in the Roosevelt administration such as Harold Ickes and Eleanor Roosevelt noted for their sympathy to black welfare (Weiss, 1983; Kirby, 1980), in general "blacks were not singled out for special attention" (Carmines and Stimson, 1989: 187). For reasons having to do with Roosevelt's personal experience and worldview as well as with the continuing domination by southern racial conservatives of the Congress with which he was compelled to co-operate on his full agenda of reforms, race *per se* played a relatively minor role in national Democratic politics through Roosevelt's presidency. Roosevelt himself consistently refused to openly support anti-lynching legislation, for example, despite widespread popular support for such a measure, because he realized the potential such issues created for dividing the congressional coalition backing his economic program (Weiss, 1983).

Nonetheless, blacks now joined the white south as loyal if not entirely compatible components of the New Deal Democratic majority. The strength of the linkage between race and partisan preferences is clear from early national surveys, as Ladd and Hadley (1978: 112) demonstrate in reviewing a large number of AIPO studies on both vote choice and party loyalty from the 1940s.[2] Increasingly after World War I, the mechanization of agriculture and the subsequent declining need for unskilled manual labor in the south had led large numbers of southern blacks to move to the urban and industrial heart of the nation, where they were able to vote; and after 1932, they voted Democratic (Lubell 1965: 98).

To the extent that race became an issue of public controversy, of course, the unity of the Roosevelt coalition was threatened. Southern whites and northern blacks were two core components of the party's electoral base, and they held opposing views on an issue of considerable importance to both. Blacks were numerically fewer, given continued restrictions on black voting in the south, but northern blacks were concentrated in highly competitive states with large numbers of electoral votes where their support could be decisive in close contests. The Second World War could be expected to stimulate black political demands by opening up economic opportunities in the mobilized war economy and by upsetting surviving perceptions that second class citizenship was inevitable or acceptable. Black demands for equal rights were reinforced more generally after 1945 both by the justification of the war as a struggle for human rights and democracy and by the need to counter Soviet propaganda about capitalist exploitation and oppression in the newly bipolar world (Bass and De Vries, 1976: 5; Woodward, 1966: 130).

The party suffered its first great shock on race in 1948. A presidential commission created in late 1946 to investigate an upsurge in racial violence in the aftermath of World War II in October 1947 sent Truman a report calling for an end to segregation and racial discrimination (Berman, 1970: 43–55); Truman's decision to support many of the commission's recommendations in a civil rights message to Congress in February 1948 caused considerable concern in the southern wing of the party.[3] When Truman reacted to the ensuing furor by approving a moderate civil rights plank for the 1948 Democratic platform, both southern conservatives and northern liberals reacted negatively (Black and Black, 1992: 94; Berman, 1970: 108). The liberals were concerned with maintaining black electoral support in the 1948 presidential election against the even more liberal alternative presented by Henry Wallace, while southern racial conservatives were increasingly concerned with becoming an outvoted minority in the national party (Berman, 1970: 85). The confrontation came to a head at the convention itself, where a floor fight led both to acceptance of a liberal civil rights plank and to a walk-out by southern racial conservatives who met three days later to create the Dixiecrat presidential candidacy of Strom Thurmond of South Carolina. Roosevelt had carried 69 percent of the southern vote in 1944, far higher than in any other region of the country and only slightly lower than his performance in his first three campaigns (Ladd and Hadley, 1978: 135). But Truman barely held a majority of southern votes, and Thurmond carried four southern states, all of them in the deep south, with 39 electoral votes.[4]

During the 1950s, the Democrats managed to keep the potentially divisive issue of race more under control. Acting much as Sundquist would suggest a party threatened by the possibility of finding itself on the wrong side of an emergent issue cleavage should act, the Democrats took steps after 1948 that had the effect of postponing the full divisive impact of their latent cleavage on race for over a decade. Stevenson was not in 1952 identified with the more activist wing of the party on race: he was acceptable to southern Democratic leaders (Martin, 1976: 554, 631; see also Huckfeldt and Kohfeld, 1989: 7), chose as his running mate a senator from the deep south, and in fact held the deep south states that had defected to Thurmond in 1948. Eisenhower maintained Dewey's gains in the outer south; the more urbanized and industrial areas of the outer south produced the largest Republican vote totals (Lubell, 1965: 118) in 1948, as southerners increasingly responded to the same set of economic concerns that produced class-linked voting and Republican support from the middle class that had long characterized the rest of the country (Sundquist, 1983: 281).[5]

As Table 4.1 demonstrates, Stevenson in 1952 in fact did relatively well among both of the opposing Democratic constituencies concerned with race: he maintained the party's advantage among blacks at the same time that he ran relatively well among southern whites. The association between race and vote choice was a healthy .40 in 1952: 75.7% of blacks voted for Stevenson, a figure well over the two-thirds used to define a group-voting norm in Chapter Three and nearly twice as large as the 38.4% support he obtained from whites. Race in 1952 was in fact more strongly associated with vote choice than were any of the indicators of social class in that year or in any year thereafter, more strongly associated than the more fragmentary pre-1952 data suggests social class was even at the height of the mature New Deal party system.

Stevenson's performance among white southerners is somewhat more complicated. On the one hand, the Dixiecrats did not re-emerge in 1952 or 1956, and Stevenson's white support was greatest among southerners: southern states provided nearly eighty percent of his total of 89 electoral votes.[6] On the other hand, Stevenson obtained the votes of barely half of southern whites and only 55.5% of the region's electoral votes.[7] The 51.5% of the popular vote Stevenson received from white southerners is certainly larger than the 36.1% of the vote he received from other whites, but the figures fall considerably short of those for the pre-war years: Roosevelt had carried about eighty percent of the southern vote and had run more than twenty percentage points better there than he did in the country as a whole in 1932, 1936, and 1940. In both of his campaigns, Stevenson's share of the southern vote was slightly over seven percent better than his percentage in the country as a whole (Congressional Quarterly, 1975: 294–5). Neither the overall proportion nor the distinctiveness of the vote would inspire one to speak of a solidly Democratic South.[8]

Furthermore, there were already clear signs in 1952 that race was undermining the Democratic coalition. The percentage of all respondents who mentioned race or race-related issues as reasons for liking/disliking the parties/candidates was a modest 7.3% in 1952, but the two traditionally Democratic groups, blacks (26.3%) and southern whites (13.4%), did so far more frequently than non-southern whites did. And the two core Democratic groups were already being driven in opposing partisan directions by the issue: blacks who mentioned race preferred the Democrats on it by better than three to one; the few non-southern whites concerned were almost evenly divided between the parties, but southern whites preferred the Republicans to the Democrats on race by better than two to one! The net partisan preference on the issue for blacks is .199, while white southerners have a mean score of –.045.[9]

TABLE 4.1
Vote Intention: Race and Region

Year	Race[a]			Region[b]		
		Percentage Democratic[c]			Percentage Democratic[c]	
	D[d]	Whites	Blacks	D[d]	White Southerners	Other Whites
1952	.40[e]	38.4	75.7	.15[e]	51.5	36.1
1956	.26[e]	37.9	53.7	.14[e]	47.3	35.8
1960	.22[e]	39.1	52.7	.07[e]	40.6	38.7
1964	.35[e]	62.6	97.4	−.18[e]	48.4	65.5
1968	.62[e]	32.8	93.0	−.02	30.5	33.3
1972	.56[e]	22.7	72.2	−.11[e]	15.2	24.7
1976	.48[e]	43.9	89.7	.03	45.7	43.5
1980	.49[e]	38.1	85.4	−.03	37.4	38.4
1984	.53[e]	32.5	76.9	−.10[e]	23.4	34.6
1988	.44[e]	37.2	74.2	−.02	37.8	35.1

Notes: a. Race is a dichotomous variable, with only whites and blacks included as valid cases.
b. Region is a dichotomous variable, with the eleven states of the old Confederacy defined as southern and all others defined as non-southern; only whites are included.
c. Percentage Democratic is the percentage of those intending to vote who intended to vote Democratic. The remainder intended to vote Republican, intended to vote for minor party candidates, or did not yet know for whom they would vote.
d. D is Somer's D asymmetric between race or region and vote intention, with vote intention dependent.
e. Indicates statistical significance at .05.

For blacks, race is part of a more general preference for the Democrats on issues: their approximately three to one favoring of the Democrats on racial issues in 1952 is actually smaller that their overwhelmingly Democratic preference of 58.5% to 10.5% on non-racial issues. For southern whites, in contrast, preference for the Republicans on race was not part of a more general Republican orientation: their two to one Republican preference on race co-existed with a modest Democratic advantage of 42.1% to 36.9% on other kinds of issues. Blacks in no sense had to choose between their racial concerns and other issues: because racial issues and non-racial issues tended to reinforce each other, it was quite easy to cast a vote that simultaneously expressed Democratic preferences on both; 17.0% had reinforcing scores on the two types of issues and only 4.1% were cross-pressured; among white southerners, the reinforcing (6.2%) and cross-pressured (4.5%) are much more evenly balanced. The south may well have been the most Democratic part of the white electorate in the 1952 presidential election, but there is no reason to see racial issues as a source of Democratic strength. Race was already undermining the traditional Democratic strength of the white south, well before the region turned to the Republicans on other types of issues or began voting Republican presidentially.

The fifties were in fact an era in which the strong link between race and vote choice weakened somewhat. During the Eisenhower years, the lack of a Democratic president increased the visibility of the party's congressional leadership, most of it racially conservative southerners who had attained their positions through the lack of electoral challenge in the solid south and the rigid working of the seniority system. Within the Senate, there were more Republicans liberal on race than Democrats liberal on race (Carmines and Stimson, 1989). Furthermore, the Republicans, deliberately or not, took steps that made them more attractive to black voters: the Supreme Court's decision to declare school segregation unconstitutional was written by a Chief Justice who had himself been a Republican governor of California and Republican vice-presidential candidate before being named to the court by a Republican president; Eisenhower avoided any overt support for that

TABLE 4.2
Race as an Issue: 1952–1960

Salience[a]

Year	Total	Blacks	Southern Whites	Other Whites
1952	7.3	26.3	13.4	3.5
1956	10.4	26.7	24.0	4.9
1960	10.3	29.7	19.9	5.0

Party Preferred on Race[b]

Year	Total Dem.	Total Rep.	Blacks Dem.	Blacks Rep.	Southern Whites Dem.	Southern Whites Rep.	Other Whites Dem.	Other Whites Rep.
1952	3.7	3.2	18.7	5.5	4.1	8.4	1.7	1.9
1956	4.4	4.7	13.0	12.3	7.9	11.1	2.5	2.1
1960	5.1	3.7	17.4	11.6	7.4	6.7	2.8	1.8

Net Partisan Preference on Race[c]

Year	Total	Blacks	Southern Whites	Other Whites
1952	.011	.199	−.045	−.002
1956	−.003	.027	−.044	.004
1960	.010	.076	−.010	.008

Notes: a. Salience is the percentage of each group mentioning race or racial issues as a reason to like or dislike either of the parties or candidates.

b. Preference is the percentage of each group with a net pro-Democratic or net pro-Republican preference on race; it is computed by adding the number of pro-Democratic and anti-Republican mentions and subtracting the number of anti-Democratic and pro-Republican mentions.

c. Net partisan preference is the mean net preference score for each group.

decision (Woodward, 1966: 163), but he did in his second term send federal troops to desegregate the schools of Little Rock against the opposition of Arkansas' Democratic governor.

It may therefore not be surprising that the D between being black and voting Democratic falls from its .40 in 1952 to .26 in 1956 to .22 in 1960. Blacks remain far more Democratic than whites in each year: but the percentage certain they will vote Democratic falls from around three-quarters to just over half, a change less due to a rise in Republican vote intentions than to a rise in the percentage uncertain at the pre-election interview as to how they will vote. The events of the Eisenhower years seem to affect black perceptions of the parties and candidates on race as well: the clear Democratic net preference of 1952 (.199) almost disappears in 1956 (.027), reappearing on a considerably smaller scale in 1960 (.076).

Among whites, southerners remain disproportionately Democratic in 1956, with a D between southern residence and Democratic vote choice of .14 essentially unchanged from 1952. The salience of race among white southerners increases, with partisan preference on racial issues remaining slightly Republican at a time when preference on issues other than race remains slightly Democratic. In 1960 the relationship between region and vote choice falls to .07, with non-southerners slightly more Democratic than in 1956 while white southerners' percentage Democratic decreases. Religion provides a more likely explanation than race in pushing the normally Democratic but overwhelmingly Protestant white south away from Kennedy in 1960 (Converse, 1966a): southern whites actually become slightly less concerned with race and slightly more pro-Democratic in their open-ended comments on the subject between 1956 and 1960, a change parallel to that for non-southern whites and blacks, while their overall issue orientation becomes somewhat more Republican; there is no evidence here that change in perceptions of the parties on race is particularly responsible for the halving of the impact of region on white votes.

One last argument helps make clear how the link between racial issues and electoral alternatives blurred in the 1950s. In 1952, the NES introduces a closed-ended racial issue question concerning the government's guaranteeing blacks fair treatment in hiring. As Figure 4.1 shows, there is very little relationship between one's preferences on fair treatment and the party one favors on race more generally: those favoring fair treatment had a very slightly pro-Democratic net partisan preference on race of .03, while the mean for those wanting nothing done was a very slightly pro-Republican −.02; association between one's issue position and one's net partisan preference was only .10. In both 1956 and 1960, even this slight association disappears: those opposing the measure are the most pro-Democratic on race in both years, and the overall association between one's position and partisan preference is .00 in both years. More dramatic evidence of the same pattern is seen in the behavior of blacks. In 1952, blacks liberal on fair employment practices had a very Democratic mean net partisan preference on race of .26; the weakened association between liberal views on race and a Democratic preference reduces this net

FIGURE 4.1

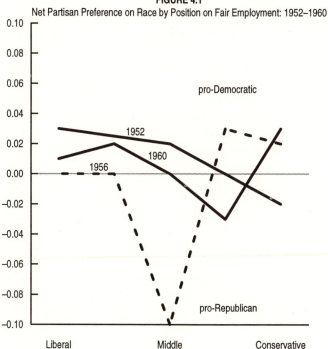

Net Partisan Preference on Race by Position on Fair Employment: 1952–1960

Note: Net partisan preference is the mean of pro-Democratic and anti-Republican mentions minus anti-Democratic and pro-Republican mentions.

partisan preference for the large majority of blacks who support the measure to .04 in 1956 and .07 in 1960.

In other words, in terms of voting behavior, partisan evaluation, and linkage of issues to party, the tie between blacks and the Democratic party erodes during the 1950s: fewer blacks are clearly Democratic in their voting preferences, and positive partisan evaluations—in general and among those with liberal views on racial issues in particular—weaken as well. White southerners remain more Democratic than non-southern whites throughout the period, although by a relatively small and decreasing margin. There is nothing to suggest that this difference is due to race: white southerners actually preferred the Republicans on race in both 1952 and 1956; in 1960, when white southerners *do* give the Democrats a small advantage on race, the percentage of them voting Democratic and the difference between them and non-southerners in vote choice both fall off. As of the 1960 presidential election, there is little reason to think that race is playing the role of dividing key elements of the Democratic coalition in a way that threatens the party's electoral fortunes. If anything, the change over time suggests a narrowing of racially-linked differences that had existed for some time.

THE ELECTORAL IMPACT
OF RACIAL POLITICS IN THE 1960s

In 1964, race moved to the center of the political agenda to a degree that is quite stunning. Years of civil rights activism, the new Democratic administration's increased sympathy with the black cause, decimation of liberal Republican ranks in Congress after 1958 (Carmines and Stimson, 1989), and emergence of clear-cut differences on racial issues in the campaign itself all contributed to a considerable increase in the number of citizens concerned with race and to considerable alteration in the distribution of partisan preferences on the issue. The number of respondents who mentioned race as one of the most important national problems with which government should deal increases to 40.8%, more than double the figure four years earlier when the question was introduced, with the increase entirely due to increased concern among whites; the percentage of white respondents who mention race as a basis for liking or disliking one of the electoral alternatives, i.e. who have a preference about which party can best handle the issue, nearly triples to 23.7%, while for blacks it doubles from a considerably higher base to 69.8%.

The difference in preferences on race increases at the same time. The association between race and net partisan preference on racial issues had been .05 in 1960, a very small association stemming from the modest Democratic advantage among concerned whites (3.9% to 2.9%) and the only slightly greater Democratic preference (17.4% to 11.6%) among concerned blacks. In 1964 that coefficient increases to .62: whites now give a solid preference on racial issues to the Republicans, by a margin of 13.2% to 9.9%; clear regional differences emerge for whites, with non-southerners quite divided in their preference (10.9% to 10.2% Democratic but with a mean of −.025) while white southerners move from the modest 7.4% to 6.7% edge they had given to Kennedy over Nixon to an overwhelming 25.9% to 5.3% preference for Goldwater over Johnson. Blacks move in the direction opposite that of southern whites: black preferences for the Republicans all but disappear, decreasing from the 11.6% of 1960 to 1.3% in 1964, while more than two-thirds of all blacks interviewed (68.6%) mention race as a basis for liking the Democrats. The mean net partisan preference score for southern whites on race increases from −.010 to −.372; the same score for blacks increases from .076 to 1.635!

Furthermore, the increased clarity on these issues noted by Pomper (1972) and Nie with Andersen (1974) emerges on closed-ended issue questions as well. Economic and racial issue positions had previously been unlinked to each other in the mass electorate (Pomper, 1972; Nie with Andersen, 1974; Nie, Verba, Petrocik, 1979). With the rise in general societal concern with the issue and with the emergence of strengthened inter-party elite differences, race for the first time became part of an integrated issue cluster with other domestic concerns. Our data show similar change with regard to the partisan implications of liberal and conservative positions on race. Figure 4.1 had shown the lack of association between position on racial issues and net partisan preference on race in the years before 1964; Figure 4.2 reports the

TABLE 4.3
Race as an Issue: 1956–1968

Salience[a]

Year	Total	Blacks	Southern Whites	Other Whites
1956	10.4	26.7	24.0	4.9
1960	10.3	29.7	19.9	5.0
1964	28.5	69.8	32.3	21.7
1968	15.9	53.7	11.7	12.0

Party Preferred on Race[b]

	Total		Blacks		Southern Whites		Other Whites	
Year	Dem.	Rep.	Dem.	Rep.	Dem.	Rep.	Dem.	Rep.
1956	4.4	4.7	13.0	12.3	7.9	11.1	2.5	2.1
1960	5.1	3.7	17.4	11.6	7.4	6.7	2.8	1.8
1964	15.9	11.9	68.6	1.3	5.3	25.9	10.9	10.2
1968	10.3	4.7	49.0	2.7	2.8	6.6	6.9	4.5

Net Partisan Preference on Race[c]

Year	Total	Blacks	Southern Whites	Other Whites
1956	−.003	.027	−.044	.004
1960	.010	.076	−.010	.008
1964	.087	1.635	−.372	−.025
1968	.102	.920	−.048	.031

Notes: a. Salience is the percentage of each group mentioning race or racial issues as a reason to like or dislike either of the parties or candidates.

b. Preference is the percentage of each group with a net pro-Democratic or net pro-Republican preference on race; it is computed by adding the number of pro-Democratic and anti-Republican mentions and subtracting the number of anti-Democratic and pro-Republican mentions.

c. Net partisan preference is the mean net preference score for each group.

same data for 1960 and 1964, showing the degree to which those with clear positions on racial policy develop strong and opposing partisan preferences. Those in favor of fair job treatment in 1964 take a strongly pro-Democratic score of .471, while those opposed take a strongly pro-Republican score of −.228; blacks are in each category far more Democratic than whites are, but the monotonic increase in Republican preferences as one turns against the fair treatment item holds for both racial groups and for both southern and non-southern whites. Similar clarity emerges when a question on integrated schools that had been asked in 1956 and 1960 is contrasted with a more general integration/segregation item that is introduced in 1964 for the first time.[10]

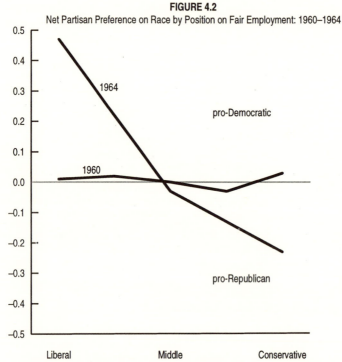

FIGURE 4.2

Net Partisan Preference on Race by Position on Fair Employment: 1960–1964

Note: Net partisan preference is the mean of pro-Democratic and anti-Republican mentions minus anti-Democratic and pro-Republican mentions.

The result of these changes is a greatly altered relationship of both race and region to vote choice that shatters the uneasy coalition of blacks and white southerners that had existed for nearly thirty years. The elections between 1948 and 1960 had allowed racially liberal blacks and racially conservative white southerners to co-exist in the Democratic coalition created by Franklin Roosevelt. But the emergence of racial issues as highly visible central elements of the nation's political agenda and the clear differences on such issues that took place leading up to the 1964 presidential election made continuation of the coalition impossible. Once the Democrats had committed themselves unequivocally to the case of de-segregation and racial equality, the racially conservative white south was antagonized; once the Republicans offered an alternative whose opposition to federal activism included opposition to governmental efforts at desegregation and racial equality, the racially conservative white south had an alternative they could support. In 1964, the percentage of blacks in the pre-election survey intending to vote Democratic increases from the 52.7% of 1960 to 97.4%; despite the simultaneous increase in Democratic voting among whites, the D between race and vote choice increases from .22 to .35 (See also Huckfeldt and Kohfeld, 1989). Furthermore, white southerners are now *less* Democratic than non-southern whites: a plurality of them do prefer Johnson to Goldwater, but the much larger percentage of non-southern whites who do so produces a D of −.18. The south, for a century the Democrats' regional base, became their weakest region in the 1964 presidential election: not only did Johnson run worse in the south than in any other region, but the deep south was the only area (except Arizona) in which Goldwater won electoral votes, carrying Mississippi, Alabama, South Carolina, Georgia, and Louisiana.[11]

One should not attribute the white southern desertion of the Democrats solely to race: Petrocik (1981: 84) points to the increasing Republicanism of middle-class southerners in the 1950s, as the south increasingly adopts cleavage patterns long established in the rest of the country; Ladd and Hadley (1978: 140) point to a southern tradition of resistance to centralized authority and the kind of early industrialization occurring in the south in the 1950s and 1960s that would naturally tend to generate opposition to the economic and social liberalism of the national Democratic party more generally;[12] Key had observed as long ago as 1949 that "the Dixiecrats...are the natural allies of northern Republicanism" (1949: 674; see also Black and Black, 1992: 155). But white southerners' partisan preferences on non-racial issues did not move sharply to the Republicans in 1964: their mean score on non-racial issues went from .002 to .120—a pro-Democratic movement that, although rather smaller than the .189 to .881 move of non-southern whites, contrasts sharply with their simultaneous shift from −.010 to −.372 on race. More than a quarter of the southern white electorate had positions on both racial and non-racial issues in 1964: 49.4% of them were cross-pressured, compared to only 31.6% of similarly situated non-southern whites and 2.8% of similarly situated blacks. The numbers involved are not large, but it is striking that of the 34 cross-pressured white southerners, 31 favored the Democrats on non-racial issues and the Republicans on race.

The Wallace candidacy in 1968 was seen at the time as the kind of proto-realignment phenomenon which for Burnham and other realignment theorists constituted a classic sign of impending system change: a symptom of the new cross-cutting issue that the New Deal coalition cannot contain. The magnitude of Nixon's 1972 victory, his carrying of the entire south, and the fact that his percentage of the popular vote roughly equaled the sum of his and Wallace's 1968 vote all reinforced the impression that Wallace had served the third-party candidate's classic role of way-station for partisans eager to abandon their traditional party who required an intermediate stop before actually voting for the opposition.

The role of race in voters' reactions to Wallace is in fact rather complicated. Race is far and away the most frequently mentioned issue when voters are asked their reactions to George Wallace: nearly a third of the electorate (31.5%) cited race as a reason for liking or disliking him, twice as many as mentioned it for the Democrats and Republicans combined in 1968 or in any other year. No other type of issue is mentioned with anything near as great frequency: the new domestic issues of social disorder and new politics are the second most frequently mentioned at only 15.7%, while all economic issues combined are mentioned by only 6.1% and foreign policy by only 7.6%.

There is no reason to think, however, that Wallace presented attractive alternatives on racial policy that had been ignored by the two major policies; the bulk of these perceptions of Wallace on race were negative. Only 5.0% of the public mentioned race as a basis for liking Wallace, while 26.7% mentioned race as a reason for disliking him: the mean net evaluation of –.248 is far larger in magnitude than any net evaluation of the Democrats or Republicans on race in any year.[13] And although the net evaluation is expectedly negative among blacks, it is negative among white northerners (–.241) and white southerners (–.079) as well. The most sympathetic of the three groups, white southerners, opposed Wallace on race by the healthy margin of 14.8% to 7.6%. The much smaller number of voters who evaluated Wallace in terms of economics or new domestic issues were in fact far more sympathetic to him: the 4.9% of the total population who supported Wallace on race is less than half the percentage who supported him on new domestic issues.[14]

Furthermore, racial considerations alone can account for but a small portion of the Wallace vote. Wallace's percentage of the vote certainly shows sensitivity both to race as a demographic characteristic and to region: almost no blacks (0.9%) voted for him, while white southerners (28.7%) were three times more supportive than white non-southerners (9.9%). And a very large proportion of the relative few

TABLE 4.4
Wallace

Percentage Voting for Wallace[a]

All respondents	12.3%
Blacks	0.9%
White southerners	28.7%
White non-southerners	9.9%

Perceiving Wallace on the Issues[b]

Issue	Positively	Negatively	Total	Net Evaluation
Economics	3.6	2.5	6.1	.009
Race	5.8	26.7	32.2	–.236
New politics	10.8	5.5	15.7	.062
Foreign	3.3	4.4	7.6	–.013

Notes: a. Entries are the percentage of each group voting for Wallace.
   b. The first three entries are the percentage of the population who mention each type as a reason for liking or disliking Wallace. The net evaluation is simply the mean number of positive minus the mean number of negative mentions. Issue areas are discussed further in Chapter 5. Codes used are given in Appendix 6.

who approved of Wallace on race did vote for him: he is supported by 43.9% of such white northerners and 58.3% of such white southerners. Yet voters sympathetic to Wallace on race provide only a small proportion of his total votes: 2.4% of the electorate consisted of those liking Wallace on race and voting for him, a figure that is actually smaller than the 3.3% liking him on new domestic issues and voting for him; and the two sets of issues together provide less than half his total vote.[15] A full discussion of the basis of support for Wallace in 1968 is beyond the scope of this project, but it would clearly be simplistic to attribute his appeal to race alone.

The 1968 election more generally shows a mixed picture of the importance of race. The large differences in vote choice between blacks and whites that emerged in 1964 continue in 1968: the 93.0% of blacks voting Democratic in 1968 is only slightly below the figure for 1964, and the combination of continued black loyalty with a large anti-Democratic shift among white voters makes the racial difference in vote choice surge from a D of .35 to one of .62. But the difference can hardly be attributed to racial issues alone: there is a considerable decrease in the salience of race as a basis for evaluating the two major parties and their candidates for both blacks (from 69.8% to 53.7%) and whites (from 23.7% to 11.7%).[16] Blacks continue their strong preference for the Democrats over the Republicans on racial issues, although at a level considerably reduced from four years earlier. And whites as a whole, although giving Humphrey only 28.4% of their vote, have an essentially neutral net major-party preference on race of .014, increased from the –.091 of 1964.

The pattern for region among whites provides even less evidence of the direct impact of race: Wallace's strong southern showing means that both Humphrey and Nixon do less well among white southerners than among other whites, but among those who do not vote for Wallace, Humphrey does only very slightly worse in the south (D of –.02) than elsewhere. Furthermore, the salience of race declines for both white southerners and other whites, in the process eliminating the greater concern with the topic among white southerners that had existed since 1952. Net preferences on race among white southerners falls from the –.372 of 1964 to a –.048 hardly larger than the mean reached in 1952 or 1956.

RACE AS PRECURSOR
OF THE SECOND MINI-REALIGNMENT

Chapter Two places the mini-realignment that produced a Republican presidential majority in 1966–1970, immediately after the dramatic 1964 increase in the salience and electoral consequences of race. The timing might well suggest that race itself plays a substantial role in *producing* the mini-realignment: it certainly produces changes in patterns of party cleavage or party coalitions of the kind to which V.O. Key directed our attention in his seminal work on critical elections (1955), producing near-unanimity in black support for Democrats, increased differences in voting patterns of blacks and whites, and a fall-off in the number of

TABLE 4.5

Race as an Issue: 1964–1984

Salience[a]

Year	Total	Blacks	Southern Whites	Other Whites
1964	28.5	69.8	32.3	21.7
1968	15.9	53.7	11.7	12.0
1972	8.1	25.4	6.8	6.2
1976	5.0	17.4	5.7	3.1
1980	4.9	23.0	1.6	2.8
1984	3.6	10.4	2.1	3.0

Party Preferred on Race[b]

	Total		Blacks		Southern Whites		Other Whites	
Year	Dem.	Rep.	Dem.	Rep.	Dem.	Rep.	Dem.	Rep.
1964	15.9	11.9	68.6	1.3	5.3	25.9	10.9	10.2
1968	10.3	4.7	49.0	2.7	2.8	6.6	6.9	4.5
1972	3.7	4.3	22.4	2.2	1.8	4.8	1.7	4.5
1976	3.1	1.6	13.8	3.1	2.5	2.9	1.7	1.1
1980	4.3	0.5	22.5	0.0	0.8	0.5	2.2	0.6
1984	2.7	0.9	9.2	0.4	1.3	0.8	2.1	0.9

Net Partisan Preference on Race[c]

Year	Total	Blacks	Southern Whites	Other Whites
1964	.087	1.635	−.372	−.025
1968	.102	.920	−.048	.031
1972	−.006	.313	−.037	−.042
1976	.017	.130	−.010	.008
1980	.050	.321	.003	.018
1984	.023	.104	.005	.017

Notes: a. Salience is the percentage of each group mentioning race or racial issues as a reason to like or dislike either of the parties or candidates.

b. Preference is the percentage of each group with a net pro-Democratic or net pro-Republican preference on race; it is computed by adding the number of pro-Democratic and anti-Republican mentions and subtracting the number of anti-Democratic and pro-Republican mentions.

c. Net partisan preference is the mean net preference score for each group.

southern votes—popular and electoral—on which the Democrats had previously depended.

It may therefore be somewhat surprising to find that race *per se* assumes a much reduced role in mass political behavior after 1968: Table 4.5 shows that the percentage of the population mentioning it spontaneously as a basis of partisan evaluation drops from the 28.5% of 1964 and the 15.9% (for the two major parties) of 1968 to only 8.1% in 1972 and to even lower levels thereafter; no more than 3.6% of whites or a quarter of blacks mention it after 1972.[17] These levels are far below even those of the racially quiescent 1950s. The perhaps surprising finding that so little of Wallace's appeal is explained in explicitly racial terms seems in part a harbinger of the reduced attention that race was to receive more generally in subsequent elections.

Differences in partisan preferences on racial issues become less distinct at the same time: concerned blacks remain overwhelmingly Democratic, but differences between them and whites are depressed by the near disappearance of such concern among whites. Positions on individual racially-related issues remain linked to partisan preference, but the magnitude of the relationship is again reduced from the levels of 1964. Figure 4.3 shows that the link between one's position on fair employment and net partisan preference in 1964 decreases somewhat in 1968 and almost disappears in 1972. To guard against the possibility that this decrease may be a function of the growing irrelevance of the fair employment question (Margolis, 1977), Figure 4.3 also graphs net partisan preference on race for different positions on the newer issue of busing. The result is the broken line that shows more polarization than for fair employment in 1972 but less than for fair employment in 1964.

Sundquist (1983: 372) maintains that the 1976 election ended the politics of race in the south, pointing to the Democrats' doing more or less as well as elsewhere in the country and to the emergence of class voting within the white southern electorate on more or less the same scale as in the north.[18] The improved Democratic vote totals in 1976 are undoubtedly a response in part to Carter's nomination: Carter does seem to stimulate some regional loyalty among southern whites, becoming the first Democrat since Kennedy to do better among them than among whites elsewhere and capturing 118 of 130 electoral votes in a region that since 1964 had been quite inhospitable to Democratic presidential candidates.

But one should perhaps see the reduction in explicit concern with race as part of a more general transformation of the role racial concerns play in American politics. The mid-1960s had been concerned with a particular form of civil rights question: desegregation, open accommodations, and voting rights all involved efforts to reverse decades of explicit political and legal inequality imposed on blacks. This first civil rights agenda sparked tremendous conflict at the time, but it was all formally in place by the middle of the decade and increasingly accepted by the early 1970s. Emergence of a new generation of moderate southern Democratic politicians, committed in principle to equal treatment of blacks, who proved capable of winning gubernatorial and senatorial elections throughout the region was a sign of the party's ability to detach itself from its segregationist past without sacrificing popular support (Bass and de Vries, 1976). Jimmy Carter's defeat of Wallace in southern Democratic primaries in 1976 is an important sign of the nature of southern political evolution on race and may have been of greater long-term significance than his election as president (see also Black and Black, 1992: 248).

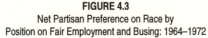

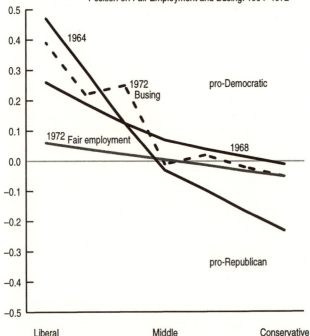

FIGURE 4.3
Net Partisan Preference on Race by
Position on Fair Employment and Busing: 1964–1972

Note: Net partisan preference is the mean of pro-Democratic and anti-Republican mentions minus anti-Democratic and pro-Republican mentions.

The concern of civil rights activists then turned to a set of issues that were much less explicitly racial: questions of economic equality and opportunity linked to more general questions of social welfare that had divided the parties for generations. At the same time, non-economic issues that assumed increased importance in the late 1960s could be seen as having racial content as well: the authors who first directed attention to the Social Issue stressed at length how such concerns should not (but might well) be confused with race. The possibility that concern with issues like crime and social disintegration might have racial content or be codewords for anti-black sentiment has been discussed at least from the initial publication of *The Real Majority* in 1971 through the Willy Horton advertisements of 1988. It is of course possible that citizens concerned with blacks and their welfare might still mention racial group benefits or refer to past legal/political changes as bases for liking or disliking the parties and candidates; but one should not be surprised if post-1968 racially-linked concerns are increasingly conflated with other types of issues (see also Carmines and Stimson, 1989).[19]

But as the explicitly racial issues that sparked the dramatic changes of 1964 become less salient, the patterns of vote choice that they generated do not disappear. Race itself remains a powerful cleavage in presidential election voting: blacks remain overwhelmingly Democratic, the gap between them and whites far larger than that for any of the other social characteristics we have examined; Ds between race and vote choice are only slightly smaller than the peak levels of 1968 and 1972, and they show only modest evidence of decline over time. For regional differences among whites, the striking change is the *lack* of any such cleavage: post-1968 elections show no evidence of either the distinctively Democratic pre-1960 white south or of the distinctively anti-Democratic south of 1964. Carter in 1976 is the only Democrat to actually do better in the south than elsewhere, but the degree to which he does so (D of .03) is quite modest; Ford wins a plurality of white southerners. After 1976, the relationship between southern residence and Democratic voting are consistently negative but consistently small: those like Black and Black (1992) who stress the poor performance of the Democrats among southern whites underestimate the magnitude of their problems among non-southern whites; only in 1984 does D reach even the modest level of −.10. The distinctiveness of southern white voters has become quite modest; and that, of course, is itself a major change from the years before 1964.

What drives Democratic electoral difficulties in the post-1968 world is a much more general phenomenon only indirectly linked to race: the Democrats are generally perceived as having moved far to the left, to a point at which they are substantially out of touch with a large segment of their own identifiers as well as with the electorate as a whole. Democratic racial activism of the 1960s undoubtedly played a role in beginning this process. But race itself plays only a minor role in the larger picture of more general Democratic ideological extremism after 1968, as one might expect once exhaustion of the explicitly political racial agenda of desegregation and voting rights leads to its replacement by concerns that overlap into questions of social welfare and social order. Race does continue to play a role in Democratic electoral failure after 1968, but it does so as part of a much more general set of ideologically-related problems.

NOTES

1. See Black and Black (1992: 87–89). Ladd and Hadley (1978: 43) and Phillips (1970: 195) attribute Hoover's success to northern in-migration and to increasing sensitivity to economic cleavages as well as to simple anti-Catholic or anti-northern sentiment. Key (1949) documents the continued Democratic strength in 1928 in areas with large black populations, where race continued to motivate the overwhelmingly white electorate; Hoover did best where there were few blacks. Weiss (1983: 10) notes that Smith made some modest gains among blacks.

2. It is striking how little attention race receives in the earlier studies of vote choice. These studies were forced by limited resources to focus on limited geographical areas, pre-

venting any full consideration of the electoral interaction of race and region. But it is still fascinating that Lazarsfeld et al. (1968) in their 1940 study of Erie County, Ohio, that focuses on the social basis of vote choice make not a single reference to race or racial issues. Berelson et al.'s (1954) investigation of the 1948 election refers to the overwhelmingly Democratic loyalty of blacks in Elmira, but race still attracts only the briefest of attention, particularly compared to the amount devoted to social class; their discussion of issues in the campaign (chapter nine) also makes only the most minimal of references to racial concerns.

3. In July 1948, Truman issued an Executive Order integrating the armed forces.

4. Thurmond was listed as the Democratic nominee on the ballots of all four states.

5. There was at the same time increasing migration of northern whites to the Sun Belt, bringing with them traditional Republican loyalties that helped make the South more two-party.

6. Four years later, he won less than half of all southern electoral votes, although they constituted more than eighty percent of his total.

7. Stevenson did particularly badly in the outer south and in the region's metropolitan areas. See Black and Black (1992: 184).

8. For a detailed state and county level analysis of Republicanism in the south, see Black and Black (1992: chapters two and three).

9. This mean score is a function both of the number of people concerned with a given issue and of the balance of pro-Democratic and pro-Republican perceptions.

10. Sullivan et al. (1978) argue quite convincingly that much of the increased constraint that Nie with Andersen (1974) observe is a methodological artifact caused by changed question formats between 1960 and 1964. Carmines and Stimson (1989: 121), equally convincingly, show that changes on race cannot be explained as a methodological artifact alone. Carmines and Stimson go on to argue that race had by 1972 become the central organizing element in mass belief systems.

11. Goldwater reverses the previous pattern in which Eisenhower and Nixon had run more strongly in the peripheral than in the deep south. See Black and Black (1992: 209).

12. They also point to a more general move to the right among white southerners after 1970 that makes their attitudes on race less isolated.

13. The .066 in 1968 is the largest absolute value the Democrats receive on race in any election; the .039 for 1964 is second largest. The –.037 for the Republicans in 1968 is second in absolute value only to the –.048 of 1964.

14. The finding would seem to support Scammon and Wattenberg's (1971) argument that social disorder and crime rather than race represented the potentially anti-Democratic issue of the late 1960s. To the extent that citizens drawn to Wallace's positions on race articulated their concern in terms of social order rather than race itself, however, these data would of course underestimate the importance of race. Carmines and Stimson (1989) are quite suggestive in teasing out possible underlying racial content of concerns expressed in nonracial terms. See also Black and Black (1992: 166); Petrocik (1987).

15. The 19.4% of Wallace voters who on balance approve of him on race is much larger than the 4.9% of the total population who do so, but it is still a small minority of his total supporters. The percentage of Wallace voters who prefer him on new domestic issues is 26.5%.

16. There is a fall-off in the salience of race as a most important problem as well (from 40.8% in 1964 to 27.7%) that occurs for both blacks and whites. On the other hand, the

upper limit of three most important problems coded combines with the extraordinarily high level of concern with Vietnam in 1968 to raise questions about whether additional racial concerns might have gone uncoded. The parallel decline of such mentions as bases for candidate evaluation does suggest that the changes are real.

17. The reduction in the number of perceptions of each party and candidate from five to three does not explain the reduced concern with race. If we limit 1968 respondents to their first three comments, omitting the fourth and fifth, the percentage concerned with race falls only from 15.9% to 14.8%. In 1976, when the questionnaire format again allows five comments, the fall-off is from 8.1% for the full set of five comments to 5.0% for the first three only.

18. Petrocik (1981) had earlier stressed an increased nationalization of party competition in the south beginning in the 1950s in which class played an increased role in determining partisan preferences of white southerners.

19. There remains, of course, considerable disagreement on how to deal with explicitly legal and political questions as well: debate over busing, affirmative action, and representation did not disappear after 1968.

5

The Emergence of the Second Mini-Realignment: Ideological Extremity and Democratic Defection*

The decline in Democratic electoral fortunes that began in 1968 has been noticed by many: the *pattern* and *stability* of Democratic failure was generally not perceived, but it was hard for even casual observers to miss the fact that the party that had won seven of the previous nine presidential elections now lost five of the next six. The burgeoning debate on realignment/dealignment undoubtedly contributed to the failure to appreciate that there was a pattern in the outcomes. Those seeking realignment saw repeated hints that a new party system was about to emerge, but the failure of all the other components of a new political order to fall into line caused them to underestimate the magnitude and stability of changes at the presidential level; those more attracted to dealignment focused on the failure of the realignment package as a whole and on the idiosyncratic 1976 election. Both failed to see that a stable pattern of presidential election outcomes could occur in the absence of the realignment package as a whole.

There was in fact considerable debate over the reasons underlying the Democratic defeats. One explanation, originating in work that appeared during the Nixon administration, focused on emergence of new issues on which the electorate was substantially more conservative than the Democratic party leadership. Kevin Phillips (1970) maintained that Democratic party elites were moving to the left on substantive issues at a time when the electorate was stable or moving to the right. Perception that the liberal policies of the Kennedy and Johnson administrations had failed created a new conservative majority which found its natural home in the Republican party. Miller et al. (1976) found that issues played a considerable (if not decisive) role in the 1972 election, with McGovern's policy positions sufficiently to the left of both the average voter and the average Democrat for issues and ideology to contribute significantly to Nixon's victory.

This first generation of works explaining Democratic presidential election failure was criticized by many who looked for and failed to find the emerging conservative majority; rather, Democratic failure was attributed to the nomination of weak candidates, especially in 1972, or to temporary ideological lapses that had no long-term consequences. Popkin et al. (1976), for example, attribute Nixon's 1972 landslide primarily to McGovern's incompetence as candidate rather than to any mass rejection of his issue positions. Miller and Levitin (1976) make a similar candidate-based argument, citing McGovern's failure to mobilize a public they claim was quite liberal on "New Politics" issues and holding out hope for Democratic victories once the party nominated candidates who could effectively tap an essentially sympathetic public opinion.[1] Kelley (1983) characterizes 1972 as a "close landslide" based on voters with relatively weak preferences for Nixon and consisting largely (if not exclusively) of candidate (rather than issue) concerns. Sundquist (1983) differs from the others in seeing Democratic defeats in 1972 and, to a lesser extent, 1968 as having ideological content, but he argues that both were due to temporary left-ward Democratic lurches effectively corrected by party leadership well before the next election (see also Gold, 1992).

Most investigators who examined survey data from later Republican victories in 1980 or 1984 also found no evidence of a general swing to the right by the electorate (Gold, 1992; Smith, 1990; Robinson and Fleishman, 1988; Kelley, 1983; but see Shanks and Miller, 1991). Abramson, Aldrich, and Rohde (1982) conclude that 1980 was a negative retrospective evaluation of Jimmy Carter based on his perceived failure to manage either the economy or the Iranian hostage crisis (Pomper 1981; Frankovic, 1981; Hibbs, 1982). Retrospective voting more generally (Fiorina, 1981; Popkin et al., 1976) provided an essentially non-ideological explanation for Republican success that meshed well with earlier voting studies skeptical of the ideological (or other) sophistication of the American electorate:[2] both 1980 and 1984 turned on evaluation of incumbent performance, with the public generally perceiving Carter as a failed president and rejecting his bid for re-election; in 1984, it contrasted Reagan's success with Carter's failure, a comparison facilitated by the Democrats' nomination of Carter's vice president, and voted to keep Reagan in office. George Bush's having been Reagan's vice president as well as the nominee of Reagan's party extends the logic of retrospective voting to 1988 (Wattenberg, 1991; Abramson, Aldrich, Rohde, 1990; see also Lanoue, 1994). Policy decisions after each of these elections may well have had an ideological character, but ideology at the elite level was a consequence of retrospective voting rather than the source of a candidate's electoral appeal.[3]

It is clear how realignment theory might in principle account for the new era of Republican domination of presidential elections that began in 1968. But it is also clear that the post-1968 world in many ways differed from what realignment theorists would have predicted: neither the substantial Republican gains in party identification nor a clear new and cross-cutting conservative issue agenda on which the Republicans were dominant emerged, and the limited Republican gains in sub-presidential elections were delayed until 1980 and then proved temporary. And yet an argument that Republican domination is due solely to a series of favorable retrospective evaluations seems initially unlikely as well. Retrospective voting shares with dealignment theory a sensitivity to the short-term that should produce considerable volatility in election outcome over time: the working of the business cycle, the sheer complexity of modern government, and the inevitable coalitions of disaffected minorities should put limits on either party's ability to sustain a retrospective advantage.

The argument made here is that there are two distinct eras of Republican domination of presidential elections after 1968, both of them at least partially retrospective in character. The interplay of respondents' own issue positions and their perceptions of the Democrats/Republicans provides an ideological explanation for Democratic losses between 1968 and 1980 despite a lack of across-the-board increase in mass conservatism: perceptions of Democrats as relatively extreme, rooted initially in the liberal activism of the mid-1960s and extended by the McGovern nomination in 1972, created conditions under which they suffer disproportionate losses even in their partisan/ideological core. But the Republicans' advantage in issue space comes to an end at the beginning of the Reagan era: after 1980, Reagan's pushing images of the Republicans to the right eliminates their ideological advantage. Continued post-1980 dominance is due largely to a more conventional set of retrospective evaluations, rooted in the Carter economic failure of the late 1970s and extended by the Reagan economic success of the early 1980s. The inherent fragility of such purely retrospective considerations is in fact what sets up the (temporary?) Democratic resurgence in 1992.

IDEOLOGICAL EXTREMITY
AND THE ASYMMETRY OF PARTISAN DEFECTION

Existing literature is sufficient to establish that no simple across-the-board increase in mass conservatism is responsible for the Democrats' failure between 1968 and 1988. That need not mean that ideological factors play no role in the Democrats' decline. If they are at work here, however, they operate in a way much more subtle than a simple general shift in mass opinion to the right.

It is nonetheless clear that *something* was preventing the Democrats from realizing victories that their long-time advantage in party identification would otherwise seem capable of providing them. Between 1952 and 1980, a solid majority of the electorate thought of themselves as Democrats, a group sufficient to produce electoral victory by itself if Democratic and Republican identifiers simply supported their own party/candidate equally. Table 5.1 shows both the Democratic advantage in party identification over time[4] and the higher Democratic defection rates in every election except 1964.[5] Even in 1984 and 1988, when the party identification edge narrows and Democratic identifiers no longer exceed fifty percent, a simple balance of defection rates would have produced comfortable Democratic victories. In fact, they lost seven of the ten elections and won two of the others with margins far less than equal defection rates would have provided.[6]

More revealing than the difference in defection rates *between* the parties are differences in the pattern of defection *within* the parties. Each group of partisans

TABLE 5.1
Party Identification and Defection

| Year | Identifiers[a] | | | Defection Rates[b] | | | |
| | Dem. | Rep. | Ratio (D/R) | Narrow[c] | | Broad[d] | |
				Dem.	Rep.	Dem.	Rep.
1952	57.8	35.0	1.65	21.3	3.1	43.8	17.9
1956	51.9	38.9	1.33	18.1	2.6	40.3	18.5
1960	52.9	37.0	1.43	17.7	2.6	41.7	18.1
1964	61.6	30.5	2.02	7.0	26.7	27.0	46.0
1968	56.1	33.1	1.69	17.5	5.0	53.2	26.2
1972	52.3	34.4	1.52	37.1	3.0	60.5	18.7
1976	52.0	33.3	1.56	19.8	9.9	44.9	35.2
1980	52.1	32.8	1.59	15.8	10.1	48.8	36.2
1984	48.7	40.2	1.21	20.4	4.8	42.2	21.1
1988	47.7	41.5	1.15	13.6	8.1	36.3	28.2

Notes: a. The total percentage of Democratic and Republican identifiers (strong, weak, and leaners) and the ratio of Democrats to Republicans.
b. The percentage of each group of partisans that defects.
c. Narrow defection is the number of each group that votes for the opposite party expressed as a percentage of all identifiers who plan to vote.
d. Broad defection is the percentage of each group who fails to vote for its party's nominee by either defecting in the narrow sense, by voting for third party candidates, or by abstaining.

can be divided into a core whose ideological orientation is consistent with the dominant tendency in the party (liberal Democrats and conservative Republicans) and a potentially disaffected non-core (conservative Democrats and liberal Republicans) whose preferences would both generate dissatisfaction with the party's dominant ideological tone and predispose citizens to find the major party alternative relatively attractive.

Figure 5.1 presents a first simplified overview of the relationship between ideological placement and defection rates using aggregate data from the full ten-election period. Responses to each closed-ended issue[7] in each year have been standardized, i.e., each value has been recoded to reflect its distance in standard deviation units from the mean for all such partisans with valid scores on the item in order to indicate how extreme it is for that population in that year. The 1972 survey, for example, contains a question on whether the government should guarantee citizens medical care and another on using busing to achieve school integration: in each case, respondents are offered a seven point response scale ranging from the most liberal position at point one to the most conservative position at point seven. The question on medical care has a mean score for Democrats of 3.50, with a standard deviation of 2.44; the question on busing has a very conservative mean of 6.06 and a relatively small standard deviation of 1.79. The difference be-

FIGURE 5.1

Percentage Defecting by Ideological Extremity

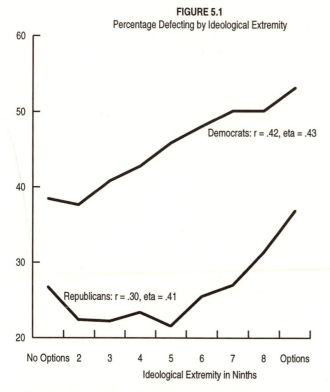

Note: No options: no ideologically attractive major party defection attractive. Options: Ideologically attractive major party alternative exists.

tween standardized scores of −2.83 on busing and −1.02 on medical care reflects how much more liberal the left-most position on busing is than the same absolute score on medical care.[8]

For ease of presentation, the Figure ranks the standardized issue scores for each response category of each question from the most liberal, i.e., furthest to the left from the population mean, to the most conservative, i.e., furthest to the right of the population mean. This ranking is then divided into equal ninths in an attempt to create sufficient categories to show variation across (and within each side of) the ideological continuum while retaining a sufficient number of cases in each category. The resulting Figure is set up so that the left of the ideological extremity continuum contains core constituencies who have no ideologically attractive major party alternative (liberal Democrats and conservative Republicans), while the right contains those for whom the other major party should seem more attractive (conservative Democrats and liberal Republicans). The Figure then presents the mean percentage of those in each category who fail to support their party's nominee in order to show how positions at different levels of ideological extremity are related to defection.

Figure 5.1 makes clear that the lower level of Republican defection indicates in Table 5.1 extends across the full range of ideological extremity: the Democratic curve is substantially above the Republican curve for each of the nine categories. Furthermore, each core population is more loyal than its corresponding non-core: the amount of defection generally increases as one moves across Figure 5.1 from left to right. What is unexpected is the different defection patterns within the two cores. After a very modest downward tick in moving from the most liberal to the second most liberal ninth, Democratic defection rates increase at a fairly constant rate as one moves from the core toward the center. For Republicans, this is not the case: the percentage defecting at the core end of the continuum is 26.7%, and as one moves toward the center the defection rates are a consistent and relatively low 22.4%, 22.3%, 23.4%, and 21.6% (see also Converse et al., 1965). The correlation

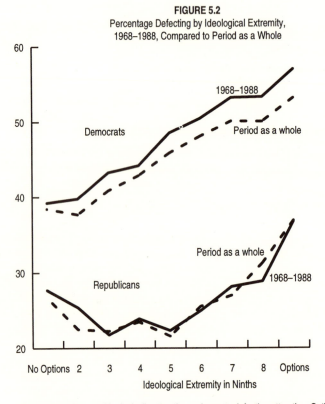

FIGURE 5.2
Percentage Defecting by Ideological Extremity,
1968–1988, Compared to Period as a Whole

Note: No options: no ideologically attractive major party defection attractive. Options: Ideologically attractive major party alternative exists.

between defection rate and degree of ideological extremity for the five categories is
−.13, compared to .26 for the parallel segment for liberal Democrats. A 11.7% gap
in percentage loyal when Democratic liberals are compared with Republican conservatives rises to 24.3% for centrists.[9] For Democrats, the almost identical values
of r and eta indicate that the relationship in Figure 5.1 is almost entirely linear
across the full range of ideological extremity; for Republicans, the curves on the
two sides of the midpoint look rather different.

These differences become even more intriguing if one looks at how the relationships change over time. One might expect from location of the second mini-realignment around 1966 that the higher rate of Democratic defection would become even greater after that year. Figure 5.2 shows post-1966 data together with
the original curve to demonstrate that is in fact the case.

The two Republican curves in Figure 5.2 show that the overall link between
ideological extremity and defection is much the same over time. The two curves
overlap each other substantially across the full range of ideological extremity: there
is neither a general increase in Republican defection nor an increase at any individual segment of the ideological extremity continuum. The 1968–1988 period
shows the same distinctive flat (or slightly downward) slope for conservative Republicans combined with a clear-cut upward slope as one moves from centrists to
liberals.

Such Republican consistency contrasts with considerable Democratic change
after 1968. Democratic defection rates increase over time across the full range of
ideological extremity: each category shows a higher level of defection in 1968–
1988 than for the period as a whole. The overall shape of the two Democratic curves
is very much the same, but the modest changes which do occur make the slope for
Democratic liberals slightly greater for 1968–1988 (.31) than for the period as a
whole (.26). For 1968–1988, the 12.1% gap between defection rates of the most
liberal Democrats and conservative Republicans more than doubles to 26.2% at
the middle of the continuum and declines slightly to 20.2% when the most conservative Democrats are compared to the most liberal Republicans. The distinct defection patterns of Democrats and Republicans in Figure 5.1 become slightly more
distinct in the latter half of the period in which Democratic electoral performance
deteriorates.

Three findings emerge from these aggregate data. First, at each level of ideological extremity, Democrats are less loyal than Republicans. Second, the two sets of
partisans have distinct *patterns* of loyalty. Democrats are sensitive to ideological
extremity across the full range of categories, from most liberal to most conservative; the effect is fairly strong and almost entirely linear. Republican liberals look
much like Democrats, with defection increasing with ideological proximity to the
opposition. Republican conservatives are the distinctive group, with their defection rates almost entirely *in*sensitive to ideological extremity. Third, Democrats
and Republicans respond differently to the passage of time: Republicans act much
the same in both time periods; Democratic defection increases, however, in each

category other than the liberal extreme, producing an even stronger linear relationship between ideology and defection that makes the contrast between liberal Democrats and conservative Republicans, supposedly trapped in a similar way by the lack of an ideologically acceptable major party alternative, even more striking.

TABLE 5.2
Individual-level Ideological Extremism and Defection: Comparison of Core Populations

Year	Liberal Democrats	Conservative Republicans
1952	.15	.16
1956	.04	.10
1960	.14	.07
1964	.11	.18
1968	.33	−.10
1972	.39	−.01
1976	.08	−.09
1980	.18	.17
1984	.14	.03
1988	.06	.02

Note: Entries are product-moment correlation between ideological extremity in ninths and voting behavior for core partisans: liberal Democrats and conservative Republicans.

Table 5.2 shifts the focus to the individual level, constructing an ideological extremity measure for each respondent by summing his or her standardized scores on all of the individual issue variables[10] and looking at core populations in each year separately. The result is if anything a more powerful version of the aggregate analysis finding of different defection rates of the two core populations.[11] There is no difference between the cores early in the period: the mean correlation between ideological extremity and defection for liberal Democrats in 1952–1964 (.11) is actually slightly smaller than that for conservative Republicans' (.13). But dramatic differences appear in 1968: in both 1968 and 1972, a substantial positive correlation for core Democrats is paired with a modest negative correlation for core Republicans; in 1976 the coefficient for the Democrats falls off, but it is still modestly positive at a time when the Republicans' is modestly negative. Differences between the parties decrease further at the very end of the period, an important point to which we will return below, but for 1968–1976 they are substantial.[12]

PARTISAN IDEOLOGICAL ASYMMETRY:
PERCEPTIONS OF ELECTORAL ALTERNATIVES

Why should there be such asymmetry between liberal Democrats and conservative Republicans? Why should the ideological cores of the two parties defect at such different rates and respond so differently to ideological extremity? Assuming that

Democratic presidential candidates throughout this period have been more liberal than their Republican counterparts, each core would seem to be tied to its own party by ideology as well as partisanship. For the Democrats, holding their larger core would seem to be the first step towards transforming a partisanship plurality into an electoral plurality. Yet Democratic defection is higher across the ideological continuum, and Democrats suffer disproportionate losses within their ideological core.

Surely it is the Republican pattern that is natural. As one moves from the conservative extreme to the center, a Republican should find the Democratic candidate increasingly acceptable. But there is no reason to think he or she would find the candidate sufficiently attractive to consider a Democratic vote: one would expect a Republican anywhere on the conservative side of the ideological mid-point to feel closer to his or her own candidate, albeit not necessarily as close as an even more conservative fellow partisan. Unless our assumption about placement of candidates in ideological space is faulty, Republicans of differing degrees of conservatism would vote for their own party's candidate with varying degrees of enthusiasm, but they would all vote for their party's candidate. And this seems, for the most part, to be the case.

Liberal Democrats behave quite differently. Movement from the liberal extreme toward the center produces increased defection; moderately liberal Democrats defect at rates higher than those of very liberal Democrats. The fact that liberal Democrats share with conservative Democrats and liberal Republicans an upward slope in Figures 5.1 and 5.2 might initially make the flat slope of conservative Republicans seem distinctive and unusual. But the logic of the link between self-placement and proximity to the candidate in issue space makes clear that it is the liberal Democrats whose behavior requires special explanation. That moderate liberals might be closer in issue space than their more liberal fellow Democrats to the Republican candidate is not surprising; that they actually defect to such an extent *is* surprising. And such defections obviously hold part of the answer to why the majority party has done so badly in winning presidential elections.

This pattern of defection is consistent with a variant of the argument that ideology underlies the Democrats' problems. Perception of Democratic electoral alternatives as relatively extreme, i.e., located toward the far liberal end of the issue continuum (Phillips, 1970; Kirkpatrick, 1976), would help explain the relative attractiveness of the Republican electoral alternative to Democratic centrists and, therefore, the impact of ideological extremity in the liberal half of the Democratic ideological continuum that contrasts so markedly with the flatness of the parallel curve for Republican conservatives. Furthermore, the literature is full of factors like the Kennedy/Johnson domestic policy activism (Ladd, 1989; Nie with Andersen, 1974; Pomper, 1972), intense intra-party conflict (Weisberg and Rusk, 1970), and disruptive nominating conventions dominated by liberal activists rather than traditional party elites (Kirkpatrick, 1976; Ladd, 1982; Polsby, 1983), which could be responsible for such change after 1964 (see also Dionne, 1991).[13]

Pursuing the possibility that the Democrats suffer in the late 1960s and 1970s because they are perceived as ideologically extreme is facilitated by the introduction of a new kind of National Election Study closed-ended issue question in 1968. NES surveys have used a number of different question formats since 1952 to determine respondents' issue positions (Smith, 1989; Aldrich et al., 1982; Fiorina, 1981), but since 1968 increased use has been made of the seven-point closed-ended issue questions cited above in illustrating creation of our measure of respondent ideological extremity: two alternate positions are defined as end-points of a seven-point continuum, and respondents are then asked to indicate their preferred outcome; the middle position is available to indicate neutrality.[14] Once respondents become familiar with the format, it can easily be used to ask them where they perceive candidates and parties to stand on some of the issues that they themselves were asked. One can therefore measure respondents' perceived distance from electoral alternatives based on their self-placement relative to their placement of the parties and candidates (see also Page and Jones, 1979; Page, 1978). Although there are problems with perceived distance,[15] it has a considerable advantage for study of the link between ideological extremity and defection in that it measures the magnitude of differences and orders them along a left-right continuum analogous to our measure of respondent ideological extremity: we can therefore determine whether respondents see themselves as more liberal or more conservative than the electoral alternatives, as well as the degree to which they do so.[16]

Table 5.3 therefore reports the mean perceived distance to each of the electoral alternatives for both sets of partisans for each election between 1968 and 1988. Perceived distance is given as a proportion of the total *possible* distance between a

TABLE 5.3
Perceived Distance: Respondents' Perceptions of Electoral Alternatives Over Time

Year	Democratic Identifiers		Republican Identifiers	
	Perception of Democratic Party/ Candidate	Perception of Republican Party/ Candidate	Perception of Democratic Party/ Candidate	Perception of Republican Party/ Candidate
1968	−.044	.088	−.122	−.009
1972	−.092	.125	−.273	−.040
1976	−.095	.118	−.304	−.093
1980	−.080	.218	−.310	.014
1984	−.016	.296	−.259	.054
1988	.012	.267	−.242	.039

Note: Positive scores indicate respondents are more liberal than the target party/candidate; negative scores indicate that respondents are more conservative. Entries are mean summed distance scores expressed as a proportion of total possible distance (to standardize for number of questions asked in each year). A respondent who gave the most liberal answer to each question and who placed both Republican candidate and party at the most conservative end of the continuum would take a score of +1.000.

respondent and a given party/candidate: scores range from 1.000 if a respondent is at the most liberal end of each issue continuum and sees the target party/candidate at the most conservative end on each issue to −1.000 when the opposite occurs. Such a measure is a useful way to summarize information on a number of individual issues in any given year, and it greatly facilitates comparison of perceived distance over time.

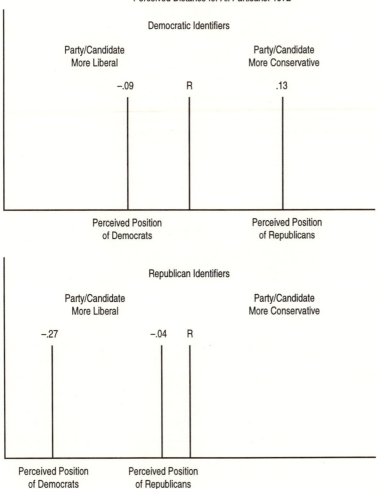

FIGURE 5.3
Perceived Distance for All Partisans: 1972

Note: Figures show mean perceived position of both electoral alternatives for Democratic and Republican identifiers separately.

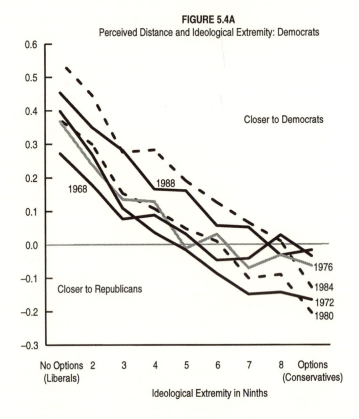

FIGURE 5.4A
Perceived Distance and Ideological Extremity: Democrats

Page (1978) has argued that the seven-point perceived distance questions are subject to considerable voter projection, placement of a favored candidate near oneself and an opposed candidate far away, but Table 5.3 shows two clear ways in which perceived distance distinguishes partisans in a way quite helpful to the Republicans, at least from 1968 through 1980. First, Democratic identifiers are consistently more distant from their own party/candidate than Republican identifiers are from theirs: in 1972, for example, both groups of partisans are more conservative than their own party/candidate, but Republican identifiers (−.040) are well less than half as distant as Democrats (−.092) are. In 1976, the difference is small, but in other years the Democrats are between 2.4 and nearly six times more distant. Second, Democratic identifiers feel much closer to the opposition than Republicans do; in 1976, for example, the average Democrat's distance to the Republican party/candidate is .118, while the average Republican's distance to the Democratic party/candidate is a far larger −.304.

Figure 5.3 uses 1972 data to illustrate how a *comparison* of the two electoral alternatives provides a much stronger incentive for a Republican to remain loyal

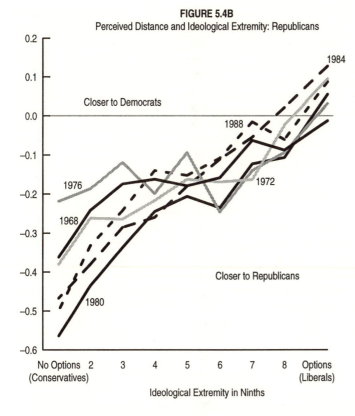

FIGURE 5.4B
Perceived Distance and Ideological Extremity: Republicans

than for a Democrat to do so. As is routinely the case between 1968 and 1980, Democratic identifiers in 1972 position themselves *between* the two partisan alternatives, more liberal than the Republican and more conservative than their own, and they are only modestly closer to their own party/candidate than to the opposition. Republican identifiers perceive themselves as more conservative than *both* electoral alternatives, but they are much more conservative than the Democrat and only slightly more conservative than the Republican; there is no ideologically-based incentive for the average Republican to defect in Figure 5.3.

Figure 5.4 demonstrates the link between perceived distance and ideological extremity more generally, graphing net perceived distance at each level of ideological extremity for both Democratic and Republican identifiers in each year. The net perceived distance measure indicates how much closer one feels to one's own candidate (or to the opposition) based on a comparison of distances to each separately.[17]

Figure 5.4 makes clear the extent to which perceived distance provides a much greater incentive for loyalty for centrist and core Republicans than it does for similar Democrats. Both groups of partisans on the extreme no-options side of the ideological extremity continuum feel much closer to their own party/candidate than to the opposition. Such preferences become less clear-cut for both groups of partisans as one moves towards the middle of the ideological extremity continuum, but the rate of change is far greater for Democrats: as one moves away from the liberal extreme, the fairly large downward slope of the curves produces essentially neutral perceived distance scores ranging from –.02 to .03 for centrist Democrats. The contrast with Republicans is strong: as one moves from their conservative extreme to the center, perceived distance becomes only slightly more Democratic. Each year's Republican centrists clearly prefer their own party to the opposition, with scores ranging from –.08 to –.20.

Figure 5.5 reproduces Figure 5.3 for centrist identifiers only, again using 1972 data to show the clear-cut advantage centrist Republicans have over centrist Democrats in their proximity to the parties.[18] Republican centrists look much like Republicans as a whole: they are slightly more conservative than their own party, but the Democrats are so much more liberal still that there is no ideological incentive to defect. Democratic centrists, like Democrats as a whole, are located between the two electoral alternatives and relatively close to each; but whereas Democrats as a whole are at least slightly closer to their own party to their left (–.09) than to the opposition on their right (.13), centrist Democrats are actually closer to the opposition (.06) than to the party with which they identify (–.12)! The average Democrat in 1972 may have only a modest ideological incentive to remain loyal to his or her party; the average centrist Democrat actually has a modest ideological incentive to defect.

It is important here to separate 1984 and 1988 from the four elections that preceded them. As Table 5.3 and Figure 5.4 make clear, the Reagan re-election campaign marked a break in the tendency for Democrats to be disadvantaged in perceived distance. The Democrats remain somewhat stable in ideological issue space in 1980: Democratic identifiers see the party moving slightly towards the center between 1976 and 1980, while Republican identifiers see it moving very slightly to the left; but neither change is very large. Reagan's conservatism, however, had an impact on perceptions of his party even in 1980: Table 5.3 makes clear that both Democratic and Republican identifiers saw the Republicans as having shifted substantially to the right between 1976 and 1980. For Democratic identifiers the perceived distance nearly doubles, from .118 to .218, while an even larger absolute shift moves the Republican party/candidate from somewhat more liberal than the average Republican identifier (–.093) in 1976 to slightly more conservative (.014).

The Reagan administration seems to have had even greater effects than the Reagan campaign: whether because of the President's own actions or those of Republicans in Congress (Hurley, 1989, 1991), of Republican party activists (Bruzios, 1990; Miller and Jennings, 1986), or even of a largely Republican-nominated Supreme Court (Mishler and Sheehan, 1993), images of the Republicans continue to move to the

FIGURE 5.5
Perceived Distance for Centrist Partisans: 1972

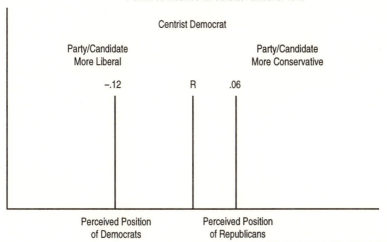

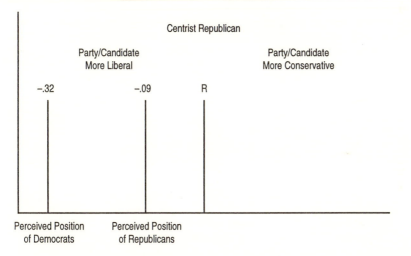

Note: Figures show mean perceived position of both electoral alternatives for Democratic and Republican identifiers separately.

right between 1980 and 1984 at a time when images of the Democrats are moving to the center (see also Gold, 1992).[19]

The net impact of these changes for net proximity to the electoral alternatives and for ideologically based incentives for loyalty or defection can be seen in Table 5.3, which shows the disappearance of the Republican advantage in issue space after 1980 for Democratic and Republican identifiers as a whole. Figure 5.6 repli-

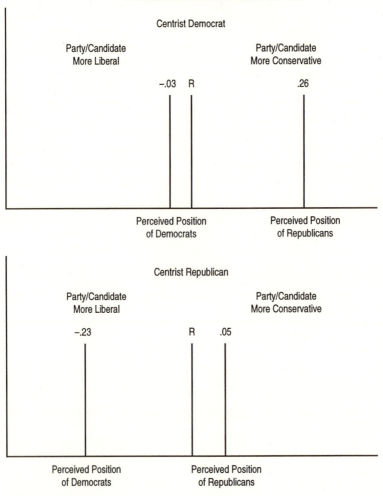

FIGURE 5.6
Perceived Distance for Centrist Partisans: 1984

Note: Figures show mean perceived position of both electoral alternatives for Democratic and Republican identifiers separately.

cates Figure 5.5 for 1984 to show the even more dramatic impact these changes have for centrist partisans.

For centrist Republicans, the impact of these changes is relatively small. The mean centrist Republican has moved from a point slightly to the right of his/her party and candidate (−.09) to one slightly to the left (.05). The fact that the direction to the party/candidate has changed is far less important that the fact that the absolute distance remains extremely small; and although the centrist Republican's mean distance to the Democratic party/candidate has decreased somewhat, from −.32 to −.23, it remains sufficiently large to place them considerably closer in issue space to their own party/candidate than to the opposition.

For Democrats, however, the changed perception of the parties and candidates in issue space has rather profound consequences. Table 5.3 indicates that the distance between Democrats as a whole and their own party/candidate is smaller than it has been since the perceived distance data first became available in 1968; and the move of the Republicans to the right creates a situation in which the average Democrat is for the first time substantially closer to their own party/candidate than to the competition. Comparison of Figures 5.5 and 5.6 makes clear how dramatic these changes have been for centrist Democrats. Centrist Democrats' perception of their own party/candidate decreases from −.12 to −.03; more dramatically, their distance to the Republican party/candidate increases from .06 to .26. Figure 5.5 had shown centrist Democrats located between the electoral alternatives, closer to the opposition than to their own. Figure 5.6 shows centrist Democrats in a situation quite similar to that of centrist Republicans: very close to their own party and candidate, very far from the opposition. Figure 5.5 showed a situation in which centrist Republicans had a strong ideologically-based incentive to stay loyal while centrist Democrats had at least a modest ideologically-based incentive to defect. Figure 5.6 makes clear that by 1984 the ideological basis for disproportionate Democratic defection has disappeared.

PARTIES AND CANDIDATES

Separating perceptions of parties from perceptions of candidates contributes to a somewhat fuller understanding of how these images evolved over time. In particular, it permits us to see how two candidates perceived as ideologically extreme— George McGovern and Ronald Reagan—had profound impact on the evolution of popular images of the two electoral alternatives.[20] Table 5.4 shows each group of partisans' perceived distance to the parties and candidates separately for each of the elections between 1968 and 1988.

The very partial 1968 data is limited to perceptions of candidates alone and deals only with the two issues of urban unrest and Vietnam. The 1968 data in Table 5.4 are therefore identical to the entries in Table 5.3: they show Democrats twice as distant from Nixon on their right as from Humphrey on their left. This certainly encourages Democratic loyalty, but nowhere near as strongly as a similar comparison provides for Republican identifiers whose position is almost identical to their placement of Nixon (−.009) and considerably more conservative than their perception of Humphrey (−.121).

The 1972 data presents a first opportunity to observe changing perceptions of candidates and the link between perceptions of candidates and parties, both of which center on the considerable negative impact that images of McGovern had for the Democrats. McGovern was generally perceived as positioned *extremely* far

TABLE 5.4
Perceived Distance to Parties and Candidates Separately Over Time

| | Democratic Identifiers | | | |
Year	Proximity to Democratic Party	Proximity to Democratic Candidate	Proximity to Republican Party	Proximity to Republican Candidate
1968	—	−.044	—	.088
1972	−.061	−.149	.116	.130
1976	−.122	−.083	.119	.084
1980	−.078	−.088	.196	.225
1984	−.020	−.015	.280	.313
1988	.015	−.002	.263	.260

| | Republican Identifiers | | | |
Year	Proximity to Democratic Party	Proximity to Democratic Candidate	Proximity to Republican Party	Proximity to Republican Candidate
1968	—	−.121	—	−.009
1972	−.230	−.322	−.045	−.031
1976	−.361	−.284	−.083	−.108
1980	−.317	−.313	−.001	.029
1984	−.254	−.260	.039	.068
1988	−.230	−.258	.035	.039

Note: Positive scores indicate respondents are more liberal than the target party/candidate; negative scores indicate that respondents are more conservative. Entries are mean summed distance scores expressed as a proportion of total possible distance (to standardize for number of questions asked in each year). A respondent who gave the most liberal answer to each question and who placed both Republican candidate and party at the most conservative end of the continuum would take a score of +1.000.

to the left: he is more distant from his own party's identifiers (−.149) than any Democratic or Republican candidate is from his own partisans in any election, three times more distant than Democrats had been from Humphrey in 1968. He is seen as much further to the left than is his party (−.061). Although Democrats' perceived distance to Nixon had increased somewhat as well since 1968, the 1972 average Democrat was actually closer to Nixon on his right than to McGovern on his left.[21] The relatively conservative self-placement of the average Republican makes the impact of McGovern's perceived extremism even greater: Republicans' distance to the Democratic candidate also nearly triples, to an extremely large −.322 that is considerably greater than their distance to the Democratic Party.

It would be hard to exaggerate how ideologically unrepresentative a candidate George McGovern was in 1972. Not only is he more distant from his own party's identifiers than either the Democratic or Republican Parties are from their own identifiers in any election, but fully 15.2% of all Democrats placed themselves to the left of their party while still being more conservative than McGovern. Only Reagan in 1980 generates anything like so unbalanced an ideological package, and even then only 10.9% of Republican identifiers take the parallel position of seeing their party to their left and their party's candidate to their right. Perceived distance to McGovern is unusually sensitive to Democrats' ideological extremity as well, far greater than for any other group of partisans in any year. The most liberal Democrat has a larger net perceived distance preference for McGovern (.479) than they do for their party (.354); as one moves to the right, the net preference for McGovern decreases rapidly, however. Among the most conservative Democrats, McGovern is much less favored than his party: net comparative perceived distance shows a strong proximity to Nixon of −.306 but only a modest net Republican Party advantage of −.096.

Jimmy Carter would seem to be precisely the kind of candidate that the Democrats might seek in order to reverse the effects of the McGovern nomination and to reduce popular perceptions of the party as ideologically extreme. Carter ran as a moderate Democrat in the primaries largely on a pragmatic issue-less appeal of trust and honesty, and his regional links might prove attractive to those driven away by the ideological conflicts of the previous eight years (Sundquist, 1983: 418; Pomper, 1977: 11).

Table 5.4 makes clear that such a Carter strategy was at least partially successful in 1976. Carter moderates images of the Democratic candidate, but he does not slow the damaging left-ward drift in perception of his party. Both Democratic and Republican identifiers see Carter as far less extreme than McGovern in 1972, with Democrats' perceived distance to their nominee only half what it had been four years earlier. But Table 5.4 at the same time makes clear that Carter's moderation does not prevent an increasingly radical image of his party: if the Democratic package in 1972 was an unbalanced package in which McGovern was far more liberal than his party, the unbalanced 1976 package has the party far more liberal than its candidate. Democrats in 1976 see the party twice as far to their left (.122) as it had been four years earlier, and further to their left than they saw Carter (.083). For Republicans, perceived distance to the Democratic Party increases even more strongly, from .230 to .361.

The net impact of these changes is only modest improvement of the Democrats' overall position in issue space. Ford's being perceived as more liberal than Nixon reduces the gains Democrats might have expected from Carter's moderation: Carter may be only −.083 to the left of the average Democrat, but Ford is only .084 to his partisans' right; both candidates are far closer to their own partisans in issue space than the candidates of 1972 had been, and the Democrats' net gain is slight. And the movement to the left in perceived placement of the Democratic party produces only modestly improved Democrats' image of the parties in issue space (.076 to .092) while producing a substantial increase (from −.132 to −.204) in the Republicans net proximity to their own party.

Carter as president failed to continue the moderation of mass perception of the Democrats that Carter as candidate had begun. Democrats' image of Carter changed little during his presidency: they saw him as very slightly more liberal in 1980 than in 1976, while Republican identifiers report a shift of Carter to the left that made him almost as ideologically extreme in their eyes as McGovern had been in 1972, equally as far to their left as the Democratic Party. The Carter years do moderate somewhat both groups of partisans' views of the Democratic Party, but in 1980 images of the Party are still further to the left among both Democrats and Republicans than they had been in 1972.

The much more dramatic change in 1980, of course, stems from the Republicans' nomination of Ronald Reagan. Both groups of partisans place Reagan considerably farther to the right than Ford, with consequences that increase the ideological incentive for loyalty for both of them. For Democrats, perceived distance to the Republican nominee increases from a modest .084 in 1976 to .225 four years later, making the average Democrat far closer to his own candidate than to the opposing candidate for the first time since 1968. An equally dramatic change shifts the average Republican from being somewhat more conservative than Ford had been in 1976 (−.108) to slightly more liberal than Reagan in 1980 (.029); the 10.9% of Republicans who see themselves more conservative than their party but more liberal than Reagan is the largest group of Republicans to be in so unbalanced a position and is second only to McGovern's degree of imbalance in 1972. But the decreased distance to their own candidate is more important than the change in direction. Reagan's strongly conservative image in 1980 coincides with a smaller but considerable move of perceptions of his party to the right as well.

The Reagan administration continues the Republican move to the right. Both Reagan himself and his party are perceived to be further to the right in 1984 by both partisan groups, with Reagan continuing to be seen as more conservative than the party.[22] Republican identifiers see their party as more conservative than they are in 1984 for the first time. Although Bush is seen as slightly less conservative than Reagan had been in 1984 by both Democrats and Republicans, images of the Republican Party remain quite conservative. For both groups of identifiers, there is the slightest movement of the Republican Party back to the center. Reagan had been seen as more conservative than his party in both 1980 and 1984. The changes in 1988 leave party and candidate in balance, but far to the right of where they had been before Reagan.

PERCEIVED DISTANCE
AND INDIVIDUAL ISSUE TYPES

The analysis of perceived distance to the parties and candidates on different types of issues is hampered by the limitations of individual NES surveys. Appendix 3 lists the limited number of issues on which usable perceived distance measures are available for each year. For the general measure of perceived distance, this limitation is not a major problem: there are at least six questions asked in each year (after 1968) about a fairly broad range of issues. Within an individual issue area, however, the number of items available is rather small, and the effects of availability or of change over time become more serious. In 1976, for example, there is no foreign policy question for which perceived distance measures were asked.[23]

Examination of the particular types of issue concern on which perceived distance mattered is nonetheless a fruitful exercise. Table 5.5 shows perceived distance to each of the two electoral alternatives separately for each of the four types of issues for which appropriate items are available. The four issue areas are: economics and social welfare; race; new domestic issues, a combination of Scammon and Wattenberg's (1971) Social Issue and Miller and Levitin's (1976) New Politics; and foreign policy/defense.

TABLE 5.5

Perceived Distance on Different Types of Issues Towards Each Party/Candidate Separately

Year	Overall	Economics/ Social Welfare	Race	New Domestic	Foreign
			Distance to Democrats		
1968	.078	—	—	−.151	−.012
1972	.164	.053	−.306	−.114	−.234
1976	.183	−.215	−.276	−.070	—
1980	.185	−.192	−.243	.001	−.215
1984	.127	−.175	−.149	−.103	−.070
1988	.100	−.169	−.185	.077	−.075
			Distance to Republicans		
1968	−.044	—	—	.047	.036
1972	−.051	.135	−.077	.076	.139
1976	−.014	.078	−.159	.056	—
1980	−.113	.109	.068	.239	.052
1984	−.176	.149	.083	.128	.237
1988	−.149	.147	.057	.211	.135

Note: Entries are perceived distance to a given party/candidate expressed as a proportion of the total possible distance. Positive scores mean that respondents are more liberal than the target party/candidate; negative scores mean that respondents are more conservative than the target party/candidate.

Foreign policy conforms to the classic expectation that voters will situate themselves between a too liberal Democratic party on their left and a too conservative Republican party on their right. The differences are quite small in 1968: the single issue of Vietnam conforms to the muddled picture of the electoral alternatives that Page and Brody (1972), among others, have pointed out; Humphrey is seen as slightly more dovish than the average voter (−.012), Nixon is only slightly more hawkish (.036), but the direction of placement is far less striking that the very small distance to each. More substantial differences emerge thereafter: in 1972, the Democrats are seen rather far to the left (−.234) while the Republicans are seen a somewhat lesser distance (.139) to the right. Table 5.6 shows the resulting sizable Republican advantage in net perceived distance (−.063) that nearly doubles eight years later when the Democrats essentially retain their position on the left (−.215) while the Republicans move back towards the center (.052).

TABLE 5.6
Net Comparative Perceived Distance on Different Types of Issues

Year	Economics/ Social Welfare	Race	New Domestic	Foreign
1968	—	—	−.036	−.018
1972	.002	−.082	−.007	−.063
1976	−.016	−.012	.027	—
1980	−.074	−.082	.122	−.105
1984	−.022	.016	.043	.061
1988	−.018	.006	.087	.010

Note: Entries are net preference in perceived distance as a proportion of total possible distance. Negative scores indicate a pro-Republican preference; positive scores indicate a pro-Democrat preference.

If foreign policy shows the distinctive Democratic disadvantage in issue space in 1968–1980, it also shows the impact of the Reagan administration in eliminating such disadvantages thereafter. The 1984 data show a marked change in perceptions of the parties/candidates. The Republicans are now the extremists: their distance score increases from .052 to .237; at the same time, the Democratic distance score decreases from −.215 to −.070. The parties retain their directional placement relative to the voter, but the perceived distances to them are greatly altered. The result is a net issue distance advantage for the Democrats in 1984 as large as the one the Republicans had enjoyed in 1972. Bush's perceived moderation in 1988 makes his party's score less extreme, and the net advantage the Democrats enjoy on the issue all but vanishes. But the slightly pro-Democratic net comparative perceived distance score in Table 5.6 for foreign policy still contrasts considerably with the sizable disadvantages from which the Democrats had suffered in 1968–1980.

The combination of two somewhat different *types* of issues under the heading of new domestic complicates any examination of popular perceptions or of net partisan advantage: the issues included in the NES survey shift from the types more associated with Scammon and Wattenberg's Social Politics (1971) to those included in Miller and Levitin's New Politics (1976) over time. But even in the earlier part of the period these issues are striking for their failure to provide the expected benefit to the Republicans.

The public is in fact more liberal than the Republicans on both types of new domestic issues: the distance involved is relatively small before 1980, when the items used primarily refer to issues like legalization of marijuana, rights of the accused, and responses to urban unrest; but the Reagan campaign and the simultaneous shift to questions about abortion rights and women's equality begin a period in which the Republicans are seen as relatively extreme. New domestic issues in 1980 and 1988 and foreign policy in 1984 are the issue areas on which the Republicans are seen as *most* extreme: none of the entries for economics or for race approach the .200 level that the entries for new domestic issues exceed. In no year are the Democrats seen as far to the left on new domestic issues as the Republicans are seen to the right in 1980 and 1988: the sole question on response to urban unrest in 1968 produces the their most extreme score (–.151), but in other years one finds smaller or even negative scores—the latter indicating that the average respondent sees the Democrats as too conservative!

The result of the increasing perception of the Republicans as conservative on new domestic issues in 1980 is a modest shift in the net partisan impact of such issues. In 1968, net advantage in perceived distance was a modestly pro-Republican –.036; thereafter it steadily becomes more Democratic, peaking at .122 in 1980 before producing smaller Democratic advantages thereafter. In 1972 there had been a considerable generational impact on new domestic concerns: respondents under thirty were the only pro-Democratic age group, distinctive in both their proximity to the Democrats and in their considerable distance from the Republicans. But after 1972 the Democratic preference cuts across all age groups. Even in 1976, when questions asked included such Social Issue concerns as legalization of marijuana and rights of the accused as well as (for the first time) women's equality, the electorate had a slight Democratic preference on new domestic issues; by 1980, with the classic Social Issue concerns dropped, the Democratic preference is considerably stronger.

Economics and social welfare are of course often seen as core issues underlying the Democratic dominance of 1932–1968: the Depression that began under Herbert Hoover and the New Deal of Franklin Roosevelt combined to produce the class-based cleavage system and policy focus on the role of the federal government in the economy that produced a generation of Democratic presidential election victories. It is an issue area in which the pattern of partisan difference and change over time are rather distinctive.

In 1972, the voters actually see the Democrats to their right on economics, albeit modestly: the 1972 Democratic ticket was seen as well to the left on race, new domestic issues, and foreign policy; but the general perception did not extend to economics, and McGovern does not suffer the net disadvantage on economics in Table 5.6 that exists in each of the three other issue areas. By 1976, however, perceptions of the Democrats on economics had moved to the left as well, producing a quite large distance score of −.215. The perceived extremity of the Democrats decreases after 1976, but it does so at a very gradual pace. What is striking is that there is no evidence for economics of the move of the Democrats to the center in response to Reagan that was seen for foreign policy issues or for perceived distance as a whole: the Democrats are still seen further to the left (−.169) in 1988 than the Republicans had been seen to the right in any year.

Placement of the Republicans in ideological issue space on economics follows a less volatile pattern. The Republicans are consistently seen as more conservative on economics than the average voter, but the absolute level of conservatism is never extreme: in no year are the Republicans positioned as far to the right on economics and social welfare as they are on new domestic issues in 1980 and 1988 or on foreign policy in 1984. In 1980, the net placement of the Republicans on economics is only .109, less in absolute distance than the −.192 for the Democrats and less even than the .135 Nixon received in 1972. The Reagan administration has considerable impact on this placement, pushing it to .149. But mostly as a result of the relatively modest changes in placement of the Democrats on such issues over time, Table 5.6 shows economics as an area of continuing Republican advantage in comparative ideological issue space even after 1980. In both 1984 and 1988, each of the three other issue areas saw the public slightly closer to the Democrats than to the Republicans in issue space, with economics the *sole* area in which Bush and the Republicans had a net advantage.

In Chapter Four, the re-emerging significance of race as a basis of political cleavage in 1964 was discussed in some detail. The Kennedy/Johnson racial activism of the early 1960s and the opposition to it by Barry Goldwater produced a considerable increase in racial polarization in vote choice. Such polarization was masked by the sheer volume and magnitude of other pro-Democratic forces in 1964, but the general fall-off in Democratic strength between 1964 and 1968 revealed a racial gap that was extraordinarily large. At the same time, a decrease after 1968 in the spontaneous mention of race as a basis for evaluating parties/candidates and in the degree to which preferences on racial issues are linked to vote choice suggest that the increased importance of race might be a temporary phenomenon of the 1964–1968 period rather than a core component of long-term electoral change of the type that Phillips (1970) discusses. Sundquist (1983: 372), for example, argues that Carter's election ended the politics of race in the south. Yet there continue to be large differences in the vote choice of blacks and whites through 1988; and while these may of course be due to factors other than specifically racial policies, Carmines and Stimson (1989) and Huckfeldt and Kohfeld (1989) have argued for continued importance of race *per se* as a major source of cleavage in American political life. It is certainly possible that the perceptions citizens have on specific racial questions play a role in the image of the Democrats as ideologically extreme that emerges so powerfully after 1964, despite the fall-off in salience of race as a basis for candidate evaluation after 1968.

The data on perceived distance in Table 5.5 makes clear that the partisan consequences of race persist in this way through 1980. The Democrats are seen as far to the left on race in every year for which perceived distance data exists: the degree of extremity does decrease over time, but its absolute magnitude remains large. In 1972, perceived distance to the Democrats on race is −.306, the largest for any issue type in any year. The net impact of this perception is softened somewhat by the fact that the public saw the Republicans to its left on race in 1972 as well: their −.077 combines with the Democrats −.306 to produce a net Republican advantage of −.082, the largest of any issue type in 1972 but far from the largest in Table 5.6.

The Republicans' advantage on race in 1976 is very modest: the public sees itself considerably more conservative on race in 1976 than it sees either of the electoral alternatives to be, with only a small net preference for the Republicans; the Democrats are perceived as slightly less extreme than they had been in 1972, while images of the Republicans move even further to the left over time. The location of both parties so far to the same side of the ideological continuum is unmatched by any other issue area in Table 5.5.

The Reagan effect of pushing the Republicans to the right holds for race in 1980, moving the Republicans from considerably more liberal than the average respondent on race to slightly more conservative. The declining absolute distance to the Republicans combines with a continuing but very gradual decrease in Democratic extremism to produce another considerable net Republican advantage. Perceptions of the parties' positions on race, in other words, created the basis for continued Republican electoral advantage well after the frequency of open-ended comments about race as a basis for evaluating parties and candidates dropped off considerably; well after race was salient enough to generate the spontaneous responses required for open-ended questions, citizens still positioned the parties and candidates in issue space in a way that placed the Democrats in an extreme location that carried with it negative electoral consequences.

In 1984 and 1988, however, the Democrats' disadvantage on even this aspect of racial politics disappears. The average voter sees the Republicans to his right on race and the Democrats slightly further to his left. Although the interaction of the two distance measures produces very small Democratic advantages, the size of the small Democratic edge is less important that the disappearance of the rather sizable Republican advantage from 1972 and 1980.[24] Images of the Democrats as extreme weaken over time, and the net Republican advantage disappears. But even in 1988, race is the type of issue on which the Democrats are perceived as most extreme.

The problems with the number and range of available perceived distance for individual issue areas should make one treat these conclusions cautiously. But the differing impacts of the different types of issues make some sense in terms of the overall pattern of perceived distance discussed above. In no year do all four types of issues provide a net advantage to the same party. The early part of the period is dominated by race and foreign policy, both of which provide a strong Republican edge in 1972 and 1980. But both race and foreign policy become neutralized or provide a slight Democratic edge by 1984. The new domestic issues provide the Republicans with modest advantages in 1968 and 1972, but by 1976 they are providing modest gains for the Democrats. Economics is the odd case: it alone provides a Democratic edge, albeit extremely small, in 1972; it alone continues to provide support for the Republicans after 1980.

PARTY SYSTEM VIa:
PERCEIVED IDEOLOGICAL EXTREMITY
AND DEMOCRATIC DEFECTION

The interplay of respondents' issue concerns and perceptions of the parties/candidates provides a substantial ideological basis for Democratic electoral performance at the presidential level between 1968 and 1980, despite the lack of increasing conservatism among Democratic partisans. Liberal Democrats had even before 1968 defected more often than conservative Republicans; beginning in 1968, however, the rate of defection increases markedly as one moves from the most liberal Democrats to the Democratic center, while there is no such change as one moves from conservative to centrist Republicans. The reason is not some dramatic shift in the public's own position on policy questions: Page and Shapiro (1992) generally and the set of authors cited at the beginning of this chapter more specifically are quite convincing in arguing that dramatic short-term shifts in public opinion do not and did not occur. Rather, the change in the mid- and late 1980s occurs at the elite level, with the Democratic Party/candidate perceived relatively far to the left in issue space, causing even moderate liberals to find themselves situated *between* the candidates and, therefore, relatively vulnerable to opposition appeals. Such perceptions were in place by the time the first fragmentary perceived distance measures became available in 1968; the McGovern nomination exacerbates the leftward movement, a process that Jimmy Carter only partially and temporarily offsets. The Republican Party/candidate, on the other hand, is seen as centrist, with center/conservative Republicans positioning themselves to the right of *both* candidates but much closer to their own. The result is Republican defection rates quite insensitive to degree of ideological extremity and, therefore, considerable asymmetry in defection rates of the two parties' ideological cores.

The pattern persists until around 1980. Ronald Reagan, to some extent as candidate in 1980 and even more as incumbent in 1984, pushes perceptions of the Republicans substantially to the right. George Bush is a somewhat more moderate figure than his predecessor, but he is nonetheless personally placed far to the right of the Republican nominees of the 1970s, and the intervening Reagan years have had a substantial impact on mass perceptions of the Republican Party. The result is elimination of the Democrats' perceived distance disadvantage: comparisons of distance in issue space to the electoral alternatives no longer leave Republicans closer to their own nominee than Democrats are; conservative Republicans' issue distance becomes more sensitive (and liberal Democrats' becomes slightly *less* sensitive) to ideological extremity.

If one looks at ideological bases for electoral change in the interaction of party identification, ideological extremity, and perceived distance, one can claim that ideology was what drove Republican electoral performance between 1968 and 1980. Yet the Republican advantage in such matters clearly disappears between 1980 and 1984: if such ideological factors were driving voting behavior after 1980, Walter Mondale and Michael Dukakis would have been elected president. The shift of perceptions of the Republicans to the right after 1980 eliminates the distinctive conservative Republican insensitivity to ideological extremity; the combination of a more distinctively conservative Republican image with a less distinctively liberal Democratic image creates a situation in which Democratic identifiers are located as close to their own party's nominee as Republican identifiers are to their nominee. Combined with the continuing, if reduced, Democratic party identification advantage, the Democrats should have started winning presidential elections in 1984 rather than 1992. The period after 1980 clearly requires a very different explanation.

NOTES

* An earlier draft of this chapter appeared in the June 1994 issue of the *Political Research Quarterly*.

1. The New Politics is in some ways similar to Inglehart's (1977) post-materialist ideology: concern with self-realization, environmentalism, and direct involvement in the political process, particularly among the young and well-educated, that could provide a non-economic basis for Democratic voting among those relatively high in socio-economic status. Inglehart elaborates his treatment of post-materialism at great length, most recently in book-length (1990) and journal (Inglehart and Abramson, 1994) treatments; for the most incisive of the many critiques of Inglehart's notion, see Flanagan (1987).

2. For a recent powerful statement that aggregate public opinion has a stability and a coherence that is lacking at the individual level, see Page and Shapiro (1992), especially chapters one and two.

3. Even Fiorina (1981) himself, however, found considerable impact of prospective issue questions on individual vote choice; see also Miller and Shanks (1982), who argue for prospective as well as retrospective bases for Reagan's initial victory. None of the comments about the lack of an ideological basis for Reagan's electoral triumphs, of course, is meant to deny that the Reagan administration produced a substantial change in public policy.

4. As one would expect from Keith et al. (1992), leaners behave much like other identifiers; the analyses that follow all show much the same results regardless of whether leaners are included or excluded. In order to maximize numbers of cases, all three types of identifiers are included. Omitting leaning identifiers would reduce the percentage of Democrats to less than a majority in each year except 1964.

5. Defection is measured both narrowly (percentage of voting Democrats or Republicans who actually vote for the other party) and broadly (percentage of all Democrats or Republicans who fail to vote for their own candidate due to either defection or abstention).

The narrower version of defection produces findings generally quite similar to those reported here. Because of these broadly similar findings, because *either* abstention or actual voting for the opposition represents the failure to mobilize a partisan base that is the theoretical focus here, and for simplicity of presentation, the broader measure is presented hereafter. See also DeNardo (1980).

6. For a similar argument about presidential popularity, see Lanoue (1989).

7. The only questions omitted are valence issues (Stokes, 1966), which are particularly vulnerable to projection and rationalization, and the ideological self-identification scale, the meaning of which in general and in relation to specific issues has been convincingly challenged (Conover and Feldman, 1981). More general problems with such closed-ended issues questions have received considerable attention; see Achen (1975), RePass (1971), Converse (1970). Appendix 2 reports the full list of issues used for each year: the aggregate data reported here consist of all response categories which included at least thirty respondents.

8. Similarly, the most conservative Democrat on medical care in 1972 takes a standard score of 1.43 ((7–3.50)/2.44), while the most conservative Democrat on school busing takes a much lower positive score of .53 ((7–6.06)/1.79); the difference between 1.43 and .53 indicates how much more conservative relative to other Democrats a respondent who places himself at point seven on medical care is than someone who does so on busing. Direction is corrected so that negative scores indicate relatively liberal positions and positive scores indicate relatively conservative positions.

9. For the non-core half of the distance measure, Republicans are somewhat *more* sensitive to extremity, with the 24.3% gap between for the two groups of centrists reduced slightly to 16.3% when the most liberal Republicans are compared to the most conservative Democrats.

10. Individual-level scores are a simple summing of a respondent's standardized scores on individual variables; the split-sample design of the 1972 survey is handled by creating a form-specific measure. Requiring a minimum response rate of 75% for inclusion of individual issue questions for each party separately strikes a happy medium between maximizing the number of respondents (i.e., avoiding missing data) and the number/breadth of issues; Appendix 2, again, reports issues used for each party in each year. This procedure does create an unfortunate tendency for more issues to be used for Republicans than for Democrats, particularly in 1972, 1976, and 1980; several issues that miss the 75% cut-off for Democrats pass it and are therefore included for Republicans. To test whether one was thereby distorting inter-party comparisons so essential for the rest of the argument, revised Democratic ideological extremity measures were created on the same basis used for the Republicans, with no regard for missing data implications: the number of valid cases did suffer, falling by 21.0% in 1972, 25.4% in 1976, and 34.3% in 1980; but the original and revised measure for those respondents who were valid on both were intercorrelated at the very high levels of .98 in 1972, .93 in 1976, and .92 in 1980. The rather minor changes in the scores on ideological extremity would not seem to justify the elimination of a substantial number of cases that a more stringent eligibility criterion would demand.

11. Vote choice at the individual level consists of three values: those intending to vote Democratic are in one extreme category, those intending to vote Republican are in the other. For the narrow measure, the middle category consists of those intending to vote but unsure which major party candidate to support; for the broader measure reported here, the middle category consists of all respondents who did not intend to vote for one of the major party candidates. Replicating the Table with leaning identifiers omitted produces quite similar results.

12. The differences would hold for 1980 as well if not for distortion caused by the third party candidacy of John Anderson. For the narrow defection measure, excluding third party voters, the correlations are .22 for liberal Democrats and .06 for conservative Republicans.

13. All of these might be expected in a party system approaching its fortieth anniversary, increasingly riven by new issues that fit uneasily with those that had shaped the old system. It is likely that the heightened level of constraint in mass belief systems noted by Nie with Andersen (1974) (*pace* Sullivan et al., 1978) created a more coherent, unidimensional ideological extremity which interacts with perceived distance in a new and powerful way.

14. The question is combined with a filter designed to legitimize non-response if the respondent has no real pre-existing position on the issue.

15. Perceived distance is unavailable before 1968, and in 1968 it is limited to perceptions of candidates on only two items (Vietnam and urban riots). It suffers the classic problems of closed-ended questions, limited to a small number of pre-selected topics that might miss highly salient individual concerns that open-ended like/dislike questions can pick up (RePass, 1971). A valid perceived distance measure requires five distinct pieces of information (placement of oneself, the parties, and the nominees) from each respondent for each issue; missing any one of them prevents assigning a score. Use of a large number of issues minimizes exhaustiveness while exacerbating missing data. Questions are included if at least half the total population had valid scores for Democrats *or* Republicans. Appendix 3 lists the issues used in each year to construct the perceived distance measure. Large numbers of respondents have missing data on perceived distance, but many of them are also missing ideological extremity or vote choice as well. For 1980, for example, 25.7% of all respondents have a valid perceived distance score; but they constitute 48.7% of those with valid ideological extremity and vote choice scores. Basing a perceived distance measure on perceptions of parties or candidates separately would add relatively few cases and would distort the choice respondents actually make. Appendix 3 lists the questions for which perceived distance information is available in each year. More generally on issue questions, see Aldrich et al. (1982); Fiorina (1981), chapter 7; and Page (1978).

16. An alternate way to get at perceptions of parties and candidates would be to look at the open-ended likes/dislikes of parties/candidates that Michigan has used since 1952. Constructing a measure of issue orientation from such questions allows us to look at party and candidate images for a longer period of time than perceived distance does. But issue orientation determines neither magnitude nor direction of preferences: it therefore cannot distinguish instances in which a respondent finds himself to the left of a party on one issue and to the right of it on another to an equal and off-setting extent from instances in which dislikes are cumulative (see also Rabinowitz and Macdonald, 1989). Since the period after the second mini-realignment corresponds to the period in which the perceived distance measures are available, they will be used here. Issue orientation and perceived distance are associated with each other, but less so than one might expect. Correlation between them ranges between .42 in 1968 and .70 in 1984; if one excludes 1968 due to the small number of issues for which perceived distance is measured, the smallest D is .54 in 1972. In each year except 1968, voters favoring the Democrats on issue orientation are more likely to favor the Republicans on perceived distance than vice versa.

17. If both Democrats and Republicans are placed on the same side of the respondent, net perceived distance is simply the difference between the two distance scores. If the respondent is between the two electoral alternatives, net perceived distance is the absolute value of distance to the nearer subtracted from the absolute value of the distance to the further.

18. Category-by-category year-by-year comparisons show that Republicans are somewhat closer to their party/candidate than Democrats are to their party/candidate even in the "no options" ninth in 1968 and 1980, and their advantage becomes larger over the remaining eight categories. In 1972 and 1976, Democrats have an initial advantage at the no-options extreme of the continuum, but the advantage decreases rapidly as one moves towards the center; by category two (1972) or category four (1976), a Republican advantage exists. A similar Figure for issue orientation would show a weaker version of the same pattern. Once again, eliminating the leaning identifiers has minimal impact.

19. It should be remembered that the perceived distance measure used here is relational: it involves the link between respondents' own position and their perception of the parties and candidates. The Republican shift to the right is largely due to Reagan's having been perceived as much more conservative than Ford had been; the continuing shift between 1980 and 1984 is partially due to continuing perceived movement of the Republicans to the right and partially to a shift in mass opinion to the left that makes the Republican position relatively more extreme. A simultaneous decrease in perception of the Democrats as leftist between 1980 and 1984 is more due to increased mass liberalism that places the average voter closer to where the Democrats had previously been than to real changed perception of where the Democrats are located.

20. The focus on the candidates is not to suggest that respondents are referring to them only as individuals; but it may nevertheless make sense to distinguish between them and the party of which they are a part, precisely to deal with the question of representativeness and to chart a sequence of change over time.

21. Page (1978: 95) argues that McGovern was perceived further to the left that he really was, a misperception he attributes to some of McGovern's earlier, more radical positions and to citizen reliance on cues from some of the candidate's more radical supporters. Miller and Levitin (1976: 144) point out McGovern's failure to do very well even with those whose issue positions were close to his.

22. In only two of ten possible instances does a group of partisans see their nominee as ideologically distinctive relative to his party across the full range of ideological extremity. One of these is 1984, when Republicans at each level see Reagan as more conservative than his party; the other is 1972, when Democrats across the ideological extremity continuum see McGovern as more liberal than his party. For Reagan in 1984, the differences are relatively small: .029 among the most liberal Republicans, .013 among centrists, .067 among the most conservative. For 1972 Democrats, the differences are far larger: .117 among the most liberal, .042 among centrists, .262 among conservatives.

23. Race is represented by a single issue in 1980, 1984, and 1988, as are new domestic issues in 1984 and 1988.

24. The changing pattern of net distance holds for both northern and southern whites: neither ever position themselves closer to the Democrats than to the Republicans, but the degree of proximity to the Republicans for both varies much as the described for the general population; white northerners are consistently slightly closer to the Democrats. In 1988, white northerners' net proximity score on race is –.036, while white southerners are at –.076. Blacks show a consistent pattern of proximity to the Democrats, with no particular pattern of increase or decrease over time; their net perceived distance is .280 in 1972, .230 in 1980, and .244 in 1988.

6

The Fragile Extension of the Second Mini-Realignment: Retrospective Voting and the Politics of Prosperity *

The interplay of ideological extremity and perceived distance to parties and candidates in issue space accounts nicely for important aspects of presidential election competition between 1968 and 1980. Perception of the Democrats as ideologically extreme explains disproportionate Democratic defection in general and the very different patterns of defection of the two parties' ideological cores, with perceptions of George McGovern and Ronald Reagan particularly helpful in accounting for the ebb and flow of relative perceived distance over time. And yet the intertwined effects of ideological extremity and perceived distance no longer account for disproportionate Democratic losses after 1980: Reagan's driving perceptions of the Republicans to the right destroys the ideological basis for the higher level of Democratic defection. If citizens voted on the basis of the ideological factors discussed in Chapter Five, Democrats would have won the 1984 and 1988 presidential elections. The attentive reader will note that they did not.

THE PECULIAR ROLE
OF PROSPECTIVE ISSUES IN THE 1980S

The failure of such ideological considerations to explain voting behavior and election outcome in the 1980s is striking, but it is not the only evidence that citizen attitudes one might expect to predict vote choice no longer do so. Table 4.1 demonstrated that Democrats retain an advantage in numbers of partisans, albeit to a lesser extent, through 1988. And the more numerous Democratic identifiers also appear to be more intense in their party loyalty: there are 1.21 Democrats for each Republican in the 1984 electorate; if we exclude the weakest identifiers, the Independent Democrats and Republicans, the ratio increases to 1.37. It may well be that the Republicans maintain a candidate orientation advantage sufficient to allow them to overcome these apparent problems with issues and partisanship. But

Wattenberg (1991: 76) has argued persuasively that popular images of Reagan's personal popularity are greatly exaggerated: Reagan was certainly more popular than his opposition in 1980 and 1984, as was Bush in 1988, but neither had the clear domination enjoyed by winning candidates in the past; Reagan, in particular, seems to have produced quite divided reactions, generating more negative comments from both supporters and opponents than other winning candidates.

Such data suggest that the Democrats have assets in terms of public opinion on core elements of political evaluation that they are unable to translate into votes: popular attitudes after 1980 are no less supportive of the Democratic party and candidates than they are of the Republican party and candidates, but the Democrats are unable to translate equally supportive attitudes into commensurate levels of voter loyalty.

Table 6.1 manipulates scores on the three classic attitudinal variables originally introduced in *The Voter Decides* (1954) (party identification, issue orientation, and candidate orientation) and the coefficients estimated for them by a probit analysis of vote choice t show the striking extent to which the Democrats fail to achieve gains from their apparent political capital.[1] The first and last columns of Table 6.1 give the predicted loyalty of Democrats and Republicans for a party identifier (all partisans in Table 6.1a, the core constituencies in Table 6.1b) with mean scores on all three independent variables. In 1952, for example, a Democrat with the mean

TABLE 6.1A
Manipulating Predicted Loyalty: All Democrats and Republicans

Year	Democratic Values[a] Democratic Coefficients	Republican Values[b] Democratic Coefficients	Democratic Values[c] Republican Coefficients	Republican Values[a] Republican Coefficients
1952	56.8	69.9	76.7	85.5
1956	64.1	77.9	77.9	84.9
1960	61.8	85.1	74.9	87.2
1964	76.7	65.2	77.0	56.8
1968	44.8	61.0	68.8	78.8
1972	35.6	71.2	73.2	83.7
1976	56.0	57.9	69.2	69.2
1980	51.2	51.2	64.1	67.0
1984	61.4	61.0	87.2	84.1
1988	68.1	67.0	78.2	75.8

Notes: a. Entries in columns one and four are predicted loyalty for mean Democratic and Republican identifiers derived from probit analyses of each partisan group separately.

b. Column two uses coefficients for Democrats but substitutes values on independent variables of the mean Republican.

c. Column three uses values on independent variables of Democrats but coefficients for Republicans.

TABLE 6.1B
Manipulating Predicted Loyalty:
Core Constituencies (Liberal Democrats and Conservative Republicans)

Year	Liberal Democratic Values[a] Democratic Coefficients	Conservative Republican Values[b] Democratic Coefficients	Liberal Democratic Values[c] Republican Coefficients	Conservative Republican Values[a] Republican Coefficients
1952	61.8	77.3	80.5	90.2
1956	71.6	82.6	82.1	87.5
1960	71.6	88.1	78.0	88.7
1964	84.4	80.0	88.3	81.1
1968	62.2	69.9	80.5	83.9
1972	61.8	81.9	82.9	87.5
1976	60.3	62.6	73.6	74.2
1980	53.2	61.8	67.0	76.4
1984	78.2	73.9	94.7	91.0
1988	77.9	77.9	84.4	84.9

Notes: a. Entries in columns one and four are predicted loyalty for mean Democratic and Republican identifiers derived from probit analyses of each partisan group separately.
   b. Column two uses coefficients for Democrats but substitutes values on independent variables of the mean Republican.
   c. Column three uses values on independent variables of Democrats but coefficients for Republicans.

Democratic score on strength of partisanship, issue orientation, and candidate orientation and who relates these attitudes to each other and to vote choice in the same manner as Democrats as a whole would have a 56.8% probability of voting Democratic; the mean Republican doing the same would have an 85.5% probability of voting Republican. There is an obvious large difference between the two probabilities which may be due to different scores on the attitudinal variables (i.e., that Republicans' party, issue, and candidate scores are simply more Republican than the Democrats' scores are Democratic) or to the different ways in which the scores are combined and affect vote choice (i.e., that Republicans are more loyal despite roughly similar scores on the three attitudinal determinants of vote choice).

The two middle columns are an attempt to determine how well the two possibilities explain differences in loyalty. Column two reports the estimated loyalty for Democrats who had the same scores on the independent variables as the average Republican; it makes use of the coefficients probit produced for Democrats, but of means on the independent variables actually possessed by Republicans.[2] If Democrats are less loyal only because they take less powerful scores on the independent variables than Republicans do, the estimated probabilities in column two should entirely eliminate the difference between the real Democratic probabilities in column one and the real Republican probabilities in column four; Democrats, in other words, would combine partisanship, issue orientation, and candidate orientation in the same way Republicans do, and their lower rates of loyalty would be due entirely to their being less positively oriented towards their party and its candidates than Republicans are towards theirs.

Column three is the exact opposite of column two. It reports estimated loyalty for Democrats using their own mean scores on the independent variables but combining them according to the Republican probit coefficients. If the third column eliminates differences between columns one and four, it would be because Democrats are equally as Democratic as Republicans are Republican in their party affiliation, issue orientation, and candidate orientation, but for some reason these factors do not contribute as powerfully to a Democratic vote as they do to a Republican vote; Democrats combine equally favorable scores in ways that produce less loyalty.

The periods on either side of 1964 show somewhat different patterns in the relative impact of scores and coefficients. In 1952–1960, the general pattern is for both values and coefficients to narrow differences in loyalty considerably, with neither factor consistently more effective than the other. Only in 1960 does either *entirely* eliminate differences in defection rates: changing values increases Democratic loyalty from 61.8% to 85.1%, the latter nearly as large as the 87.2% loyalty rate of Republicans; changing coefficients has a smaller (if still considerable) impact. In 1968–1980, scores have considerably less impact: coefficients explain a larger percentage of the difference in each of the eight cases. In 1968, for example, a Democratic probability of 44.8% rises to 61.0% when values are changed and to a considerably higher 68.8% when coefficients are changed. Neither comes particularly close to the 78.8% figure for Republicans, but both narrow the difference, and the way the values are combined is more responsible than the values themselves.

The relative importance of values and coefficients becomes even more extreme after 1980, in a way strikingly parallel to the relationships among ideological extremity, perceived distance, and vote choice in Chapter Five. In 1984, differences in predicted loyalty are solely and entirely due to coefficients: changing values produces no reduction in the loyalty gap, while changing coefficients eliminates it. The decrease in the importance of values and the increased importance of coefficients is a continuation of trends over the full ten-election period, but the clarity and the starkness of the results in 1984 and 1988 are striking. The 61.4% predicted loyalty for Democrats in 1984, for example, actually falls to 61.0% when Republican values are substituted, while substituting Republican coefficients produces a predicted loyalty of 87.2% that is greater than the 84.1% predicted for the Republicans themselves. For liberal Democrats, the findings are even more dramatic; an initial loyalty of 78.2% falls to 73.9% when values are changed and rises to 94.7% when coefficients are changed. In other words, Democrats in 1984 and 1988 have values on party, issues, and candidates as conducive to party loyalty as are the values Republicans have; but the values are combined in ways that do not add up to a similar level of loyalty.[3]

The post-1980 period is therefore very strange. Differences between Republicans and Democrats in previous years were at least in part explainable in terms of the interplay of ideological extremity and issue distance and in terms of Democrats' less favorable scores on the key attitudinal determinants of vote choice. Just as the Democrats after 1980 fail to benefit from changes in issue distance, they also fail to benefit from improving scores on the attitudinal sources of vote choice more generally. Sometime around 1980 both of these disadvantages disappeared; comparative defection rates do fall somewhat, yet electoral performance does not improve.[4]

The paradox is resolved, to a large extent, by broadening our way of thinking about issues. The classic studies of the American electorate (Campbell et al., 1960; Nie, Verba, and Petrocik, 1979) had focused on prospective issues: policy questions that would be decided as a consequence of the election result. Prospective issue voting consisted of choosing among electoral alternatives based on an overall preference for one candidate's policy proposals; such issues would seem to be central to the presumed role of elections on democratic theory—that citizens governed themselves indirectly through the mechanism of elections by voting for candidates whose policies they favored.

Joseph Schumpeter (1966) had argued in 1943 that most citizens have little ability to live up to requirements of classical democratic theory: they have no detailed knowledge of policy; they cannot meaningfully interpret, compare, contrast, or critically evaluate the competing claims of candidates. What ordinary citizens *can* do, argued Schumpeter, is evaluate consequences of government actions: they can evaluate the *results* of government actions in terms of whether they themselves are better or worse off at the end of a given administration.[5] Such retrospective evaluations allow voters to reward or to punish incumbent administrations for success or failure in producing political *outcomes*, without requiring citizens to understand what exactly the government did to produce such outcomes.[6] In 1981, at about the time that ideological considerations were losing their ability to explain the electoral outcomes, Morris Fiorina drew on work of V.O. Key, Jr. (1966, 1961) and Anthony Downs (1957) to incorporate such arguments into the empirical literature on vote choice.[7]

Retrospective issue voting clearly demands less of a citizen than prospective issue voting does. But it was precisely its less demanding nature that made it attractive after generations of scholars had produced fairly overwhelming evidence that Schumpeter, writing before the classic studies of electoral choice, had been to a large extent correct: most ordinary voters were simply not capable to living up to the more demanding requirements of prospective voting. Retrospective voting is a softer, less demanding test of voters, but it is a test that they are far more likely to pass.

Retrospective voting also allows effective citizen control of government. Schumpeter had argued that retrospective voting creates incentives for authorities to deal with the problems that their constituents face: elected officials know that voters will eventually choose to retain them (or their partisan successors) in office or to throw them out in favor of the opposition based on their degree of satisfaction with the state of political affairs on the next election day. An opposition party in a retrospective or Schumpeterian world gains office not because of its own campaign promises but because of the failures of its opponent; but it knows from the moment it assumes office that it will be judged at the next election for its own achievements, giving it an incentive to identify and advance talented candidates who will be able to succeed if a failed opposition gives them an opportunity to govern. In a Schumpeterian world, the selfish quest to retain office produces a virtuous cycle of elite competition and accommodation (see also Page, 1978: 220).

Many (Barber, 1984; Pateman, 1970; Bachrach, 1967) of course argue that elite competition is insufficient to make government responsive to public needs, that satisfying such needs is not the most likely way to generate popularity sufficient to produce re-election, that Schumpeter ignores the consequences that exercise of democratic citizenship has traditionally been thought to have for the full development of individual capabilities, or that a world of divided government, coalition governments, multiple opposition parties, and primary elections necessarily clouds the neat attribution of credit or blame on which Schumpeterian democracy rests.[8] But just as retrospective voting generally is a less sophisticated form of issue voting to which one might turn if one believes that most Americans simply do not have the ability to vote in the more traditional prospective way, so Schumpeter's mechanisms of popular control might be a second-best way for an unsophisticated electorate to monitor and exercise control over those who govern them.

If 1980 is a key transitional year in decreasing the importance of ideological explanations of Democratic failure in presidential elections, it is likely a key year in increasing the impact and partisan consequences of retrospective evaluations as well.[9] The worst election-year economic circumstances since the Depression would be expected to provide a powerful basis for anti-incumbent voting. Sundquist (1983) has argued the limited staying power of such issues: unless reinforced by clear-cut party differences on related policy questions, retrospective evaluations are likely to weaken over time as the out-party takes positions designed to cut losses from past failures and the new administration is forced to take responsibility for government performance. Issues like Vietnam and the Social Issue undoubtedly contributed to Nixon's election, for example, but they rapidly lost their electoral impact as the Democrats adopted dovish and tough-on-crime proposals after 1968 while the new administration had to take responsibility for policy (Sundquist, 1983: 303, 379–394). What might make the economic legacy of Jimmy Carter different is two-fold: first, that the American public four years later combined memories of Carter's failure with the perception that Reaganomics had been a smashing success; second, that the particulars of Carter's failure would do lasting damage to images of the Democratic Party that had been an area of strength since the Depression and New Deal.

Reagan's 1980 triumph is due in part to the kinds of ideological factors that had underlay Republican success over the preceding decade and in part to the powerful negative retrospective evaluations which Carter had generated in office. Yet at the very time that his economic policies are providing the basis for a decade of Republican electoral domination, Reagan is also inadvertently continuing the destruction of the ideological underpinnings of past Republican victories from which he himself had benefited in 1980. By 1984, the Republican advantage in ideological issue space is gone, and Republican electoral fortunes rest entirely on comparative retrospective evaluations. It is not accidental, perhaps, that Wattenberg (1991) observed the emergence of what he calls performance-based voting in 1984, with retrospective judgments becoming a more powerful determinant of vote choice than the policy preferences associated with ideological extremity and perceived distance.

Not only do retrospective considerations account since 1980 for the outcomes of individual elections; they also account for the recent failure of models of vote choice involving conventional measures of issue orientation or of perceived distance. Specifically, they explain why the Democrats have not been able to translate their impressive improvement on the kinds of perceived distance measures discussed in Chapter Five into presidential election victories. Retrospective judgments are unlikely to be caught sufficiently (or at all) by conventional measures of issue concern: neither conceptually nor empirically do they fit into the left-right ideological space of perceived distance measures, and their impact is likely to be understated by an issue orientation measure that weighs individual likes/dislikes equally.[10] Their emergence as powerful pro-Republican forces would likely increase defection among Democrats, decrease defection among Republicans, and show up neither in the interplay of ideological extremity and issue distance in Figure 5.4 nor in the probit analysis of Table 6.1.[11]

ECONOMICS AS AN ELECTORAL ISSUE

Economic conditions have of course long been seen as a source of electoral behavior. The earliest academic voting surveys included questions about economic experiences (satisfaction with one's financial situation, recent unemployment) and policy positions (to what extent the government should manage the economy) that might underlie evaluation of parties and candidates. Later studies included closed-ended prospective issue questions about services for citizens (generally or in specific areas such as medical care) or guaranteeing jobs. Yet others have used closed-ended retrospective questions that tap perceptions of recent changes in the economy or government/incumbent success in managing economic problems (Abramson, Aldrich, and Rohde, 1986; Fiorina, 1981). Innumerable aggregate data studies have demonstrated how change in objective economic conditions such as inflation, unemployment, or per capita real income affect election outcome (Lewis-Beck and Rice, 1992; Weisberg and Smith, 1991; Abramowitz and Segal, 1986; Kiewiet and Rivers, 1985; Rosenstone, 1983; Monroe, 1979; Goodman and Kramer, 1975; Meltzer and Vellrath, 1975; Tufte, 1975; Kramer, 1971) or considered the conditions under which personal economic problems are perceived as political in origin or solution

(Kinder et al., 1989; Abramowitz, Lanone, and Ramesh, 1988; Kiewiet, 1983; Feldman, 1982; Schlozman and Verba, 1979; Sniderman and Brody, 1977).

Economics has also long been identified as the key issue underlying Democratic dominance of the New Deal System. A public that held an incumbent Republican administration responsible for the Depression and credited the Democrats with both economic recovery and creation of the welfare state made the Democrats the majority party from 1932 on (Campbell et al., 1960: 45; Sundquist, 1983; Kelley, 1988). Scammon and Wattenberg (1971) saw economics as the issue that people cared most about and which they believed Democrats could handle better than Republicans.

And yet by the late 1960s, the rise of new and at least potentially cross-cutting issues caused many to argue that the importance of economics as an electoral issue was declining. Scammon and Wattenberg (1971) argued that such issues had been eclipsed in the mid-1960s by concern with rising crime rates, drug use, disruptive political protest, sexual and other permissiveness—all of them aspects of a per- ceived social disintegration that ordinary citizens found threatening. They explic- itly argued that the Democrats were threatened by the decline in salience of eco- nomic concerns on which they had been preferred since the Depression and by the simultaneous the rise of this new Social Issue on which the Republicans were seen to take the more popular tough position. Miller and Levitin (1976) agreed with Scammon and Wattenberg about the declining importance of economic issues, but they argued that sympathy with the emerging counter-culture and hostility to the agents of social control would provide a new non-economic basis for a re-defined liberal and Democratic majority; their argument was bolstered by Inglehart's (1977) investigation of the emerging concern with self-expression and political activism that he called post-materialist ideology as a dominant mode of political thinking among younger age cohorts in the wealthy industrialized nations. Ladd and Hadley (1978), Nie, Verba, and Petrocik (1979: 99), and Petrocik (1981: 98) were less likely to see a clear-cut partisan direction to the changing salience of different kinds of issues, but they agreed that economic concerns decreased in importance in the 1960s and 1970s as the social welfare program of the New Deal was accepted by both major parties and newer cross-cutting issue concerns emerged.

As both Scammon and Wattenberg (1971: 40) and Sundquist (1983: 441) ob- serve, however, economics is an issue of fundamental underlying political impor- tance: it may possibly decline in importance when times are good, but it is likely to be easily re-activated when conditions worsen. The decline of class as a basis of political cleavage need not reduce popular concern with economic issues or condi- tions: the prosperity and distractions of the 1960s may well have created a tempo- rary lack of explicit political focus on economics, but circumstances of the late 1970s would seem to have been capable of returning the issue to the center of the electoral agenda. Many have argued that it did so: Pomper (1981: 88) wrote that "economic grievances were at the heart of the [first] Reagan vote" (see also Hibbs, 1982), while Quirk (1985: 170) wrote that citizen belief "that his economic pro- gram had been an outstanding success was, without doubt, one of the principal reasons for Reagan's easy [second] victory...." Economics was the only one of the four issue areas in Chapter Five on which the Republicans retained an advantage on perceived distance in issue space in 1984 and 1988.

The most straightforward way to capture the voter's response to a broad diverse range of economic perceptions is through intensive examination of open-ended questions about likes/dislikes of parties/candidates which have provided the basis for such well-known analyses as levels of conceptualization (Campbell et al., 1960), party image (Trilling, 1976), voter decision rules (Kelley, 1983), partisan disaggregation (Wattenberg, 1984), schematic assessments of presidential candidates (Miller, Wattenberg, and Malanchuk, 1986), and the issue orientation measure used briefly above. Although they are expensive to administer, complicated to code, and sensitive to articulateness as well as substance (Smith, 1989), they can catch the salient atypical attitude that might be missed by pre-determined closed-ended questions, provide an (almost) consistent stimulus over time, and generate a rich set of perceptions that can be analyzed in a variety of different ways to deal with a variety of different substantive questions (RePass, 1971; Miller and Wattenberg, 1985; Geer, 1988). The very scholars who used such items to demonstrate the inability of ordinary citizens to formulate highly structured belief systems (Campbell et al., 1960) found that they tapped widespread perceptions of parties and candidates in terms of their impact on specific subgroups of the population or in producing good or bad times generally, both of which are likely to involve a large number of essentially retrospective comments about explicitly economic concerns.

Table 6.2 reports responses to the open-ended survey questions that show economics as a subject of widespread popular concern throughout the 1952–1988 period. The 1952 election shows more than three-quarters of the electorate concerned with some kind of economic problem. The figure falls somewhat thereafter, a drop not inconsistent with the rise of competing other issues and the combination of rising affluence with class depolarization discussed in Chapter Three. But even in the 1960s, with an increase in popular concern with new non-economic issues of race, social order, and Vietnam, economics remains a concern of well over half of the electorate. And this level of interest rises somewhat thereafter: there is a very slight increase in the frequency of economic concern in the 1970s and an upsurge in 1984 that temporarily brings it back to 1952 levels.

More interesting than an undifferentiated notion of economics is to divide the comments into four components designed to tap distinct ways in which citizens might react to economic problems and policies. The four dimensions of economics are:

1. Fiscal/monetary policy, which includes references to taxes, government spending, budget deficits/surpluses, interest rates, etc.
2. Class, which includes references to economically-defined social groupings such as economic group-benefits from Campbell et al.'s (1960) levels of conceptualization or six-variable model of partisan choice.

TABLE 6.2
Salience of Economic Concerns

Year	Any Economic Mentions	Fiscal and Monetary Policy	Class and Economic-based Groups	Social Welfare	Prosperity
1952	75.3	34.0	42.0	15.6	44.4
1956	62.9	14.5	42.4	8.8	28.4
1960	61.5	20.9	39.2	14.2	23.3
1964	62.7	17.1	36.7	32.7	12.6
1968	59.5	20.6	33.5	21.6	17.4
1972·	63.2	24.0	36.2	30.5	18.2
1976	65.7	31.0	38.6	25.8	25.3
1980	65.1	26.4	33.1	26.0	29.7
1984	74.7	40.6	34.2	43.5	30.0
1988	65.4	33.2	36.1	40.3	20.0

Notes: Entries are percentages of the total population mentioning economics in general and each of the four dimensions of economics as a basis for liking either of the parties/candidates.

FIGURE 6.1
Net Partisan Preferences: Dimensions of Economics

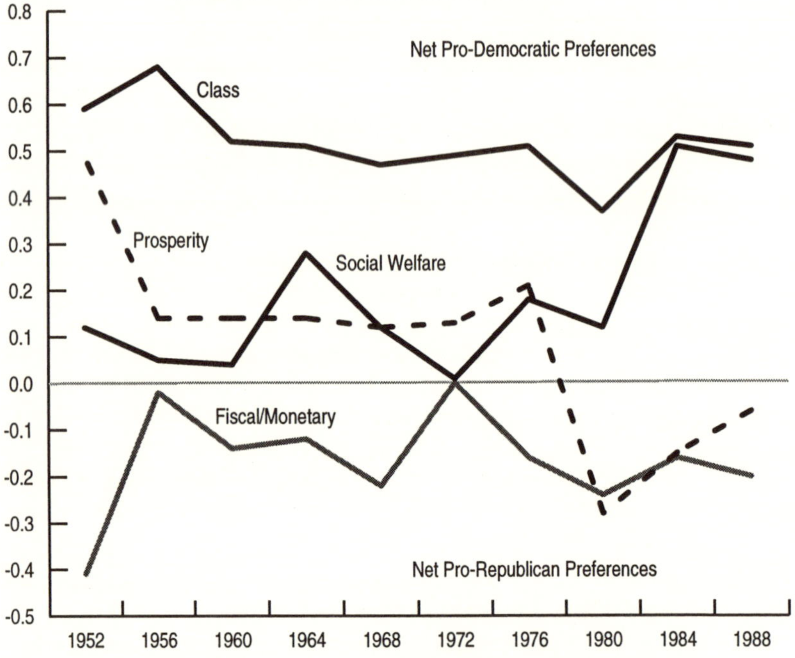

Note: Entries are net partisan preference on each dimension: the mean of pro-Democratic and anti-Republican minus anti-Democratic and pro-Republican mentions.

3. Social welfare, which includes references to citizen's economic problems/needs and to government programs, existing or proposed, to deal with them.
4. Prosperity, which includes references to inflation and unemployment, and to good or bad times of the kind that figured in the third of Campbell et al.'s (1960) levels of conceptualization—the nature of the times.[12]

The four dimensions of economics in fact behave quite differently over time in ways that are highly useful in explaining electoral change.[13]

Fiscal-monetary policy is most frequently mentioned at the very beginning of the period and toward its end, its ebb and flow mirroring that for economics as a whole. Figure 6.1, which reports the public's net partisan preference on each of the dimensions,[14] shows that it is the sole dimension that provides a consistent source of Republican strength throughout the period. As Table 6.3 shows, the Republican bias of fiscal-monetary concerns has been less due to the Republicans' being evaluated positively than to a consistent pattern of negative attitudes toward the Democrats. Even Democratic identifiers had a negative overall attitude toward their party on these issues in four of the ten elections. In 1956 and 1972, both Republican re-election landslides, the parties are essentially even on fiscal/monetary policy. Reagan's re-election landslide (–.16) is more typical of the period as a whole.

The frequency of class-linked references to the parties and candidates, in contrast, is rather stable, varying only between 33.1% and 42.4%. For the bulk of the period it is the most frequently mentioned component of economics, and its relative eclipse in 1984 and 1988 is due to the increased salience of other dimensions rather than to a fall-off of its own. The slight fall-off in its salience after 1956 is quite consistent with data in Chapter Three about the rising affluence and decreas-

TABLE 6.3

Mean Evaluation of Each Party: Dimensions of Economics

Year	Fiscal/Monetary		Class, Etc.		Social Welfare		Prosperity	
	Dem.	Rep.	Dem.	Rep.	Dem.	Rep.	Dem.	Rep.
1952	–.22	.19	.35	–.24	.11	–.01	.28	–.21
1956	–.02	.00	.39	–.29	.05	.00	.16	.02
1960	–.10	.04	.30	–.22	.04	.00	.15	.01
1964	–.05	.06	.29	–.22	.16	–.13	.11	–.03
1968	–.13	.09	.27	–.20	.11	–.01	.08	–.04
1972	–.02	–.02	.24	–.26	.01	–.02	.07	–.06
1976	–.07	.09	.27	–.24	.11	–.07	.17	–.05
1980	–.11	.13	.19	–.18	.07	–.05	–.18	.10
1984	–.13	.04	.23	–.30	.22	–.30	.05	.20
1988	–.16	.04	.29	–.24	.35	–.13	.05	.11

Note: Entries are mean scores on each of the aspects of economic policy for each party separately. The mean is a simple average of the sum of positive mentions minus negative mentions for all respondents.

ing class polarization of the electorate, but identification of the parties with the economic well-being of subgroups of the population that originated in the Depression and New Deal remains quite widespread even in 1968 and increases somewhat thereafter. Furthermore, a strong pattern of sustained partisan advantage held for class, with preferences strongly Democratic: the 1980 election sees a modest and temporary erosion, but 1984 and 1988 values return to previous levels (see also Wattenberg, 1984: 66).

The Democratic advantage on class has two mutually reinforcing sides to it: Republicans are consistently evaluated negatively and Democrats are consistently evaluated positively. Mean Republican Party/candidate score never exceeds –.18, and mean Democratic Party/candidate score never falls below .19, both in 1980. The –.30 Reagan received in 1984 is the lowest for the party in all ten elections. Republican identifiers evaluated their own party negatively on class in five of the ten elections.

The two other dimensions show more complex and significant trends. References to social welfare showed particularly dramatic changes: mentioned by no more than 15.6% of citizens through 1960, it increased to 32.7% in 1964 and ranged between 21.6% and 30.5% thereafter before surging to 43.5% in 1984. It is the least frequently mentioned dimension in 1952–1960 and the most frequently mentioned in 1984 and 1988. The 1964 and 1984 surges are both disproportionately increases in comments about candidates rather than parties, although party-based perceptions generally increase as well after 1956: the 23.3% who mention parties on social welfare in 1984 is higher than for any previous year, and the 29.5% in 1988 is greater than the 22.0% who mention candidates.[15]

For 1952–1960, years in which social welfare concerns elicited relatively little voter interest, it provided modest advantages to the Democrats. In these years, very few respondents evaluate the Republicans at all in terms of social welfare; evaluations, positive or negative, are of the Democrats. The surge in salience in 1964 aids the Democrats. Evaluations of the Democrats become much more positive than in any previous year, while those of the Republicans assume a distinctly negative overall tone (–.13) for the first time. Both changes are due almost entirely to changes by Democratic identifiers. Democrats become much more positive toward their own party (.10 to .28) and more negative towards the opposition (–.02 to –.21). The Democratic edge in social welfare is smaller in 1968–1980, but exists for each year except 1972.

Buried in Walter Mondale's 1984 defeat and in its widespread attribution to Republican domination of economic issues (Plotkin, 1985) is a considerable Democratic gain on social welfare. The 1984 increase in salience consists largely of pro-Democratic preferences, with a net partisan preference of .51 dwarfing even the .28 of 1964. As in the past, Democrats are more distinctive in their responses: Democrats' evaluation of their own party is .47, while their evaluation of the Republicans, previously most negative at –.21 in 1964, reaches –.61! Republicans give their own party a net evaluation of .03 and the Democrats a modest –.06. The Democrats' gain is especially great in comparison of candidates, with Mondale increas-

ECONOMICS AND VOTE CHOICE:
BIVARIATE RELATIONSHIPS

Each dimension except social welfare in 1952 demonstrates at least a moderately strong zero-order association with vote choice,[18] but the differences in net partisan evaluation and the considerable variation in the relative strength of the relationships over time mean that they in fact have very different electoral implications. And although bivariate relationships must be subjected to more complete multivariate analysis that controls for interrelationships among dimensions of economics and for the role of potential confounding variables such as other issues, candidate orientation, or party identification, several of the zero-order findings are worth pursuing briefly.

Figure 6.2 does this by graphing the net vote advantage for each dimension: the percentage casting a Democratic vote consistent with each economic issue area minus the percentage casting a Republican vote consistent with it.[19] The combination of salience, preference, and zero-order impact of fiscal-monetary policy, for

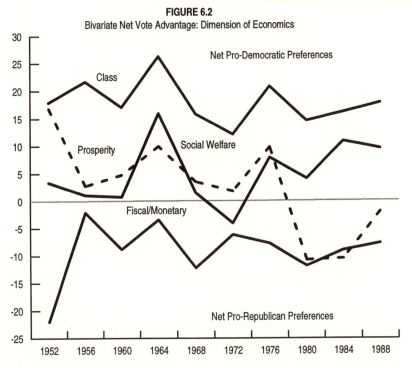

FIGURE 6.2
Bivariate Net Vote Advantage: Dimension of Economics

Note: Entries are percentage favoring the Democrats and voting Democratic minus percentage favoring the Republicans and voting Republican.

example, produces a constant Republican advantage on the first of the four dimensions: the advantage is small in 1956 and 1964, but in each other year citizens with Republican preferences on fiscal-monetary policy voting Republican outnumber Democrats on fiscal-monetary policy voting Democratic by at least 6.1%.

Class is of course the most Democratic issue-area in preferences in each year. But that advantage is partially offset by the relative tendency of those with Democratic preferences to fail to vote Democratic. In every year except 1964, for example, those preferring the Democrats on class are less likely to vote Democratic than are those favoring the Democrats on prosperity. Nonetheless, the Democrats' net advantage on class never falls below 12.2%, and in most years it is considerably higher.

Through 1960, social welfare is a relatively weak source of vote choice even for the relative few who care about it, and it therefore makes only a very modest contribution to Democratic vote totals. The 1964 surge in both salience and Democratic preference generates a net vote advantage of 16.0%; but both fall off thereafter, and the highest Democratic net vote advantage on social welfare in 1968–1980 is only 8.0%.

The 1984 resurgence in salience and Democratic preferences helps Mondale, but rather less than one might expect. The percentage of those who care about social welfare voting consistently with it in 1984 is a relatively low 71.6%—making it the only one of the four dimensions to become a less powerful basis of vote choice for the relevant issue public between 1980 and 1984; only class, the other Democratic dimension, is weaker in absolute terms.[20] Net Democratic vote advantage is therefore only 11.0%, less than in 1964 despite higher salience and more Democratic net preference. Modest declines in salience, Democratic net preference, and in the impact of Democratic preferences on vote choice produce an even smaller net vote advantage of 9.7% in 1988.

In 1952, prosperity exerted considerable impact on the vote of those for whom it was salient. Nearly eighty percent of those concerned (a full third of the total electorate and 62.2% of all Democratic voters) cast a 1952 vote consistent with preferences on prosperity, the highest of any issue area in any year: the large Democratic net vote advantage of 16.9% on prosperity in 1952 is only slightly short of that provided by class. But the percentage of voters casting a ballot consistent with prosperity drops monotonically thereafter, from 33.3% in 1952 to 11.1% in 1964, and the contribution to Democratic vote totals falls to modest levels as well: between 1956 and 1976 prosperity consistently aids the Democrats, but with a smaller net vote advantage.

The turnaround in net preferences on prosperity in 1980 is a catastrophe for the Democrats. Only two-thirds of those preferring the Republicans on prosperity actually vote Republican, a figure lower than the corresponding 84.7% for the Democrats, which makes the damage less than would have otherwise occurred. The proportion of the electorate preferring the Republicans on prosperity and voting Republican is 16.3%, higher than the Democrats had enjoyed since 1952. The corresponding 1980 figure for the Democrats, four years after a figure of 16.0% had suggested revitalization of New Deal-based associations with prosperity, was 5.6%. The 1976–1980 shift in net vote advantage on prosperity is as large as any in Figure 6.2 and transforms a 9.9% Democratic advantage into a 10.7% Republican advantage.

The 1984 data are equally bad for the Democrats. Net preference had shown a reduction in the Republicans' advantage from −.28 to −.15, as the Democrats' recovery from 1980 exceeded the simultaneous Republican improvement. But those who favor the Republicans on prosperity in 1984 are far more likely to vote Republican than they had been in 1980 (85.0% rather than 67.3%); the impact of a Republican preference increases at a time when impact of a Democratic preference falls slightly. The resulting Republican net vote advantage of 10.4% is only slightly lower than it had been four years earlier (see Ferguson and Rogers, 1986: 33).

The continuing decline in Republican advantage on prosperity affects vote advantage more dramatically in 1988. In 1988, one finds a relative weakening in the impact of Republican preferences on vote choice: the percentage of those favoring the Republicans on prosperity who actually vote Republican falls in 1988 to 74.1%, approximately half-way between the low level of 1980 (67.3%) and the high level of 1984 (85.0%), while the effectiveness of a Democratic preference increases slightly. The changes in preferences and in impact reduce net Republican vote advantage on prosperity to only 1.8% from 10.4% four years earlier.

In net vote advantage as well as preferences, then, the pattern is one of erosion of the dramatic 1980 Republican gains in subsequent elections. For preferences, the erosion begins in 1984 with recovery in net evaluation of the Democrats from the particularly dismal levels of 1980. For vote advantage, the erosion is delayed until 1988 by the unusually great impact of unusually positive evaluations of Republicans on vote choice in 1984.

But even the eroded advantage contrasts clearly with the pre-1980 pattern. The Democrats' decline in net vote advantage on prosperity between 1976 and 1988 is 11.7%. The figure is considerably smaller than the 20.3% decline between 1976 and 1984 but is nonetheless sizable. The large and potentially compensating shift in net advantage from social welfare in 1984 only partially makes up this loss: the Democrats' gain is 7.8% in 1980–1984 and 6.5% in 1980–1988. If one avoids excessive reliance on an individual base year by using the mean for the four-election sequence of 1964–1976 instead, the Democrats' loss in net vote advantage on prosperity through 1988 is nearly twice as large as their gain on social welfare. Eight years after the Reagan-Carter contest, the sharp discontinuities it produced in the impact of prosperity as an electoral issue survive. The shift in the focus of such concerns from transitory individual candidates to the parties themselves at least partially offsets the weakening in the overall Republican advantage. George Bush had every reason to think at the beginning of his presidency that concern with prosperity continued to provide a basis for continued Republican electoral success.

ECONOMICS AND VOTE CHOICE:
MULTIVARIATE EFFECTS

The language used above assigns causal significance far too easily. Assuming that economic issues are truly causes of voting behavior would seem reasonable given the central role that they have been assigned in accounts of the New Deal party system. Changes in salience, preference, and zero-order association with vote choice further suggest that the open-ended questions are tapping real citizen concerns rather than picking up widespread projection or rationalization of preferences generated by other factors. Projection and rationalization cannot be ruled out, of course, but if they are being employed it is with a subtle attentiveness to electoral context and circumstance.

One must explicitly test, however, whether assertions of impact on vote choice hold under more demanding circumstances: when the four dimensions are introduced simultaneously and when one controls for other attitudinal components of the voting decision. Do the zero-order effects survive, substantively and statistically, once the potentially confounding effects of other variables are introduced?

Additional variables to include in a fully-specified attitudinal model of vote choice are the three components of the classic model Campbell et al. introduced in *The Voter Decides* (1954): party identification, issue orientation, and candidate orientation. The only modification required is that issue orientation in this context must mean issues other than economics. Party and other issues, in particular, provide powerful competing bases for vote choice: party identification should be particularly important given the close association of economic concerns with partisanship since the New Deal (Campbell et al., 1960: 184, 201; Nie, Verba, and Petrocik, 1979: 353; Kelley, 1988: 192). Other issues would include non-economic domestic issues such as race and social order that Scammon and Wattenberg (1971), Miller and Levitin (1976), Petrocik (1981), and others saw replacing economics in salience and impact on vote choice in the late 1960s, as well as long-standing foreign policy and defense concerns.

The small number of categories on the dependent variable of vote choice make ordinary least squares inappropriate for such analysis (Aldrich and Cnudde, 1975). Table 6.4 therefore presents results of a probit analysis in which the dependent variable is dichotomized vote choice (voting Democratic) and the independent variables are the four dimensions of economics, other issues, candidate orientation, and party identification.[21]

Table 6.4 produces a revealing picture. Six of the forty coefficients for economic variables fail to survive the introduction of other economic and control variables: their ratio of coefficient to standard error falls below the 1.65 that defines statistical significance at the .05 level for a one-tailed test. In four cases (1952, 1956, 1964, 1968) this occurs for the weakest of the four dimensions at the zero-order level: social welfare in years of its low salience (1952 and 1956), prosperity in 1964, and social welfare again in 1968. The two other instances are both fiscal-monetary policy

TABLE 6.4
Probit Analysis of Vote Intention: Economic and Other Attitudinal Variables

	1952	1956	1960	1964	1968	1972	1976	1980	1984	1988
Fiscal/monetary	.46[a]	.16	.31[a]	.28[a]	.20	.28[a]	.37[a]	.18[a]	.38[a]	.18[a]
Class	.63[a]	.40[a]	.24[a]	.33[a]	.38[a]	.58[a]	.46[a]	.18[a]	.42[a]	.40[a]
Social welfare	.07	−.14	.28[a]	.38[a]	.16	.35[a]	.43[a]	.29[a]	.32[a]	.27[a]
Prosperity	.76[a]	.76[a]	.33[a]	.00	.62[a]	.36[a]	.51[a]	.43[a]	.47[a]	.25[a]
Other issues	.59[a]	.60[a]	.31[a]	.80[a]	.76[a]	.64[a]	.38[a]	.56[a]	.61[a]	.49[a]
Candidates	.64[a]	.74[a]	.81[a]	.85[a]	.84[a]	1.02[a]	.89[a]	.75[a]	.71[a]	.53[a]
Party identification	.80[a]	1.05[a]	.74[a]	.58[a]	.70[a]	.65[a]	.68[a]	.58[a]	.71[a]	.73[a]
Constant	−.84[a]	−.84[a]	−.56[a]	−.06[a]	−.79[a]	−.98[a]	−.38[a]	−.42[a]	−.82[a]	−.47[a]
Percent correct	89.0	90.0	90.1	91.0	87.0	88.8	87.7	84.3	87.7	86.3
Null prediction[b]	59.5	61.0	60.1	65.9	60.7	71.2	51.7	56.1	62.7	57.2

Notes: Entries are probit coefficients from an analysis in which Democratic vote intention is dependent and preference variables are trichotomized.

    a. Indicates statistical significance (one-tailed test) at .05.

    b. The null prediction is the percentage that would be correctly predicted if one simply predicted the modal category.

(1956 and 1968). In the remaining 34 of 40 instances, however, impact of the economic dimension survives introduction of control variables.

One of the striking findings in Table 6.4 is the relative weakness of the most reliably Republican economic variable. Fiscal-monetary policy has a statistically significant impact on vote choice in eight of the ten elections: but one of them is the aberrant 1972 contest when the electorate did not have a Republican preference on it; and in five of the seven remaining years its magnitude is the lowest of the statistically significant coefficients.

Class and prosperity show more sustained patterns of considerable impact. Class satisfies the 1.65 cut-off for every year, and the magnitude of its coefficients is consistently fairly large: only 1980 shows a (temporary) weakened impact of class-linked concerns on vote choice. Class is a consistently salient issue area of sustained Democratic advantage that consistently contributes to Democratic electoral fortunes.

Social welfare, even after its salience increases to levels comparable to that of the other dimensions in 1964, produces a more mixed profile: its coefficients are largest in 1964, 1972, and 1976—the second year in which it was only modestly Democratic—while in 1968 it failed to meet the 1.65 requirement for statistical significance. In 1984, the year in which the great Democratic surge in net preference provides a possibility of its off-setting Republican gains on prosperity, its coefficient of .32 was the lowest of the four dimensions.

Prosperity demonstrates a strong link to vote choice in every election except the year of its lowest salience (1964): its probit coefficients are larger than any other dimension in seven of the ten elections, reaching as high as .76 in 1952 and 1956.

And although they never reach that level again, prosperity provides considerable advantage to the Democrats in other years.

When prosperity becomes a Republican issue area in 1980, it continues to maintain this considerable impact on vote choice. Three of the seven previous elections (1956, 1968, and 1972) saw no economic dimension with a pro-Republican net preference have a statistically significant impact on vote choice; in three of the other four years, fiscal-monetary policy had provided a (Republican) contribution that was the weakest of the statistically significant coefficients. In 1980, prosperity strongly favors the Republicans, and its probit coefficient of .43 is fifty percent greater in magnitude than for any other economic variable. In 1984, the coefficient for prosperity is .47, and it is, again, the largest for any of the four dimensions.[22]

Table 6.5 offers a first look at the extent to which the Republicans benefit from transformation of prosperity from a Democratic to Republican issue area in 1980, with a focus on how the simultaneous Democratic gains on social welfare fail to compensate for such losses in 1984. The Table reports the probability of voting Democratic in both years for a variety of combinations of the seven independent variables in Table 6.4. In each case, the left entry shows the probability for a combination of Democratic preference on prosperity and neutrality on social welfare with various scores on the five other variables. The middle entry is the probability of voting Democratic for the same combination except that prosperity is now made Republican rather than Democratic. The right entry keeps prosperity Republican but now adds a potentially compensating change on social welfare from neutral to Democratic.[23]

The first example gives results for a Democratic identifier who prefers his or her own party on class, prosperity, and other issues but prefers the Republicans on candidate orientation. In 1980, such a voter's probability of voting Democratic is a very high .74. Simply changing preference on prosperity from Democratic to Republican reduces the probability of a Democratic vote from .74 to .39, and a subsequent changing of social welfare to Democratic increases the probability to a relatively small extent (.51) that clearly fails to compensate for losses on prosperity. The change in preference on prosperity alone reduces the probability of voting Democratic by nearly half, while the subsequent change in social welfare from neutral to Democratic restores approximately one-third of the loss. In 1984, the change in prosperity reduces the probability of a Democratic vote from .73 to .35; the offsetting change in social welfare raises the probability to .50, making up 39.5% of the fall off.

Examples (b) through (d) show similar results. Manipulating scores on class, other issues, and candidate orientation produces initial probabilities of a Democratic vote generally well over .50 that fall to well under .50 when prosperity is made Republican. The potentially compensating simultaneous change of social welfare to Democratic raises the probability, but only partially. In 1980, examples (a) through (d) average a decrease of forty-six percent in probability of voting Democratic once prosperity is made Republican; changing social welfare from neutral to Democratic makes up just over a third of the loss. In 1984, the probit coefficients

TABLE 6.5

Probability of Voting Democratic:
Effects of Manipulating Prosperity and Social Welfare

1980

	fm	c	sw	p	oi	co	id	As Given[a]	Prosperity Becomes Republican[b]	Social Welfare Becomes Democratic[c]
a)	—	d	—	d	d	r	d	.74	.39	.51
b)	—	—	—	d	—	—	d	.82	.49	.61
c)	—	—	—	d	d	r	d	.67	.31	.42
d)	r	d	—	d	r	d	d	.80	.46	.58
e)	—	—	—	d	d	—	d	.87	.59	.70
f)	—	d	—	d	d	—	d	.91	.67	.77
g)	r	d	—	d	d	d	r	.79	.45	.57
h)	—	d	—	d	—	d	r	.79	.44	.56
i)	—	d	—	d	d	—	—	.70	.34	.46
j)	r	d	—	d	d	d	—	.86	.56	.68

1984

	fm	c	sw	p	oi	co	id	As Given[a]	Prosperity Becomes Republican[b]	Social Welfare Becomes Democratic[c]
a)	—	d	—	d	d	r	d	.73	.35	.50
b)	—	—	—	d	—	—	d	.61	.24	.37
c)	—	—	—	d	d	r	d	.57	.21	.33
d)	r	d	—	d	r	d	d	.68	.30	.45
e)	—	—	—	d	d	—	d	.82	.48	.63
f)	—	d	—	d	d	—	d	.91	.64	.78
g)	r	d	—	d	d	d	r	.64	.27	.41
h)	—	d	—	d	—	d	r	.52	.18	.29
i)	—	d	—	d	d	—	—	.57	.21	.33
j)	r	d	—	d	d	d	—	.69	.31	.46

Notes: Entries are probabilities of voting Democratic for each combination of the seven independent variables. Entries are based on probit analysis of dichotomous independent variables.

a. This column reports the probability for the combination cited.

b. The second column shows the effects of changing prosperity to pro-Republican.

c. The third column shows the effect of changing social welfare to pro-Democratic.

for both social welfare and prosperity are somewhat larger than in 1980, and both manipulations therefore have somewhat larger impacts: changing prosperity to Republican reduces the probability of voting Democratic by 57.9%; less than forty percent of the loss is recovered by the simultaneous change of social welfare from neutral to Democratic. Entries (e) and (f) show the powerful effects of these manipulations in situations even more clearly Democratic in their basic structure, while the last four entries show similar effects for Republican identifiers and Independents.[24]

Table 6.6 extends the probit analysis from an illustration of the effects of changed positions on social welfare and prosperity to an estimate of the way in which the economic (and other) issue concerns contribute more generally to the distribution of the vote. The Table combines information about net preferences and the relationship each variable has to vote choice to estimate the total contribution to Democratic percentage of the popular vote. It reports the difference between the probability of voting Democratic for a citizen who takes the population mean on all ten independent variables and one who is neutral on the target variable while taking the mean score on all others: the resulting number can be interpreted as the direct impact that the public's actual score on an independent variable has on the total percentage Democratic.[25] The Table makes use of a greater amount of information that the previous one: first, it uses the actual mean score on the various independent variables rather than simply characterize them as favoring the Democrats or the Republicans; second, it breaks the "other issues" from Table 6.5 into the specific issues used in Chapter Five (race, new domestic, foreign policy), as well as a residual category of all other issues mentioned in connection with the open-ended like/dislike questions.[26]

The data in Table 6.6 show issues' having a variety of impacts on vote choice. In some cases there is little contribution even though the public as a whole strongly prefers one party to the other: the variable simply has relatively small effects on vote choice. In other cases, a variable can make a small net contribution despite its strong link to vote choice because neither party enjoys a sizable advantage in terms of net preferences: the number favoring the Democrats is much the same as the number favoring the Republicans, so although both groups vote consistently with their preference neither party receives an overall advantage. Sizable contributions to the Democrats' vote totals, positive or negative, are produced by variables on which there exist both a clear overall preference for one party and a powerful link to vote choice. In these cases, changing the net preference from the actual mean to zero is itself a considerable adjustment, and the variable's strong impact on vote choice translates the changed mean into a different expected Democratic vote.

Table 6.6 makes clear that the magnitude of contributions to electoral outcome is generally quite modest: most of the individual entries are quite small, indicating the modest extent to which most types of issues, on their own, affect vote totals once the full range of other factors that play a role in vote choice is taken into consideration. Just under half of the eighty entries for issues reach even one percent, and the absolute value of all eighty averages only 1.42%; even if we include the consistently powerful factors of candidate orientation and party identification, the average rises only to 2.16%.[27]

The eight sets of issues fall into three categories in terms of their overall contribution to election outcome. Race and the residual category produce a consistent pattern of modest impacts: in no year does either affect percentage of the vote Democratic by more than 1.8%, and their mean contributions are both below two-

TABLE 6.6

Total Contribution to Democratic Vote Totals

	1952	1956	1960	1964	1968	1972	1976	1980	1984	1988
Fiscal/monetary	-1.9	-0.3	-0.9	-0.6	+0.2	+0.0	-2.4	-1.5	-0.9	-1.1
Class	+7.4	+2.2	+2.1	+2.1	+1.3	+1.7	+4.3	+0.7	+3.5	+3.3
Social welfare	-0.3	-0.3	+0.0	+1.8	+0.2	+0.0	+1.5	+0.3	+2.4	+2.2
Prosperity	+10.2	+1.5	+1.2	+0.3	+1.1	+0.4	+3.3	-2.6	-1.7	-0.3
Race	+0.4	-0.0	-0.0	+0.9	+0.9	-0.1	+0.0	+0.7	-0.0	+0.0
New domestic	-2.6	-0.8	+0.0	-0.9	-1.2	+0.4	+1.9	+0.0	+0.6	-1.4
Foreign	-5.7	-4.8	-3.5	+0.3	-3.2	-2.9	-0.8	-2.9	+0.6	-1.4
Other	-0.0	+0.5	+0.3	+1.8	-1.7	+0.0	+0.4	-0.8	-0.0	-0.0
Candidate orientation	-5.7	-8.0	-9.4	+13.0	-2.7	-11.1	-7.2	+3.4	-4.7	-0.7
Party identification	+6.3	+3.8	+3.6	+6.6	+4.0	+2.0	+5.0	+4.2	+2.1	+2.2

Notes: Entries are net contribution to Democratic percentage of the popular vote. They are estimated by comparing predicted percentage Democratic for a respondent with mean values on all ten independent variables with the percentage Democratic predicted if a score of zero is substituted on the target variable. They can be interpreted as the change in Democratic vote percentage due to the deviation of the actual mean from zero.

thirds of one percent. Nor do even these modest impacts consistently help one party: they make a net contribution to the Democrats in some years and to the Republicans in others, with no particular pattern over time other than the consistently small value of the contribution.[28]

Fiscal/monetary, social welfare, and new domestic issues form a somewhat more powerful second cluster. New domestic issues are of course a combination of the usually Republican Social Issue and the usually Democratic New Politics. Net preference on new domestic issues varies considerably over time depending on the relative salience and net partisan preference on the two components, and their contribution to vote percentage varies considerably as well. They provide a net contribution to the Republicans as large as 2.6% (1952) and to the Democrats as large as 1.9% (1976). A probit analysis in which the Social Issue and New Politics were entered separately shows no substantial changes in results for the economic variables that are the primary concern here.

The weakness that fiscal/monetary and social welfare had previously shown in their link to vote choice produces only moderate levels of contribution to election outcome as well. They average an approximately one percent impact on vote totals between 1952 and 1988. The earlier years of the ten-election period often saw both of these concerns with very small and statistically insignificant contributions to the division of the popular vote, but they have more recently produced consistent and substantial electoral payoffs. Fiscal/monetary policy contributed to the Republican percentage of the vote in each year after 1976, as much as −2.4% in 1976; social welfare provides 1.5% of the popular vote to the Democrats in 1976 and at least 2.2% in 1984 and 1988.

The largest impacts of issues on division of the popular vote hold for class, foreign policy, and prosperity, with class (3.05%) and foreign policy (2.53%) actually making somewhat greater overall contributions to vote totals than prosperity (2.28%). Class and foreign policy are also distinctive in the consistent partisan direction of their impact: class contributes to Democratic vote totals in all ten elections, with some of the contributions substantial; foreign policy contributes to the Republicans in eight of the ten elections, often considerably, while the two exceptions (1964 and 1984) produce a very small Democratic advantage.

Prosperity, as one would expect from the discussion above, varies over time in the direction of its partisan contribution. Through 1976, prosperity consistently contributes to Democratic electoral strength, powerfully in 1952 and at levels varying between 0.3% to 3.3% thereafter. The shift in the impact of prosperity between 1976 and 1980 produces the second largest inter-election shift in Table 6.6 and the only one in which the shift is from a net contribution of some magnitude to one party to a net contribution of some magnitude to the other. Prosperity provides a net contribution to the Democrats of 3.3% in 1976 and a net contribution to the Republicans of −2.6% in 1980. Class and foreign policy produce a shift in net contribution towards the Republicans between 1976 and 1980 as well, but the 3.6% for class and 2.1% for foreign policy are considerably smaller than the 5.9% for prosperity (see also Aldrich, Sullivan, and Borgida, 1989).

The analyses in Table 6.6 can be manipulated one step further to drive home the significance of the changed impact of prosperity between 1976 and 1980. In addition to using the actual mean and a mean of zero to estimate an issue's impact on vote totals, we can also substitute mean scores from other years in an attempt to estimate how changes in net preferences over time might affect election outcome. For example, Table 6.6 shows a net contribution to the Democrats of 2.4% for social welfare in 1984; that percentage represents the difference between the estimated probability of voting Democratic for a citizen with the very pro-Democratic net preference score of .508 that voters as a whole had on social welfare in 1984 and a substituted net preference of zero. One can also, however, substitute the much weaker mean score of .117 that had existed in 1980. Doing so produces an estimated Democratic share of the vote 2.1% smaller than when the actual 1984 mean is used: the figure indicates that the Democrats received an additional 2.1% of the popular vote in 1984 because of their improved standing on social welfare.

If one carries out the same kind of analysis for prosperity in 1980, one gets an even better impression of how much changed popular perceptions on prosperity affected the election outcome. Table 6.6 indicates that prosperity deflated the Democratic vote by 2.6% in 1980. If one substitutes the 1976 mean net preference on prosperity of .214 for the actual 1980 mean of –.278, one finds a 4.4% decrease in Democratic vote totals that can be attributed to shifts on prosperity over the four years. Simply adding this 4.4% to the 41.0% that Carter actually received in 1980 produces a total of 45.4%, while subtracting the same 4.4% from Reagan's actual percentage produces a total of 46.1%! The shift in net preferences in prosperity between 1976 and 1980 would by itself seem to have produced enough new Republican votes to give Reagan an overwhelming proportion of his popular vote margin over Carter.

Prosperity is clearly not the sole factor driving Republican victories in the 1980s. Although Table 6.5 shows considerable impact of net preferences on prosperity in 1984, the less Republican net preference and the more one-sided election outcome make prosperity's total contribution to Reagan's re-election victory smaller;[29] there is a further reduction in net contribution to Republican vote totals in 1988 as well. The declining Republican net preference on prosperity gives the Democrats 1.5% more of the vote than they would have received with the even less favorable evaluation on prosperity of eight years earlier. But the Democrats do 1.4% *worse* that their favorable evaluation from 1976 would have produced. Adjusting the actual percentages Bush and Dukakis received by the 1.4% that 1976 net preference on prosperity would have produced reduces Bush's margin of victory by over a third.[30]

PARTY SYSTEM VIb:
REPUBLICANS AS THE PARTY OF PROSPERITY

The Democrats' dominance of the New Deal party system is commonly seen as based on mass perception that they could best manage the economy. Roosevelt's success in combating the effects of a depression that began with a Republican in the White House by mobilizing a majority in favor of active government management of the economy created long-term partisan benefits to the Democrats that made them the nation's natural party of government for nearly forty years (Sundquist, 1983).

Well into the 1970s, even as the Republicans began to win presidential elections quite regularly, the Democrats maintained a considerable asset in their being widely seen as better able to manage the economy. Fiscal-monetary policy was an area of Republican strength, but it proved a relatively weak basis for vote choice. If prosperity after 1952 failed to produce the strong Democratic advantages of that year (and presumably of the pre-1952 period), the party benefited from increases in both salience and preferences on social welfare and from a continuing advantage in the economic groups with which the party was identified. The 1972 election provided a partial exception to the pattern, but recession late in the Nixon/Ford administration caused the Democrats' electoral advantage on economics in 1976 to be as large as it had been since 1952.

The events of the late 1970s change this pattern in a profound way. A party that had already won but three of the preceding seven presidential elections now lost the public perception that it was the party of good times. Contrary to Shafer's (1991b) assertion that the presidency is seen as responsible for foreign policy and cultural values while the public expresses its economic and social welfare attitudes by electing a Democratic House of Representatives, it was economics that lay at the heart of Democratic presidential failure after 1978. The average American had not turned to the right on economics and social welfare; he or she was simply punishing the Democrats for failing to produce the economic outcomes that the party had long been seen as able to produce. In 1980, the Democrats were evaluated negatively in absolute terms on the prosperity dimension that had previously so helped them, and their partial recovery in 1984 was at least somewhat offset by increasingly positive evaluations of the Republicans. Prosperity was an area of substantial Democratic net vote disadvantage in 1980 and 1984, and even the erosion of the deficit in 1988 leaves the party at a considerable disadvantage compared to its pre-1980 position. The fact that the continuing Republican edge in preferences was increasingly party- rather than candidate-based suggests that it had the potential to survive Reagan's own disappearance from the electoral scene. The Democrats did make gains on social welfare in 1984, and these also are party- as well as candidate-based. But the preference gain and impact of social welfare preferences on vote choice offset only half of the Republican gains on prosperity.

Chapter Five makes clear that the ideological factors related to perceived distance provide no overall Republican advantage in 1984 and 1988 capable of explaining their victories; economics is in fact the only issue area on which the Republicans hold an advantage in issue space in 1984 and 1988, but even here the advantage is small both in absolute terms and in terms of the advantage other issues have provided the Republicans in other years. The issue orientation measure used in Chapter Five, a simple additive scale of issue-related likes and dislikes of the parties and candidates shows a similar overall Democratic advantage in 1984 and 1988.[31]

The kinds of economic factors reviewed in this chapter make clear why perceived distance and issue orientation measures missed the attitudinal basis for Republican victories. One of the advantages of the open-ended like/dislike questions is that they capture a great variety of both prospective and retrospective comments about the parties or candidates, including both purely retrospective comments on past achievements/failures and the kind of retrospectively-based prospective judgments in which past experiences are used as a cost-cutting guide to a party's future behavior (Fiorina, 1981: 12). Perceived distance measures are unlikely to be sensitive to either kind of retrospective evaluations: the key economic dimension of prosperity, in particular, is a valence issue unlikely to be seen as having an explicitly ideological character.[32] Equal importance assigned to each comment in the issue orientation measure used is likely to cause underestimation of the impact of highly salient and intensely held perceptions that co-exist among a number of less important ones. The distinctiveness of prosperity as a dimension within economics is a good example of how one kind of comment can have considerable impact that is missed by a simple additive scale.[33]

The Democrats faced a difficult task in the aftermath of the 1988 presidential election. Out-parties can do little to convince a retrospective-voting electorate of their merits. The Democrats' credibility as critics of Reaganomics was, furthermore, undermined by their claims since 1980 that such policies could not work. As long as Republican incumbents were able to avoid such disaster, there was no reason to believe that the Democrats could regain their traditional advantage.

The danger to the Republicans was two-fold: first, it is of course possible that the Democrats were correct in their analysis of Republican economic policies as short-term quick-fixes that would inevitably end in disaster; second, even if Reaganomics were fundamentally sound, the natural working of the business cycle would at some time inevitably have a presidential election scheduled at a time of national relative economic stress. Any recession would not only be likely to constitute a short-term anti-Republican force in a given election, but it would also inevitably raise at least some doubts about the long-term success of Reaganomics, reactivate at least some pre-Reagan images of the parties' abilities to manage the economy, and cause at least some voters to question the Republican ability to provide prosperity. A retrospectively-oriented electorate would certainly not be able to disentangle the competing hypotheses of a failed policy or normal and temporary slow-down. A Democratic president would then get the opportunity that Roosevelt and Reagan seized to win a series of presidential elections by showing that their parties *could* produce good times.

NOTES

* A much earlier version of this chapter appeared in the December 1991 *Western Political Quarterly*.

1. The Table reports issue orientation rather than perceived distance. Because issue orientation allows reporting of the full ten-election period and because perceived distance measures are unavailable before 1968, it seems useful to use issue orientation here. Codes used to create candidate orientation are included in Appendix 6: it is the more general candidate orientation measure reported in Lawrence (1978), a sum of open-ended likes/dislikes of the personal characteristics of candidates, whether or not the characteristics seem job-related; issue- and party-based references are omitted. Probit coefficients are from separate analyses of all Democrats and all Republicans; probit coefficients and means for all partisans and for the two cores are given in Appendix 7.

2. The original issue orientation and candidate orientation measures both use zero as a neutral score, with positive scores Democratic and negative scores Republican; the manipulation simply multiplies both variables by minus one. The original party identification variable uses the standard zero (strong Democrat) to six (strong Republican) scale; the manipulation simply subtracts the mean score from six.

3. Appendix 5 replicates Table 6.1 using perceived distance instead of issue orientation; it shows that perceived distance scores count for more than issue orientation in 1972 and 1976, as one would expect if perceived distance is sensitive to directional considerations issue orientation misses.

4. The decline in the number of citizens identifying as Democrats is of course part of the explanation for Democratic failure in the 1980s. But changed party composition is a two-edged sword: eliminating relatively conservative Democrats should bring the party the benefits of a more cohesive and more loyal membership as well (see also Hurley, 1989: 257). Our measure of extremity, a relative measure based on responses of Democratic identifiers as a whole, should therefore have shifted over time, with issue positions moderate in 1980 and before becoming relatively conservative thereafter. Such a shift would reduce the distance in issue space between remaining Democratic identifiers and their own party/candidate while increasing distance to the Republicans. Unfortunately, NES's dropping a question about when and why respondents changed party loyalty precludes our looking at 1984 and 1988 respondents who abandoned their Democratic party identification after 1980. An alternative is to look at Democrats' views on the subset of issues asked in the same format in both 1976 and 1984, the years bracketing Reagan's 1980 victory. For all respondents except the most liberal, the same combination of absolute scores does produce more conservative standardized ideological extremity scores: a Democrat who takes the middle position on each issue produces an ideological extremity score in 1976 of −.51 and in 1984 of .22; for those with the most conservative scores on each issue, ideological extremity goes from 5.07 in 1976 to 7.10 in 1984. Cohesion and loyalty should therefore rise even if the electoral alternatives remained stationary in issue space; if the Republicans were to shift to the right (as they are perceived to have done after 1980), the changed composition of their identifiers would have even more positive impact on Democratic electoral fortunes.

5. Schumpeter's claim of mass incompetence is clearly meant to apply only to the political realm. Citizens are perfectly competent in proximate areas of their private or professional lives, but they lack the skills necessary to play the role demanded by traditional notions of good citizenship. Schumpeter's citizen is entirely rational in not seeking skills that would be costly (in time and effort) to acquire and which would produce, in a country of tens of millions of voters, very little reward. Note that prospective voting focuses on the kinds of issue concerns captured at level A of Campbell et al.'s (1960) levels of

conceptualization; retrospective voting focuses on the far more common concern with consequences of government policy that was captured at level B (group benefits) or level C (nature of the times).

6. A somewhat more optimistic version of retrospective voting has citizens using past performance to make judgments about the plausibility of promises that current candidates make; see Conover, Feldman, and Knight (1987). Fiorina sees retrospective issues as a somewhat broader category of issues than the valence issues discussed by Stokes (1966): questions about which party can best achieve generally-valued (or avoid generally disliked) ends.

7. Fiorina pays only slight attention to Schumpeter himself.

8. Retrospective evaluations by unsophisticated voters may of course lead to unfair attributions of credit or blame: an incumbent may benefit from forces he neither created nor contributed to; an incumbent may be punished for problems that are not his fault or go unrewarded for having prevented even worse outcomes than the opposition might have produced. Schumpeter believes that attributing credit or blame fairly is simply beyond the capabilities of most voters: they can neither determine the linkage between policies and outcomes nor cut through partisan claims about who is responsible for what.

9. The pre-1980 data with which Fiorina deals were not designed with explicit attention to the distinction between different types of issues, forcing him to deal at considerable length with teasing out what is retrospective and what is prospective. Ironically, his considering citizens' most important perceived national problems as exclusively prospective likely causes him to underestimate the importance of retrospective concerns even before 1980.

10. The percentage of Democratic identifiers favoring the Democrats on prosperity falls from 28.2% in 1976 to 9.9% in 1980, and recovers only to 14.6% in 1988; for the core liberal Democrats, the figures are 33.9%, 8.3%, and 13.9% respectively. In 1976, 28.1% of liberal Democrats favored the Democrats in both prosperity and on the other dimensions of economics combined; only 1.8% were cross-pressured between a Republican preference on prosperity and a Democratic preference on the other dimensions. In 1980, when prosperity exerted a particularly powerful effect on vote choice, the percentage with reinforcing Democratic scores falls to 7.5% and the percentage cross-pressured rises to 12.3%; the partial recovery in 1988 produces percentages of 12.7% and 7.0% respectively.

11. For 1976–1988, the probit equation using perceived distance is less accurate for Democrats who see the Republicans better able to produce prosperity than it is for those who think their own party can best do so. Furthermore, in 1980 and 1984 the probit analysis *over*estimates Democratic loyalty for the cross-pressured and *under*estimates it for others: in other words, the data are consistent with a pattern in which the Republican preference on prosperity depresses Democratic loyalty below what a probit equation insensitive to such a valence issue would predict.

12. It may help to think of the four dimensions as differing along two dimensions: first, the extent to which they deal with policies or with outcomes, i.e., with the content of government decisions or with their consequences; second, whether they are systemic or particularistic, i.e., whether they affect the population as a whole or subgroups within the population. Fiscal/monetary consists of government policies with broad, systemic implications; class refers to particularistic outcomes, those benefiting some economically-defined subgroup in the population; prosperity refers to economic outcomes with more general, systemic consequences. The problem dimension in this scheme is social welfare, which clearly can consist of government policies or of outcomes. Any outcomes included in social welfare would involve more narrowly-defined groupings than is the case for class.

13. Appendix 6 reports the NES party/candidate codes used to construct the dimensions. See also Campbell et al. (1960): 46. For a recent discussion of the various types of economic considerations (retrospective and prospective, personal and sociotropic) that might affect vote choice, see Lanoue (1994).

14. Net partisan preference is simply the sum of pro-Democratic and anti-Republican responses minus the sum of anti-Democratic and pro-Republican responses.

15. This is one of several areas in which economic perceptions of parties defy the general pattern of increasing irrelevance noted by Wattenberg (1984).

16. Wattenberg's expectations of the decreasing salience of parties are best fulfilled by class. Over time, parties are slightly less frequently mentioned on class, although there is a sharp increase in party-based comments in 1988 from 26.0% to 31.5% that disrupts the general pattern.

17. The tensions between social welfare and class, on the one hand, and prosperity on the other is illustrated in an October 1986 CBS News/*New York Times* survey (CBS/*New York Times*, 1986) in which the public felt by 52% to 26% that the Democrats were more likely to care about the needs and problems of people like themselves while claiming at the same time by a 45% to 35% margin that the Republicans were better able to maintain prosperity.

18. Somer's D (asymmetric) ranges between .23 and .42 for each dimension and vote intention. Respondents indicating firm preferences and those leaning toward a candidate were combined. The measure is the narrower vote choice variables from Chapter Five: an intermediate category consists of those undecided between major party candidates or declaring that they did not know for whom they would vote; respondents who did not intend to vote and third-party voters are excluded.

19. More specifically, entries are the percentage of the total population favoring the Democrats on an issue and voting Democratic minus the percentage favoring the Republicans on the issue and voting Republican.

20. Bivariate analysis will of course depress the impact of issues that favor the Democrats because many voters will be cross-pressured between such variables and the other factors, favoring the Republicans, which produce the Republican victory.

21. Other issues and candidate orientation are both derived from the open-ended like/dislike questions. Candidate orientation uses comments about personal characteristics, job-related or not, of candidates. See Appendix 6 for codes used to construct these variables. Party identification is the standard seven-point CPS measure. To the extent to which party identification is a running tally of retrospective judgments (Fiorina, 1981), it may of course already "include" economic evaluations, making estimates of the impact of economics reported here conservative.

22. Kelley (1988) notices the divergence of what he calls "election's economic impact" from other New Deal issues in 1980, arguing that the divergence leaves a Democratic bias on the remainder of the New Deal agenda. His failure to explicitly link these issues to vote choice causes him to miss the relatively great impact prosperity-related concerns have on individual vote choice and, therefore, on the declining fortunes of the Democrats.

23. Entries in Table 6.4 are computed from a probit analysis in which independent variables are trichotomized into Democratic, Republican, or neutral. Dichotomized (dummy) variables are more sensitive to possible non-linear impacts but perform only trivially better: estimated Z-scores from the two techniques correlate at .98 for each year. The trichotomized model, more economical in presentation, is used in Table 6.4; dichotomized variables are used to construct Table 6.5.

24. The eroded effects of prosperity in 1988 noted above emerge in Table 6.4 as well. The probit coefficient for prosperity is .25, second lowest in the ten-election sequence. For only the second time, prosperity is less strongly linked to vote choice than is social welfare. The relative weakening of prosperity combines with lessened net preference advantage to contribute to a less damaging consequence for the Democrats than in either of the two preceding elections, but the .25 indicates a still substantial negative impact of the accumulated changes since 1976.

25. For a similar analysis using regression rather than probit techniques, see Miller and Shanks, 1982.

26. The residual issue category contains an exceptionally broad set of concerns, many of them vague statements of support (or opposition) for unspecified policies. Including it as a control therefore makes the estimates for other issue areas fairly conservative: to the extent that the residual category includes unarticulated sentiments paralleling those tapped by other issue dimensions, it would decrease the causal impact assigned to those issue areas.

27. Inclusion of candidate orientation in the probit analysis on which Table 6.6 is based probably underestimates the impact of issues. The measure of candidate orientation used includes any and all non-issue comments that respondents make about candidates, including the generalized statements of like or dislike that may well be simple re-statements of issue-preferences. One could replicate Table 6.6 using a more job-related concept of candidate orientation, but doing so would miss entirely the powerful impact of generalized reaction to candidates as individuals that clearly do play a role in vote choice.

28. Race does help the Democrats in the four years in which it has an impact. But even then the total contribution to their vote total is modest, and the four years are interspersed with others in which there is little or no net advantage. These effects are direct effects, of course. One could pursue the interrelatedness of these ten variables to tease out indirect effects as well. Carmines and Stimson (1989) make a case for substantial but subtle impacts of racial issues on election outcome.

29. Remember that probit estimates are not linear: the impact a variable has at the extremes of a distribution will be smaller than in the middle. Prosperity counts for less in 1984 in part because so many other factors helped the Republicans in 1984 to an even more one-sided victory.

30. To the extent that prosperity in 1980 or thereafter contributed to candidate orientation or to shifts in party identification, the effects reported in Table 6.6 may of course underestimate the issue effects later in the 1980s.

31. Issue orientation had been Republican in 1980 (−.300), but in 1984 (.908) and 1988 (.335) it is Democratic.

32. In each year for which perceived distance on economics is available, except 1976, prosperity is the dimension of economics to which it is least related. This includes the three elections when prosperity and perceived distance on economics both favor the Republicans.

33. Likes/dislikes on economics are less associated with perceived distance on economics than is the case for other issue areas in each year but 1976, as one would expect if there are distinctively retrospective aspects of prosperity.

7

Mondale's Revenge: Ideology and Retrospective Evaluations in 1992

The 1992 presidential election might initially seem to mark an end of the era of Republican dominance in presidential elections that dates back to 1968. Bill Clinton's victory was only the Democrats' second since 1964. And while Jimmy Carter's triumph could easily be attributed to the more-or-less accidental effects of Watergate, Clinton's seemed rooted in more fundamental and long-term aspects of electoral politics centering on core issues of economic management and prosperity. Those schooled in the classic theory of realignment would undoubtedly find the third-party effort of Ross Perot intriguing, suggestive of a failure of an existing party system to contain new cross-cutting issues associated with the budget deficit and, quite likely, indicative of Republican failure to maintain control of the issue agenda that had underlay the Reagan successes of the 1980s.

Yet in many ways the message of 1992 is one of continuity rather than change. The first, and in many ways the most important, indicator of the lack of change in 1992 is Clinton's percentage of the popular vote: Clinton of·course won with a minority of the popular vote, able to do so because Perot and Bush divided the opposition.[1] The evidence from Chapter Two provides considerable evidence that the 1992 outcome marks continuation in the pattern of recent elections which the Democrats lost: the standard deviation of Democratic percentage of the vote for a five-election sequence *falls* when 1992 is substituted for 1972 to 3.90, the lowest for any five year sequence since Roosevelt's first victory; and five of the six t statistics that mark discontinuities in Democratic election performance in Figure 2.1 through Figure 2.4 decline from already low levels. In terms of outcomes, there is no evidence that 1992 marks a break with a pattern of Democratic electoral performance that dates back to 1968.

Even more striking is the continuity of most of the attitudinal components of past elections that had favored the Democrats well before 1992: a continuing surplus of Democratic identifiers over Republicans, a continuing perception of the Democratic Party as centrist rather than ideologically extreme, a continuing modest Democratic advantage in relative proximity to voters in ideological issue space, a continuing net Democratic preference on the likes and dislikes of the parties and candidates, a continuing sense that the Democrats sympathized with the economic interests of the larger part of the population.

These factors had of course already been sufficiently Democratic to have produced electoral success since the early 1980s. If vote choice in the 1980s had been driven by party loyalty, prospective issue concerns, or economic issues like class and social welfare, President Clinton would have been accepting congratulations from President Dukakis and former President Mondale after concluding his oath of office. The party's inability to translate such apparent advantages into electoral victories because of a set of essentially retrospective evaluations of the relative success of Jimmy Carter and Ronald Reagan in managing the economy is the key to understanding recent presidential electoral politics. The Democratic victory in 1992 rested on their ability to maintain the strengths they had enjoyed for a decade at the same time that they were able to recapture the image as the party of good times that they had enjoyed between 1930 and 1978.

PARTISANSHIP AND DEFECTION IN 1992

Ross Perot's strong showing would of course be seen by dealignment theorists as evidence of continuing partisan decay in 1992. And there is some modest support for such an argument in the 1992 data on strength of party identification. Table 7.1 shows three different indicators of strength of party attachment over time. It clearly indicates both the generally recognized decline in the public's party loyalty that had begun in the mid-1960s and the end of the period of decay after 1976: the 1980 election showed no further fall in the strength of mass party identification, and the two subsequent presidential contests showed a decline in the number of pure Independents, a (small) increase in the number of those who initially were willing to call themselves Democrats or Republicans, and an increase in a crude mean level of partisanship.

Each of the three indicators in fact shows a small increase in partisan disaggregation in 1992. The change is most striking in the number of those initially willing to acknowledge a partisan tie, the indicator whose recovery after 1976 is weakest: the number of strong and moderate identifiers falls to 61.6%, lowest for the eleven elections; data for the full eleven-election period makes clear that the decline is part of a pattern of decay that began in 1968 and was interrupted, briefly (and modestly), in 1984. The two other indicators show smaller changes in 1992: the number of pure Independents rises only slightly, remaining lower than it had been in 1972–1980; and the decline in the mean partisanship indicator marks only a modest pull-back from the 1988 level to half-way between the 1988 level and that of 1976 or 1980.

Within this context of modestly resumed partisan decay, however, the Democrat's party identification advantage actually increased somewhat in 1992. As Table 7.2 shows, the percentage of the Democrats in the electorate increased very slightly,

TABLE 7.1
Strength of Partisanship in 1992: Continuing Decay

Year	Pure Independents[a]	Strong and Moderate Partisans[b]	Mean Partisanship[c]
1952	7.2	75.9	3.06
1956	9.2	75.6	3.16
1960	10.2	76.5	3.03
1964	7.9	77.0	3.07
1968	10.7	70.4	2.90
1972	13.3	64.8	2.77
1976	14.7	63.6	2.73
1980	15.1	63.2	2.74
1984	11.1	65.2	2.84
1988	10.8	63.7	2.85
1992	11.6	61.6	2.79

Notes: a. Pure Independents reports the percentage of the total population who reject declaring themselves as Democrats or Republicans even when asked if they simply lean toward one of the parties.

b. Strong and moderate partisans are those who acknowledge a link to one of the parties in response to an initial question, without requiring the follow-up question about leaning. Respondents included in neither column one nor column two are weak (or independent) partisans, those who initially denied a party loyalty but indicated that they did indeed lean to one of the parties on the follow-up question; they are the difference between the sum of columns one and two and one hundred percent.

c. Mean partisanship is a simple mean score for the population as a whole, with strong identifiers coded as 4, moderate identifiers coded as 3, weak or independent identifiers coded as 2, and pure independents coded as 1.

from 47.7% to 49.8%, while the number of Republicans fell from 41.5% to 38.6%, falling short of the forty percent mark that they had breached for the first time in 1984. The ratio of Democrats to Republicans increases from 1.15 to 1.29.

These shifts reverse the pattern of Democratic decline that began so dramatically in 1984 and continued in 1988, but they are on balance modest. The Democrats are still short of the absolute majority they had enjoyed in all pre-1984 elections, and the ratio of 1.29 remains well below pre-1984 levels, making up only half of the 1988 loss from the mean for 1968–1980. If one looks at strong and moderate identifiers alone, i.e., omits the weakest (or leaning) identifiers, the pattern is much the same: although there is no increase in the number of strong and moderate Democrats, the number of Republicans falls slightly (from 28.1% to 25.9%), and the ratio of Democrats to Republicans increases from a series low of 1.27 to a 1.38. Reagan-era gains in Republican party identification have clearly been reduced somewhat. But even at their low point the Democrats had a party identification majority sufficient to win presidential elections if all citizens cast a party-based vote, and they lost many elections between 1952 and 1980 in which their advantage was far greater than the one they enjoyed in 1992.

TABLE 7.2

1992 Changes in Party Identification

Year	All Identifiers[a]			Strong and Moderate Identifiers[b]		
	Democrats	Republicans	Ratio (D/R)	Democrats	Republicans	Ratio (D/R)
1952	57.8	35.0	1.65	48.1	27.8	1.73
1956	51.9	38.9	1.33	45.3	30.3	1.50
1960	52.9	37.0	1.43	46.4	30.1	1.54
1964	61.6	30.5	2.02	52.2	24.8	2.10
1968	56.1	33.1	1.69	46.1	24.3	1.90
1972	52.3	34.4	1.52	41.0	23.8	1.72
1976	52.0	33.3	1.56	40.1	23.5	1.71
1980	52.1	32.8	1.59	40.7	22.5	1.81
1984	48.7	40.2	1.21	37.7	27.6	1.37
1988	47.7	41.5	1.15	35.7	28.1	1.27
1992	49.8	38.6	1.29	35.8	25.9	1.38

Notes: a. The percentage of the total population who are Democratic and Republican identifiers (strong, weak, and leaners) and the ratio of Democrats to Republicans.

          b. The percentage and ratio for strong or moderate Democrats and Republicans, omitting those who initially claimed to have no party loyalty.

TABLE 7.3

Defection

Year	Narrow[a]		Broad[b]		Third-Party	
	Democrats	Republicans	Democrats	Republicans	Democrats	Republicans
1952	21.3	3.1	43.8	17.9		
1956	18.1	2.6	40.3	18.5		
1960	17.7	2.6	41.7	18.1		
1964	7.0	26.7	27.0	46.0		
1968	17.5	5.0	53.2	26.2	13.7	7.1
1972	37.1	3.0	60.5	18.7		
1976	19.8	9.9	44.9	35.2		
1980	15.8	10.1	48.8	36.2	8.2	7.1
1984	20.4	4.8	42.2	21.1		
1988	13.6	8.1	36.3	28.2		
1992	7.3	11.8	24.7	33.0	4.7	9.3

Notes: Entries at the left are the total percentage of Democratic and Republican identifiers (strong, weak, and leaners) and the ratio of Democrats to Republicans. Entries at the right are the percentage of each group of partisans that defects.

          a. Narrow defection is the number of each group that votes for the opposite party expressed as a percentage of all identifiers who plan to vote.

          b. Broad defection is the percentage of each group who fails to vote for its party's nominee by either defecting in the narrow sense, by voting for third party candidates, or by abstaining.

Defection rates in 1992 show a more clear-cut break with past trends. In only one of the ten previous elections, the highly anomalous 1964 contest, had Democrats been more loyal than Republicans. Even the Democratic victories of 1960 and 1976 had seen Democrats more likely to abandon their party's nominee than Republicans were, a pattern that of course helps explain why their margin of victory was so much smaller than their party identification advantage. In both 1968 and 1980, Democrats had also been more likely than Republicans to vote for the (very different) third-party candidates.

All three of the defection indicators in Table 7.3 show that Democratic identifiers were *more* loyal than Republicans in 1992. The 7.3% of Democrats who intend to vote for Bush is approximately half as large as the percentage who had defected to Bush four years earlier and barely a third as great as the number defecting to Reagan in 1984. The 11.8% of Republicans who vote Democratic would be low for Democrats in any year except 1964, but it is higher than all previous levels of Republican defection other than 1964. The broader defection measure shows much the same: the Democrats' defection level would be quite unremarkable for the Republicans, but it is lower than they themselves achieved even in 1964; the Republican level is within the range of previous Republican levels, albeit at the high end of the distribution.[2] Perot's supporters are Republicans by a margin of two to one, a reversal of the pattern in both 1968 and 1980. The most proximate reason why the Democrats won the 1992 presidential election is their taking advantage, to an extent not realized for over a quarter-century, of their party identification majority.

THE CONTINUING BALANCE OF IDEOLOGICAL EXTREMISM

The Democrats' ability to mobilize their nominal identifiers in 1992 was not due to improved popular images of the party in ideological issue space. The Democrats, with considerable help from Ronald Reagan, had erased their ideological disadvantage between 1980 and 1984; their failure to win the 1984 and 1988 elections cannot be attributed to their being perceived as ideologically extreme. Bill Clinton does continue a process of moderating public images of his party and its candidates, but the modest extent to which he does so is not capable of explaining changes in identifier loyalty or in election outcome.

The Democratic disadvantage in issue space in the 1970s had prevented the party from capitalizing on its continuing party identification advantage by undermining the loyalty of Democratic identifiers: their self-placement relative to the two electoral alternatives was far less supportive of a loyal vote than was that of the Republicans, producing a placement in issue space only slightly closer to their own party and candidate than to the opposition; centrist Democrats were likely to feel an ideological proximity to the Republicans in absolute terms. The first Reagan administration, in particular, reversed this ideological disadvantage, pushing perceptions of the Republicans sufficiently to the right to produce an essentially balanced set of ideological distance scores in which neither party was advantaged.

The 1992 election continues the post-1980 pattern of essentially balanced ideological bases for loyalty for the two partisan groups. Both Democrats and Republicans place themselves closer to their own party/candidate than to the opposition in issue space, to quite similar degrees: Table 7.4 shows that the mean Democrat's overall perceived distance score is .201, while that for the mean Republican is −.187. The pattern is almost identical for comparisons limited to the parties (.193 and −.178) or to the candidates (.194 and −.184) separately. Both Democrats and Republicans are slightly more comfortable with their own party/candidate (i.e., have net perceived distance scores higher in absolute value) than they had been four years earlier.

TABLE 7.4
Net Perceived Distance: Comparative Evaluations of Parties and Candidates

Year	Comparison of Parties and Candidates Combined		Comparison of Parties		Comparison of Candidates	
	Democratic Identifiers	Republican Identifiers	Democratic Identifiers	Republican Identifiers	Democratic Identifiers	Republican Identifiers
1968	.063	−.141	—	—	.063	−.141
1972	.078	−.172	.076	−.132	.052	−.214
1976	.113	−.153	.092	−.204	.110	−.140
1980	.102	−.232	.105	−.220	.081	−.228
1984	.207	−.174	.182	−.167	.224	−.171
1988	.193	−.170	.180	−.155	.186	−.186
1992	.201	−.187	.193	−.178	.194	−.184

Notes: Entries are mean comparative perceived distance scores for each group of partisans separately. Positive entries indicate net preference for the Democrats; negative numbers indicate net preference for the Republicans. The numbers themselves are proportion of total possible perceived distance: a score of +1.000 would indicate a respondent places himself at the same point as the Democrats on all available issues and as far as possible from the Republicans.

The picture of balanced differences in issue space holds if one looks at attitudes towards the two parties separately as well. Democrats place themselves extremely close to their own party/candidate (−.005) and quite distant from the opposition (.304); their ideologically-based incentive to defect is minimal. The Republican pattern is much the same: considerable proximity to one's own party and candidate (.021) and considerable distance to the opposition (−.280). For centrist identifiers, the same pattern holds: Democratic centrists are proximate to their own party/candidate (−.063) and distant from the opposition (.276), while Republican centrists are much the same (.005 and −.291). Both parties seem to have moved very slightly closer to their own partisans in issue space between 1988 and 1992

TABLE 7.5
Perceived Distance: Attitudes Toward Each Party/Candidate Separately

	All Identifiers			
	Democratic Identifiers		Republican Identifiers	
Year	Perception of Democratic Party/ Candidate	Perception of Republican Party/ Candidate	Perception of Democratic Party/ Candidate	Perception of Republican Party/ Candidate
1968	−.044	.088	−.122	−.009
1972	−.092	.125	−.273	−.040
1976	−.095	.118	−.304	−.093
1980	−.080	.218	−.310	.014
1984	−.016	.296	−.259	.054
1988	.012	.267	−.242	.039
1992	−.005	.304	−.280	.021

	Centrist Identifiers			
	Democratic Identifiers		Republican Identifiers	
Year	Perception of Democratic Party/ Candidate	Perception of Republican Party/ Candidate	Perception of Democratic Party/ Candidate	Perception of Republican Party/ Candidate
1968	−.048	.038	−.230	−.075
1972	−.120	.057	−.325	−.089
1976	−.174	−.036	−.179	−.098
1980	−.120	.181	−.301	.027
1984	−.034	.255	−.227	.045
1988	−.014	.240	−.210	.024
1992	−.063	.276	−.291	.005

Notes: Positive scores indicate respondents are more liberal than the target party/candidate; negative scores indicate that respondent are more conservative. Entries are mean summed distance scores expressed as a proportion of toal possible distance (to standardize for the number of questions asked in each year). A respondent who gave the most liberal answer to each question and who placed both Republican candidate and party at the most conservative end of the continuum would take a score of +1.000.

while moving slightly further away from the opposition; the net effect is to rein-force both parties' ideological basis for loyalty.

Table 7.5 suggests that Clinton essentially maintains the already favorable position of his party in issue space in 1992, frustrating the Republican attempt to portray him as an ideologically extreme liberal. He had certainly presented himself during the campaign as a new type of Democrat: concerned with excessive government spending and rising deficits, a former head of the Democratic Leadership Council—a group of elected Democratic officials growing out of the early Reagan years concerned with the electoral consequences of the public's image of their party as excessively liberal (Hale, 1995). And while there is no reason to think that the DLC was visible to large numbers of ordinary voters in 1992, Clinton certainly sought the image of a new, moderate Democrat. He faced primary opposition from more conventional liberals like John Kerry and Tom Harkin, and he maintained that he would have welcomed Mario Cuomo's entry into the nomination contest in order to clarify the contrast between his own centrist vision of the party and a more liberal tradition.[3]

Table 7.6 probes the success of Clinton's attempts to moderate images of his party by examining perceptions of individual parties and candidates by the population as a whole (i.e., not for Democrats and Republicans separately). The top half of the Table makes use of all the questions on perceived distance asked in each year, and it indicates both the net Democratic advantage in overall placement in ideological issue space and the change in such placement over time. The Table provides evidence of a slight polarization of perceptions of both parties and both candidates between 1988 and 1992: images of the Democrats (party, candidates, and the two combined) moved slightly to the left while images of the Republicans moved slightly to the right. But Clinton is in fact seen as slightly less liberal than his party, and of the four comparisons of parties and candidates of 1992 with 1988, the degree of increased polarization is least for the comparison of Clinton with Dukakis.

Clinton's success in moderating the image of his party in ideological issue space may in fact be somewhat understated in Table 7.6a. Comparing the degree of ideological polarization in the 1992 election with that of previous elections is in fact complicated by the limited number and range of perceived distance measures available in the later contest. There are only three issues on which the full set of seven-point perception were asked in 1992, compared to seven in 1988 and as many as nine in 1976 and 1980.[4] The limited number of items asked has the advantage of producing a relatively high proportion of respondents for whom the perceived distance variable is available; but it of course has the more serious disadvantage of allowing us to observe citizens placing electoral alternatives in ideological issue space on a much narrower range of issues. On the other hand, all three issues asked in 1992 were asked in 1980, 1984, and 1988 as well. So if we cannot tap the full range of issues of concern to voters in 1992, we can at least use Table 7.6b to look at the same limited range for the three preceding elections in an attempt to identify more clearly change on such factors over time.

For example, Clinton's mean perceived distance score of –.116 was slightly larger than the Dukakis 1988 score of –.112 shown in Table 7.6a.[5] The three issues available in both years, however, are issues on which Dukakis was placed further to the left than he was on issues not repeated in 1992; Dukakis' placement on the three repeated issues is –.164, considerably higher than the –.112 he achieves on the full set of seven, and Clinton's –.116 is therefore considerably smaller than the comparable evaluation of Dukakis.[6] Data on perceptions of the Democratic Party behave somewhat similarly: the 1992 mean placement of –.126 is an increase over the 1988 level (–.100) for all seven issues, reaching levels achieved in 1972 and 1984; but

TABLE 7.6

Placement of Parties and Candidates in Ideological Issue Space: Changes Over Time

a. All Available Variables Used

	Perception of Democrats		
Year	Candidates	Party	Combined
1980	−.190	−.185	−.185
1984	−.127	−.126	−.127
1988	−.112	−.100	−.100
1992	−.116	−.126	−.124

	Perception of Republicans		
Year	Candidates	Party	Combined
1980	.124	.098	.113
1984	.190	.160	.176
1988	.148	.144	.149
1992	.167	.175	.175

b. Variables Available in 1992 Only

	Perception of Democrats		
Year	Candidates	Party	Combined
1980	−.200	−.211	−.208
1984	−.154	−.155	−.156
1988	−.164	−.133	−.153
1992	−.116	−.126	−.124

	Perception of Republicans		
Year	Candidates	Party	Combined
1980	.097	.066	.086
1984	.204	.162	.185
1988	.152	.142	.149
1992	.167	.175	.175

Notes: Entries are net perceived distance to each party and candidate separately using both the full set of issue questions asked in each year and the more limited set of issues asked in 1992 that are available for earlier years as well. Positive scores indicate respondents are more liberal than the target party/candidate; negative scores indicate that respondent are more conservative than the party or candidate.

using the constant set of three issues reveals a continuing pattern of moderating images of the party as well, albeit to a smaller extent.

The net impact of these changes is to continue the shift in images of the Democrats toward the center that had begun in 1980. Mean placement of the Democratic party and candidate combined had moved sharply left-ward from –.078 to –.164 to –.183 between 1968 and 1976; 1980 marked a stabilization of the position at –.185, and it was followed by a nearly equally sharp move back to the center in 1984 (–.127) and 1988 (–.100). If one shifts to scores on the three questions asked in all four years, one can clearly see 1992 continuing the pattern of moderation: a mean placement of –.208 in 1980 falls to –.156 in 1984, –.153 in 1988, and only –.124 in 1992. The Clinton candidacy clearly continued the pattern of moving perceptions of the Democrats to the center that began with the election of Ronald Reagan. Clinton himself was in fact perceived as ideologically quite in tune with the increasingly moderate party that nominated him.

Popular perceptions of the Republicans underwent no such moderation between 1988 and 1992.[7] George Bush and his party were both clearly seen as having shifted somewhat to the right between 1988 and 1992, partially offsetting the moderating impact of his 1988 campaign. Bush's own mean score on perceived distance had fallen to .152 in 1988 from Reagan's .204; but Bush's time in office pushed popular impressions of him sufficiently to the right (.167) to offset nearly a third of his 1988 gain. Change in images of the Republican Party was even greater: net placement of the party increases from .142 to .175, the highest level ever reached and slightly larger than the score achieved by Bush himself.[8] Combining impressions of party and candidate produces an overall mean placement of the Republicans on perceived distance of –.175, well above their own score in 1988 and only slightly below their score in 1984.

The net effect of all these perceptions is a mean net perceived distance score in 1992 of .028: the average voter felt slightly closer to the Democrats than to the Republicans in ideological issue space. This finding might initially indicate a situation almost unchanged from that of 1988 or 1984, when the overall Democratic advantages were .020 and .025 respectively. But because use in 1984 and 1988 of the limited range of questions available in 1992 produced a more liberal image of the Democrats than the full set of variables available in those years, comparison of those years with 1992 understates the degree of the Democratic advantage in the Clinton-Bush contest. On the three questions about social services, jobs, and defense that were used in 1992, the net perceived distance score was .000 in 1984 and –.010 in 1988.[9] The .028 of 1992 therefore represents a modest improvement in the party's proximity to the issue positions of the average voter compared to that of previous elections.

The perception of the Democrats as centrist, as essentially in tune with American public opinion as a whole, undoubtedly helps Clinton in 1992. Another candidate (or another kind of nominating process) could well have reactivated perceptions of the party as ideologically extreme. But these perceptions are at best modest extensions of advantages that the party had enjoyed for some time (Ladd, 1993), through two losing campaigns that were generally considered to have been catastrophes; by themselves, these factors would not have produced victory in 1992. The Democratic defeats in 1984 and 1988 (and to some extent 1980) were not due to problems of ideological extremity; they were due to setbacks on a very different

TABLE 7.7

Net Comparative Perceived Distance: Parties and Candidates Combined

a. All Available Variables Used

Year	Candidates	Parties	Combined
1980	−.069	−.053	−.065
1984	.034	.016	.025
1988	.012	.014	.020
1992	.027	.027	.028

b. Variables Available in 1992 Only

Year	Candidates	Parties	Combined
1980	−.092	−.088	−.096
1984	.015	−.010	.000
1988	−.019	.000	−.010
1992	.027	.027	.028

Notes: Entries are net comparative perceived distance to parties, to candidates, and to parties and candidates combined. Entries at the left are based on all questions available for that year; entries at the right are for the three variables available in 1992. Positive entries indicate a net proximity to the Democrats; negative entries indicate a net proximity to the Republicans.

set of issues linked to the parties' ability to effectively manage the economy, issues with roots in the economic outcomes of the late 1970s and early 1980s.

By 1992, however, the Carter-Reagan contest was twelve years in the past. At the end of Reagan's second term, in 1988, the Republicans were still seen as the party of good times; and the perception was increasingly institutionalized, i.e., based on comparison of parties rather than of candidates alone. But it is also true that the image was also weaker than it had been since 1980. Without further Republican economic success, one would expect that the inevitable emergence over time both of new, potentially cross-cutting issues and of new voters who may have been as young as six in 1980 would dilute images of the parties' economic success further. If that natural deterioration of a twelve-year old concern were to be reinforced by an actual economic deterioration under a Republican administration, the potential for Democratic recovery would be greatly enhanced.

THE CONTINUING RELEVANCE OF ECONOMIC EVALUATIONS

In the 1984 campaign, Walter Mondale mounted a concerted attack on the Reagan administration's economic and social welfare policies, questioning whether tax cuts could stimulate stable long-term economic growth and challenging the fairness of cutting social welfare programs for those in genuine need of government assistance. His argument was not a *total* failure: Chapter Six makes clear that Mondale did succeed in raising the salience of social welfare and in convincing the electorate that Democrats were most likely to do what they wanted on it. But for the most part the strategy did fail: the economy in 1984 was strong and was perceived to be strong; the contrast between Reagan's macro-economic success and Carter's macro-economic failure was vivid, with Carter's vice-president perhaps not the person best able to argue that the contrast was unfair or misleading. Democratic claims in 1980 that Reagan's policies could not succeed and their argument in the first two years of Reagan's term that continued economic difficulties were evidence of his policies' failure made them entirely unconvincing critics of a policy that appeared to be doing quite well by 1984.

The Democratic problem was characteristic of an out-party's dilemma in an essentially retrospectively-oriented electoral system. It is hard to argue that current good times are not the achievement of the governing party; it is hard to convince the electorate that currently successful policies are short-term fixes that will produce long-term failure, particularly if you have already been predicting their imminent failure for four years; it is hard to convince the electorate that you can do better if it can remember recent history in which you clearly did worse. The out-party in a retrospective world has little choice but to wait until the incumbents, through bad luck or through genuinely flawed policies, must face the electorate when times are not so good.

Bill Clinton was the Democratic challenger who got to run for president in a weak election-year economy. Whether George Bush's economic difficulties were due to flaws of the type that Mondale had identified eight years before or whether they were the result of the normal working (and bad timing) of the business cycle was, for the 1992 election, at least, largely irrelevant. What was important is that economic reality undermined what had been a basis of Republican electoral strength for the previous twelve years. A retrospectively-oriented electorate paid Walter Mondale little attention when he claimed that the apparent prosperity of 1984 was illusory or temporary; it was similarly not going to pay George Bush much attention in 1992 when he claimed that bad times were about to end, were not his fault, or would be exacerbated by the even worse policies of the opposition. Bad times alone should produce a damaging anti-incumbent shift in votes that might well fatally wound a president initially elected with less than 54 percent of the popular vote; to the extent that they undermine a long-standing basis of the incumbent party's strength, perhaps by activating seeds of doubt about the underlying policies that had been planted in the clearly unfertile soil of 1984, their impact could be greater in magnitude and more long-term in effect.

All four dimensions of economics in fact produce more Democratic impacts in 1992 than they had in 1988. Class and social welfare remain highly salient areas of considerable Democratic strength; fiscal/monetary continues the pattern of pro-Republican impact that extends back to the beginning of the NES surveys, but the degree to which it helps the Republicans is much less than in the preceding three contests. And prosperity, an issue that had become Republican for the first time around 1980 and provided much of the basis for continuing Republican electoral victories following the simultaneous disappearance of their advantage in ideological issue space, now reverts to its pre-1980 status as a substantial net contributor to the Democrats.

As Table 7.8 shows, class continues to be an area of considerable Democratic strength in 1992. The percentage of the population mentioning class-linked reasons for liking/disliking the parties/candidates increases slightly to 37.2%, continuing a pattern of small but steady increases after 1980. And class continues to be a dimension of economics that substantially favors the Democrats: 31.5% of the population prefer the Democrats on class in 1992, compared to only 4.4% who favor the Republicans. The resulting mean preference of .542 is more Democratic than for any year since 1956. Furthermore, the impact of class on vote choice is particularly large in 1992: for the first time in the eleven-election sequence, it is the dimension of economics with the greatest net impact on vote choice, and it produces a bivariate net vote advantage of 24.2% that is larger than for any other dimension.

Social welfare was of course a less salient and less reliably Democratic component of economics in the early NES surveys. In 1984 and 1988, however, its salience exceeded that of class, and it assumed a powerfully pro-Democratic character rivalling that of class as well. This later pattern is extended even further in 1992. The salience of social welfare reaches 45.6%, the highest level any dimension reached in any of the eleven elections and the highest of the four dimensions for the third straight year.

More than a third of the population (35.3%) has a Democratic preference on social welfare in 1992, while only 8.5% prefer the Republicans; both figures are more favorable to the Democrats than in 1988 or 1984. The result is a net preference advantage of .601, higher even than that for class in 1992 or than social welfare itself had achieved in 1984 or 1988. The bivariate net vote advantage to the Democrats on social welfare is 22.5%, slightly smaller than for class only because social welfare is a slightly less powerful source of vote choice for those with a preference.

Fiscal and monetary policy has of course been a reliably Republican dimension of economics since 1952,[10] although its weakness as a determinant of vote choice meant that it often contributed little to Republican electoral success. One might suspect that the attention to budget deficits and taxation in the 1992 campaign would have stimulated public concern with this aspect of economics, a suspicion well supported by the data in Table 7.10. The 40.7% of the population who indicate concern with fiscal/monetary policy in 1992 increases from 33.2% in 1988 and exceeds even the level of 1984, the previous high.

The problems that stimulated concern with fiscal and monetary policy in 1992, however, did not work to the advantage of the party that had traditionally domi-

TABLE 7.8

Class and the 1992 Election

	1952	1956	1960	1964	1968	1972	1976	1980	1984	1988	1992
Salience[a]	42.0	42.4	39.2	36.7	33.5	36.2	38.6	33.1	34.2	36.1	37.2
Percentage favoring Democrats[b]	33.7	35.6	30.6	31.6	27.9	30.3	32.2	26.2	28.9	30.0	31.5
Percentage favoring Republicans[b]	6.1	5.1	7.2	4.3	4.9	5.0	4.9	5.3	4.2	4.7	4.4
Mean net preference[c]	.588	.677	.516	.513	.466	.493	.511	.371	.527	.519	.542
Net vote advantage[d]	17.9	21.7	17.1	26.3	15.9	12.2	20.9	14.7	16.3	18.0	24.2

Notes: a. The percentage of all respondents who mention class as a basis for evaluating the parties and candidates.

b. The percentage of all respondents with a net Democratic or a net Republican preference on class on the open-ended like/dislike questions.

c. Population mean on the sum of pro-Democratic and anti-Republican minus the sum of pro-Republican and anti-Democratic open-ended comments on class.

d. Percentage of those favoring the Democrats on class and voting Democratic minus the percentage favoring the Republicans on class and voting Republican.

TABLE 7.9

Social Welfare and the 1992 Election

	1952	1956	1960	1964	1968	1972	1976	1980	1984	1988	1992
Salience[a]	15.6	8.8	14.2	32.7	21.6	30.5	25.8	26.0	43.5	40.3	45.6
Percentage favoring Democrats[b]	12.0	5.7	8.3	23.7	12.8	14.0	17.7	15.8	31.4	28.0	35.3
Percentage favoring Republicans[b]	3.3	2.7	5.4	8.0	7.7	14.3	6.9	9.7	10.8	10.5	8.5
Mean net preference[c]	.117	.045	.036	.284	.124	.014	.177	.115	.511	.484	.601
Net vote advantage[d]	3.4	1.1	.8	16.0	1.6	-4.0	8.0	4.2	11.0	9.7	22.5

Notes: a. The percentage of all respondents who mention social welfare as a basis for evaluating the parties and candidates.

b. The percentage of all respondents with a net Democratic or a net Republican preference on social welfare on the open-ended like/dislike questions.

c. Population mean on the sum of pro-Democratic and anti-Republican minus the sum of pro-Republican and anti-Democratic open-ended comments on social welfare.

d. Percentage of those favoring the Democrats on social welfare and voting Democratic minus the percentage favoring the Republicans on social welfare and voting Republican.

TABLE 7.10
Fiscal/Monetary Policy and the 1992 Election

	1952	1956	1960	1964	1968	1972	1976	1980	1984	1988	1992
Salience[a]	34.0	14.500	20.9	17.1	20.6	24.0	31.0	26.4	40.6	33.2	40.7
Pro-Democratic Party[b]	3.3	2.800	1.6	2.2	1.1	3.0	4.2	1.3	2.5	2.7	2.1
Anti-Democratic Party[b]	21.3	4.300	10.0	6.9	11.4	4.7	11.9	7.7	8.6	12.7	13.5
Pro-Republican Party[b]	16.1	4.4	8.0	5.2	8.7	5.2	9.8	8.4	8.4	11.5	8.4
Anti-Republican Party[b]	2.9	4.9	4.6	1.3	2.9	6.5	5.0	2.7	6.8	9.7	9.0
Pro-Democratic Candidate[b]	.4	.5	1.0	2.1	.1	2.6	6.7	.9	6.4	3.8	6.9
Anti-Democratic Candidate[b]	.9	.3	1.4	2.2	2.2	2.8	4.9	5.0	11.4	6.6	9.3
Pro-Republican Candidate[b]	2.8	1.1	1.1	2.5	3.2	3.3	4.4	8.7	12.0	4.1	4.2
Anti-Republican Candidate[b]	.4	.7	.5	.5	.2	4.4	1.8	3.1	11.5	3.9	13.5
Evaluation of Democrats[c]	-.219	-.015	-.098	-.052	-.130	-.022	-.069	-.113	-.125	-.158	-.182
Evaluation of Republicans[c]	.187	.001	.040	.062	.091	-.023	.087	.126	.035	.040	-.104
Percentage favoring Democrats[d]	4.2	6.9	5.8	4.7	2.8	11.4	11.3	5.5	16.0	11.3	18.7
Percentage favoring Republicans[d]	28.6	7.1	14.1	11.6	17.0	11.3	17.8	19.8	22.4	19.5	18.8
Mean net preference[e]	-.406	-.015	-.138	-.115	-.221	.001	-.156	-.239	-.160	-.199	-.078
Net vote advantage[f]	-22.0	-2.1	-8.8	-3.4	-12.2	-6.2	-7.7	-11.8	-8.9	-7.7	1.9

Notes: a. The percentage of all respondents who mention fiscal and monetary policy as a basis for evaluating the parties and candidates.

b. The percentage of all respondents mentioning fiscal/monetary concerns as a reason for liking/disliking each party/candidate.

c. The mean evaluation of the Democratic party/candidate and Republican party/candidate, computed by summing the number of positive and negative comments.

d. The percentage of all respondents with a net Democratic and a net Republican preference on fiscal and monetary policy.

e. Population mean on the sum of pro-Democratic and anti-Republican minus the sum of pro-Republican and anti-Democratic open-ended comments on fiscal and monetary policy.

f. Percentage of those favoring the Democrats on fiscal and monetary policy and voting Democratic minus the percentage favoring the Republicans on fiscal and monetary policy and voting Republican.

nated such concerns. Mean evaluation of the Republican on fiscal/monetary becomes negative, falling from .040 in 1988 to −.104: only in 1972 had this score previously been negative, at a much smaller −.023. Negative comments about the Republicans are primarily made about Bush personally, not about the party: the slight deterioration in the party's performance between 1988 and 1992 is primarily due to a decrease in the number of those with favorable comments about the party, but the percentage mentioning fiscal/monetary policy as a reason for disliking Bush (13.5%) is a considerable increase from the 3.9% he received in 1988. The two most recent Republican incumbents (Bush in 1992 and Reagan's 11.5% in 1984) produce the only instances in which more than 4.4% of the population mentions such issues as a reason for disliking the Republican candidate.

Decay in evaluation of the Republicans on fiscal/monetary policy is not accompanied by any improvement in perceptions of the Democrats: overall evaluation of the Democrats on fiscal and monetary concerns falls to −.182, continuing a pattern of deterioration that goes back to 1972; only in 1952 was evaluation of the Democrats on fiscal/monetary policy worse than in 1992. Comparisons of the parties alone continue to show the long-standing Republican advantage, producing a mean of −.144 that is only slightly weaker than the −.151 of 1988 and is quite a bit larger than the −.095 of 1984. But comparisons of Bush and Clinton themselves produce a Democratic advantage of .066, the largest in the series and the only positive score other than 1972.

The overall result of such changes is that the Republicans retain their net preference advantage in 1992, but the margin by which they are preferred is relatively small. Only in 1956 and 1972, both of them years in which other Republican incumbents sought re-election, was the mean preference on fiscal and monetary policy less than the −.078 for 1992. The 18.8% who prefer the Republicans on fiscal/monetary policy is a slight decline from the 1988 figure and is essentially the same as the 18.7% preferring the Democrats; the latter figure had been 11.3% four years earlier.

In the two previous years in which the Democrats had done relatively well in net partisan preferences on fiscal/monetary policy, the issue's contribution to their electoral fortunes had been reduced by the fact that a Democratic preference on this issue had a particularly weak impact on vote choice. The result was a bivariate net vote advantage of −2.1% in 1956 and of −6.2% in 1972, the latter fairly remarkable in that more people favored the Democrats on fiscal and monetary issues in 1972 than favored the Republicans. In 1992, however, those Democratic on fiscal/monetary policies are *more* likely to vote Democratic than those with Republican preferences are to vote Republican; the result is that the modest Republican advantage in net partisan preferences is transformed into the first and only Democratic net vote advantage (albeit a small one of 1.6%) in the series.

Prosperity was of course the dimension of economics whose partisan impact changed most dramatically between 1952 and 1988. Before 1980, the population consistently reported that the Democrats could better produce good times, a perception that had its roots in the Depression and New Deal. The shift on public perceptions on prosperity around 1980 had immense partisan consequences: Democratic economic performance failure in the later Carter years produced powerful anti-Democratic perceptions on prosperity that were a primary source of Reagan's initial electoral success, and Reagan's success in managing the economy in his first term generated a perception that the Republicans *could* produce prosperity that underlay Republican electoral success for the rest of the 1980s. Modest weakening of both elements of these balanced, mutually reinforcing perceptions occurred in Bush's defeat of Dukakis, but prosperity remained a Republican issue area in 1988, with increasing evidence that it was being used to distinguish parties as well as candidates. Perceptions of the parties' relative abilities to produce prosperity replaced perception of the Democrats as ideologically extreme as the primary source of continuing Republican domination after 1980.

By 1992, Republican claims to be better able to manage the economy and to produce good times were under obvious pressure. The related problems of recession and deficit provided two problems for George Bush's re-election campaign: first, they provided the kind of short-term bad news that could hurt any incumbent administration presiding over an economic slow-down; second, and much more importantly, they threatened to undermine what had been the primary basis of Republican electoral strength for a decade. In the absence of perceptions of the Democrats as ideologically extreme that had underlay Republican electoral success between 1968 and 1980, Republicans were highly vulnerable to changed perceptions of their ability to produce prosperity. Walter Mondale may have been unable to argue convincingly that the apparent prosperity of 1984 was transitory or superficial; in 1992, widespread perception that the economy was in trouble made the Democratic argument more effectively, generating doubt about the effectiveness of Republican economic policies and increasingly negative retrospective evaluations of Ronald Reagan himself (*Los Angeles Times*, 4 November 1991). What was problematic was whether the Democrats, and Bill Clinton in particular, could transform economic discontent into Democratic votes.

The data in Table 7.11 give a clear sign of how dramatic the shift in public perceptions of the parties' ability to produce prosperity was in 1992. The degree to which prosperity is mentioned as a basis for liking/disliking the parties or candidates rises from 20.0% in 1988 to 29.4%, a level almost identical to that reached in the 1980 and 1984 elections in which prosperity clearly lay at the center of the electoral agenda. These perceptions are overwhelmingly perceptions of candidates rather than of parties: prosperity is a more frequently used basis of evaluating candidates than ever before, at 25.0% of the sample, while the 8.6% who mention prosperity as a basis for evaluation of the parties is the lowest figure for the entire eleven-election period. The contrast with 1952, the high point in overall concern with prosperity, is extreme: a far larger 44.4% of the population mentioned prosperity in 1952, but only 3.5% used it in connection with the *candidates*. The tendency for concern with prosperity to be associated with candidates rather than party in 1992 is only a slightly extended version of the pattern of 1980 and 1984, but it is a reversal of the 1984–1988 trend toward institutionalization of Republican advantages in the area.

The more distinctive shift in the role of prosperity in 1992 of course has to do with preferences rather than salience. After three consecutive contests in which the Republicans had an advantage, a large one in 1980 and 1984, 1992 sees a return to the perception that the Democrats can best produce good times: 26.0% of the sample had a net Democratic preference on prosperity, compared to only 2.9% who favored the Republicans. The figure favoring the Democrats exceeds the level reached in any year since 1952, while the number favoring the Republicans was lower only in the extremely Democratic year of 1964.

As one might expect, it is not the challenging party whose image on prosperity is transformed between 1988 and 1992. The Democrats enjoy only a modest improvement in their perceived ability to produce good times, their net score increasing from .053 in both 1984 and 1988 to .099. The improvement is entirely focused on Clinton rather than on his party: he improves slightly the percentage making both positive (4.0% to 6.8%) and negative (1.3% to .6%) comments compared to the levels achieved by Dukakis four years earlier. The number of respondents mentioning the Democratic *Party* in connection with prosperity in either a positive or a negative manner both actually decrease slightly.

The change in net preferences on prosperity between 1988 and 1992 is mostly due to changed attitudes towards the Republicans. The number of respondents who thought that the Republican *Party* could produce prosperity falls quite dramatically, from 8.9% in 1988 to only 1.0% four years later, wiping out the incipient signs of an institutionalized Republican advantage on the issue. And while the percentage blaming the party for inadequate performance on prosperity increases only slightly, from 1.8% to 4.4%, the number blaming George Bush in particular increases from 1.2% to 19.2%. The latter figure is unprecedentedly large, exceeding the 16.2% who made anti-Carter comments on prosperity in 1980! The result is an extraordinarily large negative net evaluation of the Republicans on prosperity of −.265. Even in 1952, the year in which the Republicans were previously weakest, their score was only −.209; in 1984 and 1988 it had been .198 and .110 respectively; the negative shift in net evaluation is greater than the 1976–1980 negative shift (.166 to −.182) of the Democrats.

These various components combine to produce a mean net preference score on prosperity of .364, a figure whose absolute magnitude was exceeded only in 1952. Mean preference falls short of the levels reached by class (.542) or social welfare (.598), but it returns to its pre-1980 position as an area of considerable Democratic strength. Even Republican identifiers concerned with prosperity in 1992 have a net Democratic preference on it, albeit a far smaller one (.173) than did Democratic identifiers (.535): the shift toward the Democrats and against the Republicans occurs more or less equally among the two partisan groupings.

Prosperity remains a powerful source of vote choice in 1992. Its net vote advantage for the Democrats is 17.8%, the largest of any of the eleven elections. This

TABLE 7.11
Prosperity and the 1992 Election

	1952	1956	1960	1964	1968	1972	1976	1980	1984	1988	1992
Salience[a]	44.4	28.4	23.3	12.6	17.4	18.2	25.3	29.7	30.0	20.0	29.4
Pro-Democratic Party[b]	26.6	13.3	13.1	8.3	8.3	4.8	11.0	3.7	3.9	4.3	3.4
Anti-Democratic Party[b]	5.9	1.6	1.7	.1	2.6	.8	1.7	3.7	1.1	1.8	1.0
Pro-Democratic Candidate[b]	1.8	1.6	2.5	2.2	1.1	2.9	5.6	2.2	3.8	4.0	6.8
Anti-Democratic Candidate[b]	.3	.3	.4	.1	.3	.4	.6	16.2	1.9	1.3	.6
Pro-Republican Party[b]	5.9	7.8	6.7	1.0	2.4	2.0	3.1	3.8	4.2	8.9	1.0
Anti-Republican Party[b]	21.8	7.6	5.5	3.6	5.9	5.3	5.2	1.2	1.9	1.8	4.4
Pro-Republican Candidate[b]	1.1	4.0	.5	.1	.8	3.8	3.5	7.0	17.3	2.8	1.4
Anti-Republican Candidate[b]	.7	2.1	.1	.4	.6	5.1	4.8	1.2	4.4	1.2	19.2
Mentions parties[c]	43.2	24.4	22.2	11.0	15.6	10.4	17.2	10.9	9.7	14.4	8.6
Mentions candidates[c]	3.5	7.6	3.3	2.5	2.8	11.2	12.8	23.2	24.8	8.6	25.0
Percentage favoring Democrats[d]	34.4	16.8	15.4	11.5	12.5	12.0	18.0	6.0	9.7	8.4	26.0
Percentage favoring Republicans[d]	8.0	10.3	7.1	1.0	4.6	5.5	6.3	22.9	19.6	11.0	2.9
Mean net preference[e]	.489	.138	.138	.141	.115	.128	.214	-.278	-.146	-.057	.364
Democrats' net preference[f]	.887	.391	.328	.219	.234	.245	.443	-.103	.115	.127	.535
Republicans' net preference[f]	-.062	-.172	-.128	.017	-.078	-.023	-.073	-.559	-.467	-.263	.173
Net vote advantage[g]	16.9	2.8	4.8	10.0	3.6	1.9	9.9	-10.7	-10.4	-1.8	17.8

continues

TABLE 7.11

Prosperity and the 1992 Election (*Continued*)

Notes:
a. The percentage of all respondents who mention prosperity as a basis for evaluating the parties and candidates.
b. The percentage of respondents mentioning prosperity as a reason for liking/disliking each party/candidate.
c. The percentage of all respondents who mention prosperity as a basis for evaluating the parties or candidates on the open-ended like/dislike questions.
d. The percentage of all respondents with a net Democratic or a net Republican preference on prosperity on the open-ended like/dislike questions.
e. Population mean on the sum of pro-Democratic and anti-Republican minus the sum of pro-Republican and anti-Democratic open-ended comments on prosperity.
f. Mean net preference on prosperity for Democratic and Republican identifiers separately.
g. Percentage of those favoring the Democrats on prosperity and voting Democratic minus the percentage favoring the Republicans on prosperity and voting Republican.

figure remains smaller than the bivariate advantage provided by class and social welfare, but the contrast with the three preceding contests is considerable. Such concerns in 1980 had generated a net vote advantage of −10.7%; in 1984 it was −10.4%. Class, social welfare, and even fiscal/monetary policy also produce pro-Democratic shifts in net bivariate vote advantage between 1980 or 1984 and 1992: but the magnitude of the shift, the change from sizable pro-Republican to sizable pro-Democratic impact, and the reversal of what had seemed to be an emerging area of Republican strength all point to the particular importance in 1992 of prosperity.

A MULTIVARIATE ANALYSIS OF ECONOMIC PREFERENCES AND VOTE CHOICE IN 1992

The bivariate net vote advantage data are of course suspect given their failure to deal with the various attitudinal sources of vote choice simultaneously. But several multivariate analyses that combine all four dimensions of economics, non-economic issues, party identification, and candidate orientation all confirm the impact of the shifts in perceptions on prosperity between 1988 and 1992.

Table 7.12 reports three probit analyses, differing in the way in which the independent variables are handled (population means or trichotomized to show simple preference) and how non-economic issues are dealt with (separately or combined

TABLE 7.12
Probit Coefficients: 1992

	Non-Economic Issues Separately[a]	Non-Economic Issues Combined[a]	Issues Trichotomized[b]
Fiscal/monetary	.27591	.15184	.43004
Class	.24500	.24415	.55194
Social welfare	.17258	.09576	.33820
Prosperity	.22420	.16181	.31120
Race	−.06512[c]		
New domestic	.33886		
Foreign policy	.20588		
Other issues	.25011		
Non-economic issues		.18780	.52273
Candidate orientation	.33888	.23150	.68454
Party identification	.35003	.30793	.73271
Constant	.62660	.28299	−.41863

Notes: Entries are coefficients from a probit analysis of vote choice with voting Democratic the dependent variable.

    a. For the first two columns, raw scores are used for all independent variables.

    b. For the third column, values on independent variables are trichotomized into Democratic, Republican, or neutral.

    c. The coefficient does not meet the one-tailed .05 level of statistical significance.

into a single score). What is striking in Table 7.12 is that all three equations confirm the impact changes in preferences on prosperity have on vote choice. All four dimensions of economics have sizable statistically significant impact on vote choice in all three versions of the probit equation: there is nothing like the weak impact that social welfare showed in the earliest years of this period or that fiscal/monetary had showed from time to time. Prosperity is actually the weakest of the four in the trichotomized version of the probit reported in Chapter Six, but its impact is nonetheless sizable. In the two probit equations that use mean scores it is second or third in magnitude of its probit coefficients.

The impact that the change in prosperity has on the election outcome can best be shown by using the probit coefficients to estimate the probability of voting Democratic. Table 7.13 shows a variety of not unreasonable combinations of scores on the assorted independent variables in order to demonstrate the effects of changing preferences on prosperity from Republican to Democratic. Example (a) shows the estimated probability of voting Democratic for a Democratic identifier who prefers his own party on social welfare but prefers the Republicans on both fiscal/monetary policy and on non-economic issues as a whole: a Republican preference on prosperity combines with the two Republican preferences to give this respondent only a 27.1% probability of voting Democratic; simply changing the preference on prosperity to Democratic increases the probability to 50.4%. Example (b) shows a Democratic identifier with Democratic preferences on all the dimensions of economics *except* prosperity combined with Republican preferences on non-economic issues and candidate-orientation; changing the preference on prosperity

TABLE 7.13

Predicted Probability of Voting Democratic: Effects of Changing Scores on Prosperity

Party[a]	Fiscal/ Monetary[a]	Class[a]	Social Welfare[a]	Non-Economic Issues[a]	Candidate Orientation[a]	Prosperity Republican[b]	Prosperity Democrat[b]
Dem	Rep	—	Dem	Rep	—	27.1	50.4
Dem	Dem	Dem	Dem	Rep	Rep	54.8	77.0
Ind	Rep	Dem	Dem	Dem	Rep	33.4	57.5
Ind	—	Dem	Dem	Rep	—	35.9	60.3
Ind	Rep	Dem	—	—	—	27.1	50.4
Rep	Rep	—	—	Dem	Dem	24.1	47.6
Rep	—	—	Dem	Dem	—	27.4	50.8

Notes: Probabilities are based on the probit results reported in Table 7.12.

    a. Entries indicate scores on independent variables: (Dem) indicates Democratic, (Rep) indicates Republican, (Ind) indicates Independent, and (—) indicates neutral.

    b. Entries indicate the probability of voting Democratic for a respondent who combines these attitudes with a preference for the Republicans on prosperity and a preference for the Democrats on prosperity. The difference in the entries indicates the impact of changing a Republican preference to a Democratic preference.

TABLE 7.14
Total Contribution to Democratic Vote Totals: 1976–1992

	1976	1980	1984	1988	1992
Fiscal/monetary	−2.4	−1.5	−0.9	−1.1	−0.8
Class	4.3	0.7	3.5	3.3	5.0
Social	1.5	0.3	2.4	2.2	3.9
Prosperity	3.3	−2.6	−1.7	−0.3	2.4
Race	0.0	0.7	−0.0	0.0	0.0
New domestic	1.9	0.0	0.6	−1.4	0.8
Foreign	−0.8	−2.9	0.6	−1.4	−1.1
Other	0.4	−0.8	−0.0	−0.0	1.6
Candidate orientation	−7.2	3.4	−4.7	−0.7	−1.1
Party identification	5.0	4.2	2.1	2.2	3.5

Note: Entries are net contribution to the Democratic percentage of the popular vote. They are estimated by comparing predicted percentage Democratic for a respondent with mean values on all ten independent variables with the percentage Democratic predicted if a score of zero is substituted on the target variable. They can be interpreted as the change in Democratic vote percentage due to the deviation of the actual mean from zero.

from Republican to Democratic increases the probability of a loyal vote from a bare 54.8% to a comfortable 77.0%.

Other examples demonstrate comparable impact of changing scores on prosperity for Independents and Republicans as well. An independent with Democratic preferences on class, social welfare, and non-economic issues but Republicans preferences on fiscal/monetary and on candidate orientation (example c) sees an increase in probability of voting Democratic from 33.4% to 57.5% when his or her score on prosperity shifts from Republican to Democratic. Republicans who prefer their own party on fiscal/monetary but the opposition on non-economic issues and on candidate orientation (example f) are only 24.1% likely to vote Democratic if they also prefer their own party on prosperity; a shift on prosperity alone increases the probability to 47.6%. The claim here is of course not that prosperity is the sole issue linked to vote choice; but prosperity is the variable on which popular preferences shifted most dramatically between 1988 and 1992, and a Democratic preference on prosperity does seem sufficient to push many voters otherwise predisposed to vote Republican into the Democratic column.

Table 7.14, finally, estimates the net contribution of the full range of attitudinal factors to Clinton's triumph in 1992, replicating Table 6.6. The entries use mean net preference scores and the impact of independent variables on vote choice to determine consequences of each type of issue (plus candidate orientation and party identification) on the overall probability of voting Democratic.

The Table shows some continuity with the pattern of previous elections and some change. As with any close election, there is a multitude of factors that could conceivably be seen as having produced the winner's margin or victory: eight of the ten independent variables show an increased contribution to the Democrats since 1988, so there are surely multiple factors that can claim at least partial credit for the revival in Democratic fortunes. But prosperity stands out in the magnitude of its pro-Democratic shift in a way that confirms a reading of it as central to the turning around of the 1988 result.

One of the exceptions to the pattern of increased Democratic contribution is race, which continues to show minimal overall electoral impact: for the fourth time in five elections, race provides no net contribution to either party; its value of +0.0 is unchanged from 1988. To the extent that racial issues play a role in 1992, they continue to work indirectly through economics or social issues rather than directly. The second exception is candidate orientation, where a modest fall from −0.7% to −1.1% indicates a slightly greater contribution to Republican vote totals.[11]

For two independent variables, fiscal/monetary and foreign policy, the change between 1988 and 1992 takes the form of a lessened negative impact on the Democratic vote. For fiscal/monetary policy there is a slight fall-off in net contribution from −1.1% to −0.8%, continuing a pattern of slightly decreasing net Republican contribution that began in 1976. If Bush could merely have maintained Reagan's more favorable 1980 net preference advantage on fiscal/monetary, he could have expected an additional 1.2% of the vote over what he in fact received. Foreign policy sees a similarly reduced net Republican contribution from −1.4% to −1.1%.

For three independent variables—party identification and the two economic dimensions of class and social welfare—an already considerable contribution to the Democrats in 1988 increases further in 1992. The Democratic gains in party identification in 1992 generate an increase from 2.2% to 3.5% in the variable's net contribution to the Democratic vote total, a level somewhat above that of 1984 or 1988 although still well short of most previous elections. The increase in Democratic votes from social welfare reaches the unprecedented level of 3.9%, while the net contribution for class (5.6%) had previously been exceeded only in 1952.

The three remaining independent variables actually show a change in sign of net contribution in 1992. Two of them present some difficulty of interpretation given their heterogeneity: "other" issues are by definition an unspecified grab-bag combining vague, unelaborated, and therefore uncodable likes/dislikes with either idiosyncratic year-specific concerns or with more lasting issues (like farm policy or the space program) not mentioned frequently enough to justify establishing a separate category of their own. The salience of such residual issue mentions increases from 25.6% in 1988 to 32.5% in 1992, with the surge concentrated in the two categories used to code unelaborated comments about "general domestic ideas" and "general economic ideas." The first of these categories is entirely impenetrable; the second, although clearly economic in nature, cannot be assigned to one of the four dimensions because of respondents' lack of specificity.[12] A surge in the frequency of pro-Democratic comments of this kind in 1992 causes the category to take on a clearly more Democratic character; net evaluation of the Democrats rises from

.039 to .073 at the same time that net evaluation of the Republicans falls from .044 to −.124. And this, in turn, is responsible for the transformation of the −0.0% net contribution in 1988 to one of +1.6% in 1992.

New domestic issues are of course a combination of Scammon and Wattenberg's (1971) Social Issue and Miller and Levitin's (1976) New Politics, and year to year variation in its net contribution are more likely to be due to variation in the relative salience of its rather different components. Such variation seems to be responsible for the 1988 to 1992 shift from a net Republican contribution of −1.4% to a net Democratic contribution of 0.8%. Yet it is the modest Democratic advantage that is typical of most recent elections: the Republican net contribution in 1988 was the first since 1968, and it can be rather unambiguously attributed to a surge in the salience and in the Republican character of one particular kind of Social Issue comment. Salience of new domestic issues increased from 14.9% in 1984 to 36.4% in 1988; and although net evaluation of the Republicans became only slightly more favorable in 1988 (−.015 to −.001), net evaluation of the Democrats became considerably more negative (−.032 to −.242). The surge in anti-Democratic Social Issue comments was concentrated in one code, 972, used for comments about a soft line on law and order, with special reference to criminals, organized crime, and street crime. Whereas 10.6% of the population had mentioned any social issue reason for liking or disliking the candidates in 1984; only 0.2% of them had used code 972. But in 1988, code 972 alone was used by 8.9% as a reason for disliking Michael Dukakis. The −.242 net evaluation the Democrats received on the Social Issue in 1988 is far more negative than they had received in any other year. In 1992, salience falls off somewhat, code 972 all but disappears (0.3%), evaluation of the Democrats returns to a level (−.042) more typical of pre-1988 contests, and net contribution returns to a pattern common in pre-1988 contests as well.[13]

The remaining issue is prosperity, and the shift over four years in its net partisan impact is striking. Like the three other dimensions of economics, prosperity in 1992 makes a more Democratic net contribution than it had four years previously. When fiscal/monetary policy became less Republican and class and social welfare both became more Democratic, however, prosperity shifts from providing a small net Republican contribution (−0.3%) to a sizable Democratic contribution (2.4%). The increase over four years is the largest in the Table, exceeding those for residual issues (1.6%) and new domestic issues (2.2%) as well. Subtracting out the 2.4% net Democratic contribution is sufficient to transform Clinton's comfortable 43.2% to 37.7% lead into an extremely close 40.8% to 40.1% advantage. And the impact of prosperity is probably understated by simply comparing 1988 and 1992. If one compares the impact of Clinton's .364 mean score on prosperity in 1992 with the effects of Reagan's −.278 advantage in 1980, one can see a Democratic gain on prosperity over the twelve years of +3.9%. The large single year net contribution to percentage Democratic and the clarity of its shifts in its net contribution in both 1980 and 1992 justify placing prosperity at the very heart of explanations of variation in recent American presidential elections.

PARTY SYSTEM VIc: THE PROSPECTS
FOR A NEW ERA OF DEMOCRATIC DOMINANCE?

Ronald Reagan was not elected because of a turn of the American public to the right; he had no ideological mandate. Reagan won because Jimmy Carter was perceived as a failed president. In 1982, with the economy weak, polls on Reagan's job performance showed him low in popularity and sinking further; he appeared likely to be fifth consecutive unsuccessful president, the third in a row to be defeated in a race for re-election. What saved Reagan was his willingness to act as a president in a Schumpeterian or retrospectively-voting world *should* act: he pursued policies that he believed would ultimately succeed, and when they did succeed sufficiently in advance of the 1984 election, he was able to win one of the greatest landslides in American electoral history. The contrast with his failed predecessor and his ability to argue that the difficulties of his first two years were necessary to achieve the success of his last two years make the retrospective logic even stronger. Reagan had clearly understood the power of retrospective evaluations in 1980 when he asked viewers, late in his televised debate with Carter, whether they were better or worse off than they had been four years earlier; he seems to have understood the power of retrospective evaluations once in office as well.

To a large extent, Bill Clinton entered office as Reagan did: his victory over an incumbent was due more to the incumbent's failures than to anything that he as challenger had done.[14] Clinton had of course avoided the various possible catastrophic mistakes that challenging candidates have made in the past: unlike McGovern, he had not let himself be portrayed as incompetent or as an ideological extremist; unlike Goldwater, he had managed to portray himself as an intelligent, sensitive, balanced individual. But he won essentially because George Bush lost the advantage on economic management and prosperity that had underlay Republican electoral success since 1980. That image had been central to Republican success primarily because Reagan's economic success was achieved at the cost of moving images of the party sufficiently to the right to destroy the ideological advantage the party had enjoyed since 1968.

The events of 1992 gave Clinton an opportunity: incumbents always have greater control of their own fate than challengers do. But both the general condition of incumbents in a dealigned political universe and the specific circumstances of 1992 provide limits to the use Clinton was likely to make of his opportunity. The limits imposed by the particular circumstances of 1992 flow directly from the analysis in this chapter and are fairly straightforward: Clinton's victory was largely due to Democratic re-capture of their traditional core issue area of prosperity at a time when they had escaped the taint of ideological extremity that was the legacy of the late 1960s; being able to maintain both of these conditions was Clinton's first and most fundamental goal.

Yet neither task was ever likely to be simple. Attacking George Bush's economic record was certainly easier than producing prosperity on one's own. The complex and conflicting pressures of creating job and income growth without stimulating inflation or of controlling budget deficits without cutting popular services or raising taxes confound economists as well as presidents. Bush's failure to benefit from the re-emergence of slow but steady expansion in the year before his re-election bid raises further questions about the magnitude and pace of growth necessary before an electorate begins to give an incumbent administration electoral credit. Clinton and his administration seemed by 1994 to suffer a similar inability to benefit from prosperity, as modest but steady growth and largely optimistic economic forecasts failed to impress an electorate who thought progress inadequate, thought that others (such as the Federal Reserve) might share credit with the administration, or thought that other issues on which the administration was doing less well were simply more important.

The early Clinton years also raised questions about the administration's ability to maintain the image of moderation that had been so important in 1992. One popular interpretation of the 1994 congressional election result was that Clinton had not in office been the "New Democrat" he had claimed to be as a candidate: he had failed to mold the Democratic Party into the centrist force for change he had promised, and the failure of his medical care proposals of 1993–1994 in particular had re-ignited popular perception that Democrats always favored large, expensive, bureaucratic government programs as the solutions to social ills.

Such problems take on special importance in the context of a dealigned political universe of the 1990s. Clinton's relationship with congressional Democrats were always a likely source of tension. Lacking both the strong party bonds (and the great personal standing with the electorate) necessary to link their fate to his, he lacked the ability to mold them to his new vision of the party and country; too few of them saw themselves as dependent on him for their own future success. The need to compromise with them risked dulling the clarity of his own issue agenda in an effort to reach out to a world more liberal than his own; and failure to use the newly unified federal government to effectively implement a legislative program would likely both undermine his claimed ability to end governmental deadlock and tarnish his image of effective leadership for change. Even had he been far more successful in achieving his policy ends, the dealignment-generated inability to translate immediate policy success into long-term partisan loyalties would limit Clinton's (or any incumbent's) ability to extend today's personal popularity into tomorrow's partisan domination.

NOTES

1. This is merely an arithmetic observation: it makes no assumption about how Perot voters would have behaved had their candidate not been on the ballot.

2. The same basic pattern holds for pure Independents. They give a plurality of their vote to the Democrats for the first time since 1964, by a margin of 33.0% to 16.4%. Four

years earlier, the pattern was more typical of the eleven-election period as a whole: pure Independents had supported Bush by 26.3% to 13.6%.

3. There is a certain irony here in that Chapter Five makes clear that neither Dukakis nor Mondale were perceived as particularly liberal.

4. Two of the three items used tap aspects of economics and social welfare (spending on social services and guaranteeing jobs), while one deals with foreign policy (defense spending); there are no perceived distance data available for any race, social, or New Politics concerns.

5. Even this score is smaller than any other Democratic nominee had achieved since Hubert Humphrey.

6. Margolis' (1977) complaint that continued use of identical items over time in an attempt to guarantee continuity over time does not hold in this case. We are discarding items from earlier years, not from later years: there is no chance that we are discarding the live, controversial issues that became relevant in 1992. The fact that *only* these three issues were asked in 1992 suggests that the NES authors considered them to still be relevant. Similarly, their introduction in 1980 indicates that they were felt to tap some salient issue dimensions then. As long as we retain the full set of issues for 1980–1988, there seems to be little risk in making comparisons of attitudes on an identical set of continually relevant issues over time.

7. For Republicans, the subset of 1984 and 1988 perception variables available in 1992 differed in no systematic way from the full set of items reported in Chapter Five. In 1980, the Republicans were seen as slightly more moderate on the subset of issues used in 1992 than on the full set of available items: mean placement of party was .066 instead of .098; mean placement of Reagan was .097 instead of .124; overall mean placement was .086 instead of .113. In 1984, in contrast, the more limited items produced a mean placement of the Republican party and candidate together of .185, quite similar to the .176 for the full set of variables; in 1988 both measures produced a net combined placement of .149. The data reported here are based on the more limited set of pre-1992 data, but the differences between them and those reported in Chapter Five are minimal.

8. Reagan had of course been seen as considerably more conservative than his party in 1984.

9. The same effect held in 1980: the original net score of –.065 was –.096 for the three continuously used items.

10. The sole exception is 1972, when mean score on fiscal and monetary policy was .001.

11. The possibility that candidate orientation is concealing some issue content is of course increased by its including general re-statements of positive or negative affect for candidates that respondents can not or will not articulate explicitly. The consistency with which candidate orientation favors the Republicans (nine of the eleven elections) may also merit investigation.

12. It is interesting to note that such vague references to economics probably means that estimates of the impact of our four economic dimensions underestimate of the impact that would exist if the more precise content of the unelaborated general comments could be determined.

13. The distinctive 1988 pattern on the Social Issue clearly suggests the success of the Bush campaign in using the Willy Horton episode to suggest Democratic softness on crime. It is of course interesting, given the simultaneous lack of increased importance of race in 1988, that the Horton episode was reported by citizens as a crime-linked rather than as a

racial concern. Those skeptical of the lack of racial effects here and in Chapter Four will find reason for further investigation here. It should be noted that the Republican shift on the Social Issues was confined to whites: their mean partisan preference increases from −.025 to −.306, while that for blacks moves from .028 to .041.

14. There are some important differences between the two victories as well: Reagan won by twice as great a margin and did obtain a majority of the popular vote. Reagan's victory was also far more dramatic because pre-election polls had forecast an extremely close election, and the margin of victory on election night was therefore something of a surprise.

8

Conclusion:
Realignment, Dealignment, and Electoral Change from Roosevelt to Clinton

Realignment attracted considerable attention in the late 1960s and early 1970s by providing a powerful dynamic theory of periodic, large-scale, far-reaching political change. Realignment predicted regular substantial change in mass voting behavior, party control of government, and the nature of policy outputs; it provided a rich framework for reinterpreting the whole of American electoral history. Realignment made sense of the widely perceived disruptive changes in the American party system occurring at the time: emergence of new cross-cutting issues like race, foreign policy, and social order; the decline in strength of mass party loyalties; ideological tensions and conflict within parties, culminating in insurgencies like Goldwater's or McGovern's or Wallace's.

Realignment theory made clear that the fifth party system, with its roots in the Depression and New Deal forty years before, was coming to an end, but it did not itself point to any one inevitable result of the process of change. The period around 1970 did not lack plausible scenarios. Phillips (1970) described a "black socio-economic revolution" that would drive the Democrats to the left and leave the Republicans with a centrist/conservative majority; Scammon and Wattenberg (1971) identified a Social Issue of perceived social disintegration and threatening cultural change on which their perceived permissiveness made the Democrats vulnerable and which would provide (given reduced concern with the traditionally Democratic issue of economics) the basis of a new era of Republican domination; Sundquist (1983) saw a continuation of the class-based New Deal system, with the Democrats' dominant position nationally undermined somewhat by extension of class cleavage into the previously monolithically Democratic south; Newfield and Greenfield (1972) write of an economically-based populist resurgence that a Democratic Party recommitted to its class base could make the cornerstone of a revitalized national majority; Miller and Levitin (1976) described a New Liberalism in which suspicion of the agents of social control and concern with self-expression would offer the Democrats the chance to construct a new majority not dependent on economics.

Subsequent elections offered hints that one or more of these scenarios might be on the verge of coming true, but the realignment package as a whole clearly never materialized. Nixon's 1972 victory could be attributed to his having added disgruntled Democrats who had voted for George Wallace to his own 1968 base, a classic example of a third party's acting as way-station for partisans in transit; but even in 1972, the Republicans made no substantial gains in sub-presidential elections or in party loyalty. Carter's 1976 victory, perhaps an accidental consequence of Watergate, nonetheless provided the basis for Democratic resurgence by defusing the divisive issue of race and reconciling the majority party's two regional wings; but the magnitude of Carter's 1980 defeat made clear that his administration was to be a one-shot monument to Watergate rather than a general return of his party's majority status. Reagan's 1980 landslide could be seen to mark the final triumph of the forces of which Goldwater was a premature expression, particularly because it was accompanied by Republican capture of the Senate and followed by Republican gains in party identification. But by 1986, such hopes seemed to be dashed: the rise of Republican party identification had stalled with the Democrats retaining their majority; Republican control of the Senate disappeared as soon as the class of 1980 came up for re-election; Democratic dominance of the House of Representatives continued beyond what incumbency advantage alone would suggest; and most scholars concluded that the Reagan victories had not been caused or accompanied by a substantial shift of American public opinion to the right of a kind that could lead to a new era of Republican dominance.

The apparent failure of realignment theory led in the mid-1970s to emergence of the very different theory of dealignment: dealignment argued that the incoherence which earlier scholars had seen as a temporary manifestation of an old and dying party system *was*, in fact, the new, stable, and enduring political order. The partisan glue that holds party systems together had been fundamentally weakened by an expanded mass media that generated unprecedented amounts of political information at a time when higher education levels produced an electorate sophisticated enough to interpret political events without need for trusted partisan intermediaries; both changes had enhanced impact with entry into the electorate of the first of the particularly well-educated, media-oriented, and numerous Baby Boomers in 1968.[1]

Institutional reforms exacerbated the process of partisan decay: presidential nominations were transformed from a system of relatively centralized decisions by party leadership to one in which individual candidates competed in primaries for the nomination of a party whose label they only loosely shared; the increase in independent sources of campaign funding allowed candidates to run as individuals rather than as part of a party team, giving individual local candidates the ability to distance themselves from their national party (Jacobson, 1991; Petrocik, 1991). Elections increasingly consisted of unrelated campaigns by ambitious individual politicians nominally sharing a party label who, even when successful, were unable to unite behind a common legislative program. The resulting elite-level incoherence further encouraged the decay of parties in the electorate, producing a fuzzy party image that discouraged strong partisan attachments, leading to further decline in party voting and to the increased split-ticket voting that produced considerable disconnectedness between presidential and congressional elections.

But although there emerged ample evidence of a weakening of mass partisan loyalties, of the impact of such loyalties on vote choice, and of an increased disconnectedness of presidential and sub-presidential voting, the pattern of presidential elections' outcomes failed to assume the volatility that dealignment theorists predicted. After the second mini-realignment in 1966–1970, the point at which all micro-level and many of the macro-level symptoms of dealignment are already apparent, there is a particularly stable pattern of outcomes, with standard deviations of Democratic percentage of the popular vote low enough to rival that of 1932–1948.[2] The Republicans dominate presidential elections after 1966 to a degree and with a consistency characteristic of the most stable of stable realignment-based party systems.

The combination of apparent realignment in presidential outcomes with clear dealignment of parties both as institutions and in the electorate is troubling. For strong party loyalties, unified control of government, and implementation of a clear issue agenda were seen by realignment theorists as part of an intricate interrelated package, components of which both caused and were caused by stable party-based patterns of voting. If the realignment-like consistency of presidential outcomes was not due to the decisive impact of long-term party loyalties, what else could have caused it? Changes at the micro-level in the strength and impact of party identification are indisputable signs that there has been substantial dealignment in the electorate, as is the subsequent increase in split-ticket voting and disconnectedness between branches of government; but why has the triumph of dealignment at both individual and institutional levels produced a stability of presidential election results characteristic of the most mature of party systems?

Realignment theory in fact does a fairly good job of explaining the deterioration of the New Deal party system in the years immediately following the end of World War II. The first mini-realignment is clearly a product of both types of realignment theory: the slow but constant change in social composition of the electorate produces the gradual unidirectional shift in balance of party forces characteristic of secular realignment; and new issues emerge that cut across the existing system's issue-party nexus, creating tensions that over time accumulate sufficient force to cause the dramatic and sudden changes of party loyalty and long-term voting behavior characteristic of critical realignment.

What is surprising about the emergence of such changes in the immediate postwar world is their timing. The first mini-realignment is clearly premature: the expected thirty- to forty-year life expectancy of a party system should have seen the New Deal political order survive at least another ten years beyond the 1946–1950 transition point shown in the discontinuity tests of Chapter Two. And yet speeding up of the processes of both secular and critical change makes a good deal of sense given the truly awesome transformations of American social and political life between the late 1930s and the early 1950s. World War II and the economic transformations that it stimulated produced more far reaching changes in the context in which presidential elections take place than any comparable fifteen years in modern American history.

Improved economic conditions and the erosion of their class-based partisan core make the Democrats vulnerable to a secular realignment toward the Republicans in the post-war years. Citizens' memories of the Depression and New Deal were of course still quite powerful in the late 1940s, especially when combined with a Democratic party loyalty that was itself a consequence of the cataclysmic economic dislocations of the previous decade. Images of the Democrats as the party of good times and as a party sympathetic to the plight of ordinary people survived well into the post-war world, carried into the ranks of the middle class by the new upwardly mobile. The weakening of class polarization in the post-war years actually allowed the Democrats to partially offset the shrinking size of their mass base by making gains among traditionally Republican upper-SES groups.

But the decline in the size of the social groups on which Roosevelt's majority depended is nonetheless a serious problem for post-war Democrats. The New Deal majority was based on the support of the large number of economically disadvantaged at a time of national economic crisis. Falling unemployment and rising real incomes would inevitably erode the size of the Democratic core as the crisis eased. Economic recovery had in fact begun by the end of the late 1930s, partially in response to the New Deal itself and partially in response to economic mobilization caused by the approach of World War II; and although the transition to a peacetime economy immediately after the war is initially difficult, the late 1940s and early 1950s are a period of further considerable improvement in the general standard of living. By the early 1950s, unemployment was a fifth of what it had been in 1933, while median real income had doubled: the Depression had been an extraordinary economic catastrophe, but recovery from the Depression had been extraordinary as well.

The more familiar critical realignment literature of course predicts increasing tension in the later years of a party system through the emergence of new issues, a phenomenon encouraged by an inevitable generational replacement that ensures that the electorate is increasingly composed of new voters who know the crisis and issues which formed the existing system only second-hand. And while it is certainly not inevitable that new issues cut against those underlying the existing party system, the probability that they will do so to some extent is high. The result is an accumulation over time of cross-pressured voters whose partisan allegiances, forged in the last realignment, come under increasing pressure and the falling out of groups within both majority and minority parties who were allies on the issues that formed the existing system but who are unable to agree on the issues of the new day.

The period after the war in fact sees the emergence of two sets of issues which, in different ways, cut against the dominant economic issue underlying the New Deal system. Foreign policy and defense had been major areas of public concern in the years leading up to World War II, and the United States' emergence from the war as leader of one of the world's two armed camps keeps them at the top of the post-war political agenda. What is new is a change in the partisan impact of such issues: foreign policy had provided no clearly partisan advantage in the immediate post-war world; but by 1951, following Communist victory in the Chinese civil war and American military intervention in Korea, it assumed a clearly Republican character. By the time that former general and war hero Dwight D. Eisenhower is running for president in 1952, the NES survey showed an extremely large Republican advantage on this issue, with a majority even of Democratic identifiers or of those favoring the Democrats on economics reporting that they think the Republicans can best handle foreign policy.

Race had of course been a classic example of an issue with potential to divide the Democrats ever since Roosevelt combined white southerners and blacks—groups with fundamentally opposing interests on racial issues—in his new majority coalition after 1932. As long as the political agenda centered on the economic concerns that dominated the 1930s, the Democrats were able to maintain party unity by ignoring what was a secondary issue of no immediate political significance: Roosevelt was well aware of his dependence on southern Democratic support in Congress, and he did little to antagonize those whose support he needed on the economic issues he cared most about.

But race moved inevitably closer to the top of the issue agenda in the post-war years. To some extent this is the result of an easing of the economic pressures that had forced unity on the Democrats in the 1930s; but two factors increased the absolute salience of race in the post-war years as well. First, the war itself greatly accelerated the social mobilization of blacks; second, propaganda wars against both the Nazis and the Soviet Union increased pressure to live up to America's self-professed commitment to human rights and democracy. The result was an increased pressure for desegregation and for political/legal equality for blacks that brought the Democratic majority under unavoidable intense strain. The crisis comes to a head with the party's 1948 adoption of a relatively liberal civil rights platform, generating the convention walkout by southern conservatives, the Dixiecrat presidential candidacy of Strom Thurmond, and the end of Democratic domination of the white south.[3]

The combined effect of these changes was the end of the Democrats' national majority in the first mini-realignment of 1946–1950. The degree of change in 1946–1950 is less than that of a classic realignment: the magnitude of the discontinuity coefficients in Chapter Two is smaller than that in 1894 or 1930, but the change is nonetheless clear.[4] Roosevelt had obtained a solid majority of the popular vote in each of his four campaigns. In the five elections after his death, the party received a majority only in 1964, when powerful short-term factors linked to the Kennedy assassination and Goldwater nomination worked in their favor; in two other elections the party won with less that a majority; and in 1952 and 1956, with powerful short-term factors working against them, they were decisively beaten.[5]

The second mini-realignment in 1966–1970 marks the further deterioration of the Democrats' competitive position. An accumulation of gradual changes in the class composition of the electorate continued to erode the size of the Democrats' class-based core through 1973, but the secular changes after 1966 are rather modest compared to the changes pointed to by classic realignment theory. The primary source of the second mini-realignment was the sharp leftward move in the popular image of the Democrats in the late 1960s caused by precisely the kind of ideological ferment that realignment theory predicts *should* emerge late in a party system. Goldwater's nomination was a sign of such ferment among Republicans; and Goldwater's candidacy helped produce the Johnson landslide, which in turn allowed the Democrats to implement the broad program of reform that created the party's activist and liberal image. Internal disagreement among Democrats came to a very visible head in the chaos of their 1968 nominating convention, which is itself a primary cause of the post-1968 delegate selection reforms that four years later produced a candidate who solidified the popular image of the party as ideologically extreme.

The Democratic lurch to the left produced a situation in which the party was ideologically out of touch even with centrist Democrats, creating the asymmetry in which core Democrats defected at far higher rate than core Republicans between 1968 and 1980. Centrist Democrats in 1972 actually found themselves closer in ideological issue space to the Republicans than to their own party, producing the ideologically-based incentive to defect that many pursued; centrist Republicans, on the other hand, felt quite close to their party, quite distant from the Democrats, and had neither an ideologically-based reason to defect nor a high defection rate. Perception of the Democrats as ideologically extreme extended to a broad range of issues: race was most important early in the period, but the perception extended to foreign policy and new domestic issues as well; later, when perceived extremity on new domestic issues lessened, the perception that they were out of the mainstream persisted for race, economics, and foreign policy.

Post-1968 elections settled into a stable pattern of Republican domination identical to what Campbell (1966a) and Burnham (1970) first identified as constituting a stable party system. The stability of election outcomes is indisputable, with standard deviations of the Democratic percentage of the popular vote as low as that of 1932–1948 and a clear transition from the highly competitive electoral world of 1948–1964 to one in which the Republicans are dominant. And yet, the new Republican era turns out not to be quite what realignment theory would predict. All of the factors that should underlie stability after a classic realignment were lacking: there was no clear Republican party identification majority, no Republican penetration of sub-presidential elections, no ability to establish a clear issue agenda which the Democrats opposed and on which the Republicans dominated.

The underlying cause of these changes is precisely the kind of change identified by dealignment theorists: a substantial weakening of the partisan glue that had previously provided the stability to stable party systems. To some extent the weakening in party identification is due to cross-cutting new issues that are entirely natural in the waning days of a dying party system. But such factors are exacerbated by more general societal trends that reach some critical point in the 1960s and which prevent the emergence of a new set of party loyalties that might replace the old: the rise in levels of education, increased availability of political information, maturation of the Baby Boomers, opening up of the nomination process, and rise of independent campaign organization/finance. In such a dealigned setting, new issues are not necessarily seen as having implications for party identification and the party loyalties that persist have reduced impact on vote choice. It would be a gross exaggeration to claim that party became irrelevant to electoral politics after 1966, but Wattenberg (1991; 1984) is certainly on to something when he writes of the *increasing* irrelevance of parties.

Why, then, the stability of election outcomes? How can clearly dealigned electoral behavior nonetheless produce a pattern of outcomes identical to that of a stable party system? The answer to this puzzle is in fact fairly simple. Republicans' dominance of the post-1966 world is due to two very different processes, one of which operates roughly from 1966 to 1982 and the other roughly from 1978 to 1990: they are both Republican in partisan effect and more or less the same in magnitude; and they are only accidentally linked to each other, in the person of Ronald Reagan, whose conservative activism destroyed the Republican ideological advantage while providing the image of his party as able to produce prosperity. Each of these processes lasted longer than the eight years that dealignment theorists might have anticipated, but each was far less deep and far less extensive than those produced in a classic realignment.

The Reagan administration implemented a series of conservative activist policies whose consequences were much the same as those of the Democratic liberal activism in the 1960s: it pushed images of the governing president and his party to the ideological extreme. By 1984, the Republican advantage in ideological issue space is destroyed: the Republicans are seen as having moved well to the right. The result is not a Democratic advantage in any real sense: it is not the case after 1980 that the Democrats are seen as moderates while the Republicans are seen as extremists; rather, the two parties are essentially balanced, with the average voter more or less equidistant between them and both of the partisan cores situated comfortably close to their own party and candidate. The Democratic gain lies in having removed the prime obstacle that had long prevented them from capitalizing on their continuing advantages in party loyalty.

But Democratic gains in ideological issue space after 1980 did not bring an improved level of electoral performance. The 1980 election had turned on powerful anti-Democratic retrospective economic evaluations. These issues did not merely have consequences for 1980: the magnitude of Carter's economic failure was sufficient to cause substantial changes in an image of the ability of the Democrats as the party of good times that had been established in the aftermath of the Depression, had been anchored by images of Hoover and Roosevelt, had been reinforced by continued differences between the parties on the role of the government in managing the economy and providing social welfare, and had lasted nearly fifty years. The image extended far beyond generalized references to prosperity, extending to perceptions of the kinds of people whose economic welfare the parties cared about. These images had most likely weakened somewhat by the beginning of the NES surveys 1952, but they remained on balance an area of Democratic strength on which the party could draw even in those times when other issues worked against them.

The magnitude of economic distress in the late Carter years substantially altered these long-standing party images. The Democrats' perceived ability to generate prosperity deteriorated sharply in 1980, to the point where prosperity became an area of net Republican strength. To this Democratic failure Reagan added Republican success: his economic policies, after a difficult initial period that produced the specter of yet another failed one-term president, were widely perceived by 1983 to be successful. Reagan's post-1980 accomplishment, off-setting the pushing of his party's image to the right that destroyed its long-standing advantage in ideological issue space, was to produce a perception of the Republicans as the party of good times—an image that transformed the one-sided anti-Democratic image of 1980 on such issues into the balanced, pro-Republican, anti-Democratic perceptions of 1984 and 1988. The Democrats maintained (or even increased) their advantage on social welfare and class after 1980, but their weakness on the considerably more potent issue of prosperity became an extremely important electoral liability.

This second phase of Republican electoral dominance was similar to the first in three ways. First, it produced more or less the same pattern of election outcomes: the discontinuity coefficients of Chapter Two show considerable stability of election outcome after 1966, with no sign of volatility on either side of 1980 that might suggest a break in the pattern of election results; standard deviation of Democratic share of the popular vote is extremely low for both 1968–1984 and 1976–1992.

Second, Republican electoral dominance continues to occur in a period of dealignment. The Republicans made some gains in numbers of partisans in 1984 and 1988, and the *strength* of partisanship in the electorate increased somewhat as well. But neither change is very large in magnitude: the strengthening restores little more than a third of the partisanship lost between the beginning of the dealignment era and the low point of 1976, and the Democrats retain a comfortable if reduced advantage in numbers of identifiers.[6] Republican capture of the Senate in 1980 proves temporary, and they never capture the House. The disconnectedness between party and vote choice that had existed since 1966 continues, as does the disconnectedness between presidential and sub-presidential voting; the Republicans maintain a stable pattern of electoral dominance despite their lack of a party identification majority.

And, third, the issue underlying the second period of Republican electoral dominance is temporary. Ideological extremity had provided the Republicans the basis of electoral dominance for four elections; retrospective economic evaluations does so for three more.[7] Had the economic crisis of 1979–1980 been able to generate a powerful Republican advantage on party identification while resurrecting the impact party had had on vote choice during the period of classic realignment theory, effects of the crisis might have continued to be felt long after the specifics of the later Carter years were forgotten. But in a dealigned political universe, the ability of parties to translate advantages on even powerful issues into party-linked loyalties capable of providing a long-term basis for electoral dominance is limited.

American presidential elections since 1966, then, form a history of short-lived presidential-level patterns in a generally dealigned political system. Both of the processes that drive these elections favor the Republicans. But because the deterioration of party linkages prevents either ideological extremity or retrospective economic evaluations from creating the kind of party-based dominance that might allow the Republicans to win presidential elections for a generation and to extend their gains to sub-presidential voting as well, the effects of each is limited. That there are two different processes at work with only short-term effects is perhaps obscured by the facts that both favor the Republicans, to very similar extents, and that the first flows directly into the second: Reagan initiates the era of Republican economic management at the same time that he destroys their advantage in ideological issue space.

But the Republicans' dependence on their being perceived as the party of good times was always likely to prove a somewhat fragile basis for electoral success. The economic issue of the 1980s is certainly weak when compared to the economic issues of the New Deal era: the Republicans lacked support in the related economic dimensions of social welfare and class, and dealignment prevented them from building an effective party identification majority from the economic disaster of their opposition.[8] The Republicans were therefore excessively dependent after 1980 on the ability to retain their image as the party of good times.

Incongruities between the business and electoral cycles would make it inevitable that some Republican at some time would have to run for (re-)election when the claim to be the party of good times seemed less compelling than it did in 1980 or 1984. In 1988, George Bush benefits from the same kinds of economic perceptions that helped Reagan in 1984, but they are considerably reduced in magnitude. By 1992, as the expansion of the Reagan/Bush years ends, taking with it the perception of the Republicans as the party of good times, economics becomes the major issue of the election, with class and social welfare playing an enhanced Democratic role and prosperity shifting from helping the Republicans to (strongly) helping the Democrats. The Democrats re-capture both the economic issues and the White House they had lost in 1980.

It is doubtful that the Republicans ever had a real chance to construct a classic, party-based era of domination after 1966. Perhaps if the Democrats had cooperated more, taking a more consistently left-wing posture rather than moving at least intermittently toward the center in the way Sundquist (1983) claims,[9] or if Vietnam and social order were issues that could be maintained longer, there would have been greater opportunity to built a new powerful link between issues and party that could have given the Republicans their party identification majority and their unified control of government. More likely, the changes identified by dealignment theorists made any such reconstitution of a classic stable party system impossible. By the mid-1960s, parties had moved excessively far from their position at the center of citizens' political world; one gets no sense of a tension between an existing party-issue nexus and new issues that needs to be resolved. Rather, the great national issues of the day have relatively modest consequences for citizens' party loyalties, and citizens' party loyalties had relatively modest consequences for their vote choice.

Chapter Two leaves no doubt that the post-1966 world constitutes a pattern of stable election outcomes of the kind seen central to realignment theory by Campbell (1966a) and Burnham (1970). The irony for dealignment theorists is that the volatility was not in outcomes, but in the processes driving the outcomes. Dealignment theorists would be troubled by survival of a single basis of electoral outcomes for thirty to forty years, given their accurate observation that the micro-level phenomena responsible for the stability of a traditional realignment are lacking. But what may seem to be a single period of Republican dominance was in fact two different and reasonably short patterns caused by two very different processes. Neither was sufficiently powerful to transform the party loyalties of the population or to re-create the central role party loyalties had played in an earlier age. Nor was there any necessary linkage between them: the Reagan administration undermined the first and solidified the second; but a failure of Reagan's economic program in the early 1980s might well have produced a world in which his party had lost its advantages in ideological issue space without winning any long-term advantage on retrospective economic evaluations. Instead, Reagan's economic policies were generally perceived to have been successful, and the period of Republican domination on the basis of ideological extremity flowed smoothly into the period of Republican domination based on economic management. The stable pattern of outcomes looks superficially like what realignment theorists might have expected; but a careful examination of the processes underlying stability produces a far more convincing case for the triumph of the more modest and somewhat necessarily *ad hoc* explanations of dealignment theory.

Dealignment theory *is*, to some extent, necessarily *ad hoc*. Realignment theory can make concrete predictions about the evolution of party systems over time: it can predict, for example, extended periods of party-based stability of electoral outcomes; and although it cannot predict the specific new issues that will emerge over the life of a party system, it can predict with a high degree of certainty that they will emerge and that they will fail to reinforce exactly the issues upon which the existing system rests. It can predict that these issues will produce increasing tension with party loyalties forged in the previous realignment and that, at some point thirty to forty years after the old realignment, the combination of new issues and new voters will produce tensions sufficient to cause the shifts in party identification and issues-party nexus that will underlie a new era of stable election outcomes.

Dealignment theory makes less ambitious claims: it predicts only change. In a dealigned world citizens lack the party identification anchor through which even major new issues produce stability of vote choice over time. Dealignment theory is no less precise than realignment theory on what new issues will emerge, but it is far less specific on what their effects will be and how long the effects might last. An analyst informed by dealignment theory could identify the issue at the source of Republican electoral strength in the 1980s, could observe its failure to establish the party-linked base for long-term Republican dominance, and could combine the insights of dealignment theory with some sense of economic cycles to predict that an advantage based on economic management could not last. But dealignment produces far less guidance than realignment theory about how long an individual issue will dominate the electoral agenda, how it will interact with emergent new issues, and how its period of domination will come to an end.

Dealignment theory makes good sense of Bill Clinton's election as president in terms of the Republicans' economic failure at a time when they held neither an advantage in ideological issue space nor a secure foundation in mass partisan loyalties. Whether Clinton's 1992 image of moderation could survive the strains of governing, i.e., whether policy activism would inevitably rekindle an image of a governing party as ideologically extreme (as it did for Johnson after 1964 and for Reagan after 1980) was of course one of the key questions that would determine the longevity of the 1992 outcomes; so was the ability of prosperity, buttressed for the Democrats by an accompanying advantage on social welfare and class, to prove a more reliable basis for long-term Democratic success as it was for the Republicans.[10]

Clinton's task was clearly not an easy one even before his party's 1994 debacle. Unified control of government in his first two years provided him fewer benefits than it had offered other Democratic presidents in the past: sharing a nominal party affiliation with the congressional majority no longer provides a basis for the legislative triumphs or clear legislative record it allowed Franklin Roosevelt or Lyndon Johnson. Even if the Democrats had held together well enough to allow implementation of a clear legislative program against Republican opposition, the advanced state of partisan disaggregation in the electorate made the likelihood of generating mass party loyalties that could drive elections for a generation to come would have been slim. Unambiguous *personal* success would undoubtedly have guaranteed Clinton's own re-election, but his party's deriving long-term gains from such personal success would be unlikely. And Republican capture of both houses of Congress in 1994 of course reduced Clinton's ability to establish a clear-cut party-based legislative record in any case.

A dealigned political universe does not necessarily doom Clinton in 1996 or his party in 2000; and the dramatic Republican off-year gains of 1994 certainly do not guarantee them success in future presidential elections. Mass preferences on issues and mass perception of the parties in the mid-1990s give neither party a clear-cut basis for extended electoral domination: and even if one party succeeds in resolving the current public opinion ambiguities and inconsistencies in a way that conveys clear partisan advantage, it is highly improbable that such success could be translated into the powerful multi-generational partisan loyalties that had supported the stable party systems of the past. Clever (or lucky) politicians of either party may well find a way to create stable electoral eras of twelve or sixteen years even in a dealigned political universe: the dramatic Democratic failures of 1966–1968 and 1979–1982 gave Clinton's Republican predecessors the ability to maintain their party's dominant position for longer than early dealignment theorists had thought likely. It may even be possible to concatenate two such eras, as Reagan did, to produce an extended period of one-party rule that looks superficially like a true realignment. But a truly realigned stable electoral era based on a party-issue nexus forged in the past crisis, extending to sub-presidential levels of government, and transmitted across political generations through the mechanism of salient and powerful party loyalties is highly unlikely.

The most probable best-case scenario for either party after 1996 would be the modest period of electoral domination appropriate for a dealigned age; the party systems of the early twenty-first century are likely to be at best brief and superficial. Volatility inherent in a dealigned political universe means that the longevity of any pattern of electoral outcomes will rest on the ability of party leaders to constantly re-invigorate the relatively short-term and unstable coalitions that initially put them in power. The ambiguities and inconsistencies of public opinion combine with the sheer demands of governing to make success in such an enterprise unlikely. As we stagger through the continuing post-New Deal dealigned political universe, volatility of electoral outcomes is likely, and volatility in the specific processes that drive electoral outcomes is all but certain.

NOTES

1. The new dealigned electoral universe was in large part a response to the particular changes in post-war American politics and society, but its roots could be seen in the party decomposition that Burnham (1970) saw originating in the beginning of the century and which had only temporarily been disrupted by the Depression and New Deal.

2. The first mini-realignment created a rough balance in strength of the parties, allowing each to win elections when favored by contest-specific short-term factors. Much of the *apparent* instability in election outcomes between 1948 and 1964 is due to the fact that each of the parties did control the White House for part of this period. The real volatility that existed was due largely to the highly anomalous 1964 contest rather than to any general pattern of variable outcomes.

3. Race is of course the primary example of shifts in the electoral coalitions of the two parties since the high point of the New Deal system.

4. This is in fact a very conservative conclusion based on the Democratic percentage of the total vote. All the other discontinuity coefficients—Democratic percentage of the two-party vote, Republican percentage of the total vote, and all of the four-election sequences—produce discontinuity coefficients as high in 1946–1950 as for 1930.

5. The lack of party identification data from before 1952 makes it impossible to determine if the post-war changes reduced the Democrats' advantage there as well. It is of course clear that the Democrats retained a substantial party identification advantage at a time when they were essentially even with the Republicans in electoral performance. The impact of religion is more superficial in the sense that it did not weaken the Democrats in the long run.

6. Both of these trends are reversed in 1992, with the overall strength of partisanship weakening again and the Democrats making party identification gains.

7. And this formulation generously counts Reagan's 1980 victory twice.

8. The Republicans do generally have an advantage on the fourth economic dimension: fiscal/monetary policy. But Republican in office seem to do less well with fiscal/monetary than they do in opposition: gains on fiscal/monetary no doubt come at the expense of aggravating existing weakness on class or social welfare, presumably limiting the ability of Republican administrations to follow up their fiscal/monetary hopes once in office.

9. Our own evidence, of course, suggests that the Democrats did retain their clearly left-wing image, despite the attempts at moderation Sundquist describes.

10. Furthermore, fiscal/monetary concerns were muted in 1992, as they often are when Republicans are running for re-election; they are likely to take on a more clear-cut anti-Democratic coloration in a Democratic administration.

Postscript 1996

Students of electoral behavior greet an approaching presidential contest with a combination of considerable excitement and lurking dread. For ordinary citizens and even for politicians, the worst thing that can flow from a presidential election is a victory by the wrong candidate. For those who write books like this one, the stakes are much higher: each election has the potential to devastate their intellectual universe, revealing mistakes and misunderstandings to all a few short months after the book's publication. Recognition that one is living in a dealigned political universe offers both consolation and threat to the exposed author: one can always claim that dealignment predicts change, and any change is therefore to some extent therefore expected and explainable; but one lives from year to year realizing that one's cleverly worked out understanding of the current electoral era could be shattered even before the personal satisfaction of having worked it out is fully enjoyed.

The 1996 presidential election, happily enough, pretty much reinforces the argument advanced in this book: the 1996 combination of the two parties' being ideologically balanced while one of them enjoyed a clear advantage in retrospective economic evaluations represents a continuity in the underlying process of electoral choice in the United States that has existed, for the most part, since 1980. The basic structure of the 1996 presidential election in fact looks almost identical to that of 1992. Bill Clinton won in 1996 because he managed to maintain (or recreate) his centrist location in ideological issue space, with a strong assist from Newt Gingrich and his congressional Republicans, at a time when retrospective economic evaluations continued to favor the Democrats.

The role of retrospective economic evaluations in 1996 is also to some extent a modest recapitulation of 1984, with Clinton in the role of Ronald Reagan, and George Bush in the role of Jimmy Carter. Clinton in 1992 (like Reagan in 1980) owed his initial election more to negative perceptions of his predecessor's ability to effectively manage the economy than to any widespread support for his own economic program. By 1996, Clinton (like Reagan in 1984) had created a positive evaluation of his own economic achievements that he could pair with memories of his predecessor's failures to make economics a balanced, two-sided, area of strength.

It did not, of course, always look as though Bill Clinton would be re-elected. Re-election itself and the specific forces that would ultimately produce it both seemed unlikely for much of his four years in office. Presidential actions in 1993–1994 seemed to reinforce Republican claims that Clinton was well to the left of mass opin-

183

ion and vulnerable to the comparative ideological extremity that had plagued his party in the 1970s and which he had fought so hard (and so successfully) to eliminate in his 1992 campaign. The disastrous (for the Democrats) 1994 congressional elections were interpreted by many as an ideological repudiation of a centrist candidate who had become a liberal president. And although the economy after 1992 continued its slow but steady pattern of growth, surveys consistently indicated that voters neither recognized economic conditions as favorable nor granted Clinton (or the Democratic party more generally) any electoral advantage from it.

The relationship between objective economic conditions and what the public thinks about economic conditions is of course highly inexact. I have not tried to suggest that specific levels of growth, unemployment, or inflation are either necessary or sufficient to produce the perception that times are good or that the incumbent administration deserves credit. The mass voter perception of good times is only loosely tied to actual economic conditions at any given time and is highly variable regarding which combination of factors is salient or what appropriate time lags might be. Clinton had come to office at a time when most statistics (and many economists) suggested that economic recovery had already begun, but recovery was neither soon enough nor strong enough to alter established perceptions of bad times for which voters were already blaming George Bush.

Bush's problems were aggravated by the widespread belief that bad times were due, to some extent, to the economic reforms initiated under Ronald Reagan that had once held out the promise of continued prosperity. The supply-side logic behind Reaganomics advocated cutting taxes substantially in order to generate rapid economic growth. Such growth would produce both higher levels of prosperity and, after some time lag, higher tax revenues as well; the economy would in effect grow itself out of the short-term deficits that the initial tax cuts would cause.

But by the middle years of the Bush administration, Reaganomics had led to unacceptably large deficits that seemed to demand either the cutting of popular social programs or the unpopular raising of taxes—at a time when the economy was already in recession. Objective economic difficulties, frustrated expectations, Bush's slow recognition of the public mood, and the fact that new party preferences on prosperity again fit congruently with long-standing Democratic advantages in other dimensions of economics like class and social welfare, provided considerable Democratic advantage in 1992. Initial signs of recovery in 1992 were too late and too modest to alter an established image of Republican economic failure, much to Bush's frustration. Whether these anti-Republican attitudes could be sustained over time, and whether Clinton could produce a perception of his own economic success to balance a continuing image of Republican failure, was a constant theme of Clinton's first term in office. It *was* the economy, stupid, in 1992; the question was whether it would continue to be the economy thereafter and, more importantly, whether the economy would continue to be an area of Democratic strength.

For much of his first term, Clinton must have viewed economic performance much as George Bush had by late 1992. Actual economic performance continued a pattern of slow but stable growth, but the public seemed reluctant to give the incumbent credit for achieving it. After quick abandonment of a proposal to stimulate the economy through increased government social welfare spending, Clinton devoted his attentions to an economic plan that raised taxes on wealthier

Americans as a means of cutting the budget deficit. The goal of the plan was to provide a basis for continued economic expansion by taking pressure off interest rates: steady growth, declining deficits, and relatively low interest rates did in fact characterize the rest of the first Clinton administration. But the policy itself was nonetheless a clear political liability for much of the term. Increased taxes became a target of Republican attacks in both 1994 and 1996, evidence that Clinton represented a return to the tax-and-spend liberal Democratic policies that Republicans had so often attacked in the past; and the resulting growth generated little political reward. The 1994 congressional campaign was filled with press speculation about how good economic conditions—in terms of both real economic indicators and popular perceptions—could fail to help the Democrats who were the presumably responsible incumbents.

Raising taxes was not the sole Clinton activity that threatened to undo his carefully crafted image as a moderate. Several other actions in the first two years pushed perceptions of the President and his party to the left in a way that could re-create the ideological disadvantages of the 1970s. One of Clinton's first acts as President was to try to follow through on his campaign promise to end discrimination against gays and lesbians in the military, a policy that ignited considerable controversy and which ultimately led to the compromise "don't ask, don't tell" policy that pleased neither proponents of change nor advocates of the status quo. The failure to implement a promised reform raised questions among some supporters about Clinton's steadfastness and helped create a more general initial image of a President unable to deliver on campaign commitments, despite the Democrats' unified control of government. At the same time, it helped undermine the carefully crafted image of Clinton as centrist, as part of the cultural mainstream, among many who had seen Democratic proximity to the counter-culture as a reason to abandon the party in the late 1960s and 1970s.

A second great policy debate that threatened to damage the President's centrist credentials was the debate over reform of health care. Clinton was again to some extent constrained by commitments he had made during the campaign which would have been difficult to disavow once he took office. Concern with rising costs and threatened access to care had made health care reform a major theme for the Democrats, particularly after the relatively unknown Harris Wofford was credited with using the issue to unexpectedly defeat a well-known and popular former Republican cabinet member and governor in a special election to fill a vacated Pennsylvania senate seat in 1991. Perception that this was a popular issue on which there was broad consensus about the need for reform made it a natural focus of Democratic activities in 1993.

Health care did not in fact help the Democrats in 1994. Clinton's desire to avoid a single payer plan, with its connotations of a substantial direct governmental role in providing medical services and its limited ability to control costs, led him to produce a plan based on competition by large private providers. The proposed bureaucratic structure of competing health alliances generated fears of large government-produced institutions intruding into lives of ordinary Americans on an issue they cared deeply about. If tax rises threatened to re-create the image of the Democrats as devoted to tax-and-spend, health care threatened to create an image of the party as committed to large and intrusive government. The attention that

Clinton himself directed to the health care plan—the central role it played in his 1994 State of the Union speech and the role he assigned to his wife in its development—guaranteed that the program would substantially affect the way the electorate saw the President in ideological issue space. When the program failed to win approval of a Democratic Congress, a great price had been paid in squandering the party's centrist position without any compensating gain in ability to claim that a major policy problem had been solved.

The result of these rather unfavorable developments was a catastrophic setback for Bill Clinton and the Democrats in 1994. The Republicans gained control of both House and Senate, ending the unified control of government that Clinton had promised would end the politics of gridlock. Most striking was Republican capture of the House, where a gain of more than fifty seats gave them control of the institution for the first time since 1952. Clinton himself was of course not on the ballot in 1994, but it is hard to read the election results as anything other than a repudiation of his first two years in office. By the end of 1994, Clinton's centrist position in ideological issue space and his ability to use economic performance as an effective issue both looked like ancient history, and his chances for re-election itself looked grim.

The remarkable turn-around in Bill Clinton's electoral fortunes between 1994 and 1996 can in fact be explained fairly simply. The person most responsible for re-creating the ideological balance of 1992 in 1996 was the architect of the Republican earthquake of 1994: the new Speaker of the newly Republican House of Representatives. Newt Gingrich made the classic mistake of many a landslide election winner: he assumed that the electorate, in voting for him and his party, supported the platform and program on which the party ran. Gingrich believed that the electorate had endorsed the Contract with America and its call for a conservative revolution; he expected that public opinion would support him as he turned the Contract into specific pieces of legislation and that it would support his ideological conflict with the demoralized, discredited, and apparently lame-duck Democratic incumbent President. Gingrich's subsequent actions played a major role in allowing the Democrats to re-gain the center ground in 1995 and 1996.

If, on the other hand, the election of 1994 reflected popular rejection of the Democrats' record as the majority party in a unified government—i.e., represented retrospective rejection of Democratic performance rather than prospective endorsement of Republican promises—the Gingrich strategy would be expected to fail. Conservative activism of 1994 and 1995 would produce much the same effect that similar Reagan ideological activism had produced fourteen years earlier: it would push Republican images well to the right, creating space for the Democrats to reassert the centrist credentials that their own earlier behavior had tarnished. Bill Clinton, his centrist instincts reinforced by the failures of his first two years in office, would be able to reclaim the center and to re-create the moderate image that had temporarily been lost.

For much of the 104th Congress, it was in fact perceived Republican ideological extremism that drove American public opinion. A long-standing tension between popular skepticism towards government in the abstract and support for specific social welfare programs created a profound Republican liability in 1995 and 1996: voters who opposed tax-and-spend government nonetheless reacted badly to Republican attempts to cut specific programs that they supported and from which they expected to benefit.

Three major steps in Clinton's recapture of the ideological center can be identified. First, he was able to position himself as the defender of widely supported programs like Medicare and Social Security, which he was able to portray as threatened by Republican budget-cutting initiatives. Second, when deadlock between President and Congress over a budget caused partial shutdown of the government, Clinton emerged as the voice of pragmatic moderation, defending programs (and voters) against ideologically-driven opponents oblivious to the human cost of their reforms. And, late in his term, he signed, after much visible intra-Administration debate and with obvious ambivalence, a welfare reform law that marked a substantial reduction of the long-standing government commitment to the poor. Welfare reform became a symbol of his ability both to move pragmatically to the center and to cooperate with the Republican Congress on real policy achievements when necessary.

The policy questions on which Clinton positioned himself as a centrist were of course not definitively resolved in his first term. Portraying oneself as a defender of Social Security, for example, does not eliminate the need to deal with the financial crisis the program will face in the new century; implementation of welfare reform will require considerable attention to questions of how those removed from welfare rolls might fare given their lack of marketable skills or the lack of available jobs. The way in which such issues were used by Democrats in the campaign may well complicate relations with the Republican Congress re-elected in 1996, as both parties struggle to define their position advantageously in ideological issue space and to claim credit for any policy success. But there can be little doubt that the way in which these issues were managed politically in the run-up to 1996 played a substantial role in Clinton's electoral success.

Press accounts of the 1996 election gave considerable emphasis to the role of a relatively conservative group of presidential advisors like Dick Morris in pushing Bill Clinton to the center in the aftermath of 1994, and they may well be right. But it is also important to remember that the President they were advising had reasons of his own to be receptive to their advice. First, Clinton had been aware as a candidate of a need to push the image of his party towards the center, aware of the costs its more leftist position in the late 1960s and 1970s had exacted. Cynics may complain that it is difficult to identify Bill Clinton's core beliefs about the nature of government and the purpose of public policy, but nobody could claim that the post-1994 move to the center was fundamentally out of character with his previous behavior. Second, no group of advisors had to inform Bill Clinton that the ideological enthusiasm of the conservative new Republican Congress created an opening in the center which it would be electorally advantageous to seize. By the time of the government shutdowns in 1995 and 1996, Clinton was able to present himself as the voice of Democratic pragmatic reasonableness, combating a Republican ideological intransigence that went far beyond what the bulk of the electorate could support.

The explanation for the re-capture by the Democrats of the ideological middle ground after 1994 is quite straightforward. An account of how the economy came to once again be an area of Democratic strength in 1996 is somewhat more subtle. The state of the economy did not in fact change dramatically between 1995 and 1996: a pattern of slow but steady inflation-free growth continued in much the same way as it had in 1993 and 1994. And although no theory makes credible claims about exactly how and when a particular pattern of economic performance gets translated into retrospective political judgements, two factors provide plausible explanations of why the kinds of economic conditions that failed to protect the Democrats in 1994 might nonetheless have made them a source of Democratic strength in 1996.

First, the sheer length of the expansion may have been able to provide both a sufficient level of cumulative economic benefits for which the Democrats could claim credit and a sense of economic well-being that was more stable, predictable, and reliable than it had seemed two years earlier. What in 1994 looked like a modest pattern of growth that had been in place for less than three years had survived nearly twice as long by 1996. Clinton's ability during the campaign to repeatedly cite the number of new jobs created during his administration enabled him to demonstrate the cumulative effects of four years of growth. Second, to the extent that presidents are personally given credit or blame for economic performance, the fact that Clinton himself appeared on the 1996 ballot could well have served to make economic performance more central in voters' evaluations than it might have been in the off-year election of 1994. In a relatively dealigned electoral universe, the ability of individual Democratic legislators to take credit even for a Democratic president's clear-cut successes would be limited.

The new factor that significantly reinforced the Democratic advantage on economics in 1996 was Clinton's ability to contrast his own economic record with the economic package advocated by Bob Dole. Dole in fact faced substantial problems in formulating a credible and effective economic package. The Republicans were divided between budget-cutters concerned with the perils of deficit spending and supply-siders convinced that an appropriate package of substantial tax cuts could generate the rapid economic growth that would, ultimately, generate both prosperity and tax revenue sufficient to balance the budget. Dole had long been more comfortable in the first camp, skeptical even of the supply-side measures taken in the Reagan administration, but many Republicans (including his vice-presidential candidate) were convinced supply-siders. Dole needed to unify the party at the same time that he developed an economic policy that was both intellectually coherent and politically viable.

Either Republican economic strategy was in fact likely to be of limited effectiveness. An appeal for traditional budget cutting would be undermined by Clinton's ability to point to already-declining deficits and by the fact that an effort to reduce them further or faster would require either cutting programs or raising taxes to an extent that would generate substantial voter resistance. But Dole's acceptance of an across-the-board fifteen percent tax cut as the centerpiece of his economic program produced serious problems of its own. Polls regularly showed large numbers of voters doubting that the cuts would really be made, questioning whether the program was a serious plan for economic policy or an election-year gimmick. Clinton's claims that such cuts had contributed to the deficits of the Reagan-Bush years allowed him to re-direct attention to the economic problems that had so helped him in 1992, to reinforce his claim that his own policies were reversing the effects of Republican economic failure, and, par-enthetically, to remind voters of some of the policies which had helped move im-ages of the Republicans to the right in the 1980s. Neither traditional budget-cutting nor supply-side expansion was likely to generate the broad-based economic appeal that Dole needed to successfully oppose the Clinton record.

1996 therefore does look remarkably like 1992: the intervening years had been filled with events capable of transforming the electoral landscape, but the end re-sult was a second consecutive election in which economics was an area of Democratic strength and in which the Democrats had achieved a balance (or per-haps secured a slight advantage) in ideological issue space. The Democratic cata-strophe of 1994 was central in allowing Clinton to escape his failures of 1993 and 1994, with Newt Gingrich providing essential aid in allowing the Democrat's suc-cessful re-claiming of the ideological center; continued (if gradual) economic ex-pansion then combined with the inherent limitations of either possible Repub-lican economic plan to provide sufficient retrospective economic strength to secure the President's re-election.

One must not, however, exaggerate the magnitude of Clinton's achievement. If 1996 looks like a remarkable triumph from a standpoint of 1994, it seems a modest continuation and extension of the trends of 1992. It is as important to remember how 1992 was nearly squandered as how 1994 was reversed. The outcome of the election reinforces a picture of a modest victory with limited implications for the future. Despite indications throughout the campaign that Clinton was headed for a landslide re-election, his actual margin of victory was modest: he received less than half the popular vote, and his margin of victory was well under ten percent. If one were to incorporate data for 1996 into the analysis of election outcomes in Chapter Two, one would find little change and no good news for the Democrats. Substituting 1996 for 1976 in the five-election sequence actually produces a modest decrease in both the mean and the standard deviation of the Democratic vote. The Democrats continued to average about 44 percent of the popular vote, and there is stability to their disappointing results that is quite striking in historical terms. The two Clinton victories do not mark a break in a pattern of mediocre Democratic per-formance in presidential elections, and the 1996 presidential victory was, of course, combined with Republican retention of both houses of Congress. There is little ev-idence here of a resurgence of the kind that could spark even the most optimistic Democratic activist to speak of a new or renewed Democratic majority, or even of a new or renewed Democratic presidential majority.

What, if anything, can we say about electoral politics in 2000 and after on the basis of this understanding of 1996? The obvious answer in a dealigned electoral universe is clear: not very much. Even in its most simplistic form, dealignment the-ory would allow for eight-year periods of stability. There is no reason why specific candidate-centered coalitions should not be able to secure their own re-election. What would be troublesome for a dealignment argument would be continuity in the structure of electoral politics much beyond this constitutionally-specified life-span.

The basic similarity of 1976 to 1968 and 1972 or of 1988 to 1980 and 1984 makes clear that twelve- (or even sixteen-) year periods of electoral stability are not impossible in a dealigned world. And Al Gore's closeness, personal and political, to Bill Clinton combines with his clear standing in early 1997 as heir apparent to suggest that the Democrats, at least, will offer much the same kind of presidential package in 2000 as they did in 1992 and 1996. But whether that package will in fact be delivered and how attractive it will ultimately look depend on factors like the relative ideological position of the parties after four more years of policy debate (within as well as between the two parties) and the economic success of a second Clinton administration, which will not be determined for some time.

Even if the Democrats' 2000 offering already seems reasonably predictable, the opposition they will face is very much up in the air. The Republicans have no heir apparent, and the particular package that the Dole-Kemp ticket represented is only one of several possible ways to work out their own internal divisions. The party remains divided on core economic questions between budget-balancers and supply-siders; and it faces even more fundamental internal conflict between the primarily economic focus of a modern secular conservatism and the social/cultural conservatism of groups like the Christian religious right. Neither Steve Forbes nor Pat Buchanan is likely to be the party's nominee in 2000, but each represents a wing of the party not entirely happy with the Dole campaign that will claim that its distinctive appeal offers the promise of both policy and electoral success. And although Perot's encore in 1996 fell far short of his initial performance in 1992, the potential for third-party challenges, particularly if a less successful second Clinton administration combines with continued Republican divisions, cannot be ignored.

What is fairly clear is that a stable party system of a classic sort is even more unlikely after 1996 than it was after 1992. In 1992, the return of unified government may have temporarily encouraged those who thought a classic realignment possible. In 1994, the optimists might have envisioned a Republican resurgence that would allow them the forty years of dominance that realignment promises. In 1996, ratification of continued divided government makes clear that a party-based era of one-party dominance and its extended period of policy innovation is not on the verge of being introduced. All of the other factors that underlie a dealigned electoral universe show clear signs of continuing: the failure of a clear new ideological cleavage to dominate issue debate, mass dependence on retrospective evaluations of incumbent performance, the interaction of increased educational opportunities and endlessly-expanding sources of political information, the candidate-centered organization, and financing of both nomination contests and general election campaigns.

Bill Clinton's re-election is a great triumph for Bill Clinton; it is certainly a good thing for the Democrats. But it was clearly a very personal triumph that neither generated across-the-board gains for the Democratic party in 1996 nor created a stable basis for the party's electoral success in the future. Nothing that happened in 1996 suggests that the dealigned electoral politics that have dominated the last thirty years is coming to an end. In 2000, Bill Clinton moves from electoral politics to electoral history, and the forces that twice elected him enter the uncertainty that characterizes all electoral politics in a dealigned age.

Appendix 1
Codes Used to Construct the Dichotomous Occupation Measure

The following are the codes used to construct the dichotomous occupation variable. For 1952–1980, the codes used were census occupation codes for head of household. For 1984 and 1988, codes used are 1980 census major group categories. In 1988, there is no separate coding for head of household. Where more than one occupation was coded for a household, the respondent was categorized as white collar if *either* occupation was white collar and missing only if *both* occupations were missing.

1952–1964: white-collar: 1–39
                blue-collar: 41–78
                missing: 80–99

1968–1980: white-collar: 101–395
                blue-collar: 401–785, 901–984
                missing: 810–824, 999

1984–1988: white-collar: 1–5
                blue-collar: 6–8, 10–13
                missing: 0, 9, 14–99

Appendix 2

The following are the closed ended questions used to construct measures of ideological extremity. Aggregate analysis uses all response categories for these questions that include at least thirty respondents. Entries indicate whether the item met the cut-off of 75 percent of respondents with valid scores necessary to be included in the individual-level analysis for each year:

D indicates that the criterion was met for Democrats only;
R indicates that the criterion was met for Republicans only;
B indicates that the criterion was met for both sets of partisans;
— indicates that the criterion was met by neither of the partisans,
   a blank indicates that the item was not asked in a given year.

In cases in which an old version is repeated and a new version of the same question is introduced, only the newer version was included.

	1952	1956	1960	1964	1968	1972	1976	1980	1984	1988	1992
Fair job treatment	B	B	B	B	B	D				—	B
Korea	B										
Government economic activity	B										
U.S. stay home	B	B	B		B	B	B	B	—		B
Taft-Hartley	—										
Job guarantee		B	B	B	B	B	B	—	B	B	B
Aid to education		B	B	B	B						—
Friendly to other nations		B									
Medical care		B	B	B	B	B	B		—	B	B
Fire suspected communist		B									
Integrated schools		B	B	B	B	B	B				—
Cut taxes		B						—		B	—
U.S. act tough abroad		B									
Troops overseas		B	B								
Foreign aid		R	B	B	B	B	R				
Integration/segregation				B	B	B	B				
School prayer				B	B			R	B		B
Talk with communists				B	B						

Continues

	1952	1956	1960	1964	1968	1972	1976	1980	1984	1988	1992
Integrated housing				B	B	B	B				
Open accommodations				B	B	B					
Aid parochial schools				R							
Trade with communists				—	R	—					
Vietnam				—	B	B					
Cuba				—	—						
Communist China in UN				—	—	B					
Urban riots					B	R	—				B
Protest					B						
Abortion						B	B	B	B	B	B
Women's equality						B	R	B	B	B	B
Marijuana						B	B				
School busing						B	B	B	—		
Aid minorities						R	B	R	B	B	B
Rights of accused						R	B				
Progressive taxation						B	—				
Military spending						B	B	B	B	B	B
Amnesty						B					
Inflation						B	B	—			
Pollution						B					
Recognize communist China						B					
Campus unrest						R					
Ration gasoline							B	B			
Job safety							B				
Require identification card							B				
Allow wire taps							B				
Car pollution							R				
Courts too lenient							R				
Gun control							R				
Equal rights amendment							R	R			
Social services								B	B	B	B
Nuclear power								B			
Environmentalism								R			
Ties to USSR								R	B	B	
Equal opportunity									B	B	
Central America									B		
Cut arms										B	
Oil										B	
Death penalty										B	B
Reverse discrimination										B	B
College quotas										B	B
Gay rights										B	B
Imports										—	
South Africa										—	
Nursing homes											B
Abortion: parental consent											B
Abortion: state funding											B
Abortion: notify											B

Continues

	1952	1956	1960	1964	1968	1972	1976	1980	1984	1988	1992
Child care											B
Gays in military											B
Gay adoption											B
English official language											B
Bilingual education											B
Use force internationally											B

Appendix 3

The following are the NES issue questions which were used to construct perceived distance. Questions were included if a perceived distance measure could be created for at least half of the Democratic and half of the Republican identifiers.

1968: urban riots, Vietnam.
1972: form 1: job guarantee, progressive taxation, school busing, help minorities, marijuana, rights of accused.
form 2: inflation, busing, help blacks, marijuana, pollution, rights of accused, urban riots, campus unrest, Vietnam.
1976: job guarantee, medical care, progressive taxation, school busing, help minorities, marijuana, rights of accused, urban riots, women's equality.
1980: job guarantee, social services, inflation, cut taxes, help minorities, abortion, women's equality, military spending, ties to USSR.
1984: job guarantee, social services, help minorities, women's equality, military spending, ties to USSR, Central America.
1988: job guarantee, medical care, social services, help minorities, women's equality, military spending, ties to USSR.
1992: social services, jobs, defense spending.

Appendix 4

The following are the open-ended codes used to construct issue orientation:

1952–1968, party: 100, 101, 110–115, 120–131, 140–204, 210, 211, 220–292, 300–330, 340, 342–348, 350–380, 390–392, 400–422, 431–446, 451, 453–455, 460, 461, 470–492, 493, 499, 500–601, 615–650, 660, 670, 671, 690–703, 710–750, 760, 770, 771, 788, 790, 791–799, 970–979, 982 (1968: also 390).

1952–1968, candidate: 60, 70, 80, 81, 292, 400–417, 420–422, 430–448, 450–456, 460–485, 490–492, 500–520, 530–533, 537–541, 550, 552, 553, 560, 561, 570–595, 599, 601–699, 701–703, 710–750, 760, 770, 771, 780–799, 970–979, 982, 985 (1968: also 201).

1972–1992: 220, 221, 329, 330, 405, 406, 513, 514, 519, 520, 551–554, 601–607, 608, 718, 720, 801, 829, 830, 847–849, 900–902, 904–997, 1001–1033, 1035–1040, 1101–1199, 1201–1297.

Appendix 5

Manipulating Predicted Loyalty: Perceived Distance as Measure of Issues

All Democrats and Republicans

Year	Democratic Values/ Democratic Coefficients[a]	Republican Values/ Democratic Coefficients[b]	Democratic Values/ Republican Coefficients[c]	Republican Values/ Republican Coefficients[a]
1968	46.4	57.9	77.3	82.4
1972	50.8	88.9	85.8	94.3
1976	58.3	64.1	67.4	87.6
1980	57.1	61.6	70.2	76.1
1984	71.9	76.7	91.0	90.5
1988	84.1	82.6	88.7	87.3

Core Constituencies: Liberal Democrats and Conservative Republicans[d]

Year	Liberal Democratic Values/Democratic Coefficients[a]	Conservative Republican Values/ Democratic Coefficients[b]	Liberal Democratic Values/Republican Coefficients[c]	Conservative Republican Values/ Republican Coefficients[a]
1968	57.1	62.9	82.6	84.1
1972	74.2	96.0	90.5	96.2
1976	59.5	66.3	74.9	81.6
1980	57.9	59.9	77.9	86.4
1984	87.2	88.3	96.4	95.5
1988	92.7	92.9	93.2	93.9

Notes: a. Entries are predicted loyalty for mean Democratic and Republican identifiers derived from probit analyses of each partisan group separately.
   b. Column two uses coefficients for Democrats but substitutes values on independent variables of the mean Republican.
   c. Column three uses values on independent variables of Democrats but coefficients for Republicans.
   d. Mean scores are for liberal Democrats and conservative Republicans.

Appendix 6

The following open-ended codes are used to construct the individual issue-area variables used in the text.

fiscal/monetary:
1952–1968 party: 120–131, 210, 211, 340, 342–343, 345–348
1952–1968 candidate: 80–81, 432–438, 440–448
1972–1992: 601–602, 605–606, 902–904, 926–933, 942, 1046, 1054

prosperity:
1952–1968 party: 350–380, 499
1952–1968 candidate: 450–456, 599
1972–1992: 627, 934–941

social welfare:
1952–1968 party: 220–221, 300–330, 344, 390–392, 491, 492, 671, 692, 771, 792
                  (1968: not 390–392)
1952–1968 candidate: 420–421, 430–431, 490–492, 591–594, 771, 788, 792
1972–1992: 905–916, 920–925, 994–996, 1001–1003, 1007–1009, 1025–1027, 1038–
            1040, 1047–1049, 1052–1053, 1219–1222, 1233–1234

class:
1952–1968 party: 451, 453–455, 615–650, 710–750
1952–1968 candidate: 550, 552–553, 710–750, 782, 783
1972–1992: 952–958, 1035–1037, 1205–1214

race:
1952–1968 party: 400–422, 670, 770
1952–1968 candidate: 500–520, 770, 787, 977; also 1968: 201
1972–1992: 405–406, 946–948, 991–993, 1043–1045, 1217, 1218

social:
1952–1968 party: 110–115, 470–486
1952–1968 candidate: 60, 292, 570–586, 595, 985
1972–1992: 551–554, 603, 604, 720, 847–849, 917–919, 968–990, 1019–1024, 1041–
            1042

new politics:
1952–1968 party: 431–433, 461, 982
1952–1968 candidate: 530–533, 561
1972–1992: 624, 626, 721, 723, 731, 829, 830, 949–951, 962–964, 1004–1006, 1013–
       1015, 1050–1051, 1055–1056, 1223–1226, 1235–1236

foreign:
1952–1968 party: 500–599
1952–1968 candidate: 70, 601–699
1972–1992: 220, 221, 513, 514, 519–520, 1101–1199, 1300–1303

residual:
1952–1968 party: 100–101, 140–204, 222–292, 434–446, 460, 487–490, 493, 600–
       601, 660, 690–691, 693–703, 760, 790–791, 793–799, 970–979
       (1968: also 390)
1952–1968 candidate: 400–417, 422, 439, 460–485, 537–541, 560, 587–590, 701–
       703, 760, 780–781, 784–786, 789–791, 793–799, 970–976,
       978–979, 982
1972–1992: 607–608, 801, 900–901, 943–945, 959–961, 965–967, 997, 1010–1012,
       1016–1018 1028–1030, 1059–1060, 1201–1204, 1215–1216, 1227–1232,
       1235–1297

candidate orientation:
1952–1968: 10–59, 61–69, 71–79, 82–291, 293–399, 810–861, 893, 895, 900–901
       (1968: not 201)
1972–1992: 201–219, 222–332, 334, 397–404, 407–428, 431–498, 502–508, 542,
       543, 544, 609–614, 617–624, 626–697, 701–719, 729–730, 732–733,
       797 (1972: also 541–542)

Appendix 7

The following are probit coefficients and means used to construct Table 4.1.

	Democrats			Republicans		
		Means			Means	
	Coefficients	All	Liberal	Coefficients	All	Conservative
1952:						
Intercept	.02704			−.96853		
Partyid	.27095	.744	.759	.25931	5.196	5.165
Issues	.15241	1.924	2.573	.14958	−2.189	−3.412
Candidates	.18350	.298	.543	.17448	−2.072	−2.361
1956:						
Intercept	.09207			−.07342		
Partyid	.34693	.712	.730	.08570	5.176	5.178
Issues	.16383	2.259	2.779	.13367	−2.005	−2.452
Candidates	.21873	.652	1.270	.13429	−2.913	−3.356
1960:						
Intercept	.13376			−1.13352		
Partyid	.40305	.728	.622	.28954	5.248	5.208
Issues	.15828	2.056	2.829	.09177	−2.464	−3.376
Candidates	.28637	.480	.836	.18211	−2.865	−2.887
1964:						
Intercept	.27416			−1.80763		
Partyid	.23924	.711	.677	.28627	5.177	5.346
Issues	.12597	2.687	4.167	.18666	−2.026	−3.955
Candidates	.14425	1.983	2.608	.26740	−.431	−1.536
1968:						
Intercept	−.13135			−1.97906		
Partyid	.45665	.815	.727	.41766	5.027	4.910
Issues	.13794	1.453	3.261	.12478	−2.786	−4.056
Candidates	.25757	.687	1.248	.18047	−1.814	−2.281
1972:						
Intercept	−.27036			−.60158		
Partyid	.30204	.929	.961	.21364	4.996	5.003
Issues	.20058	1.618	3.324	.11973	−1.440	−2.127
Candidates	.53034	−.262	.374	.21366	−1.602	−1.984

Continues

205

		Democrats			Republicans	
		Means			Means	
	Coefficients	All	Liberal	Coefficients	All	Conservative
1976:						
Intercept	−.03206			−1.64403		
Partyid	.21366	.932	1.000	.32950	4.987	5.057
Issues	.13489	2.372	3.173	.17326	−1.093	−1.600
Candidates	.19443	.321	.398	.19940	−1.541	−1.762
1980:						
Intercept	.02209			−1.48754		
Partyid	.45936	.879	.978	.27518	4.945	5.067
Issues	.14219	1.184	1.703	.17562	−2.477	−3.495
Candidates	.27439	.892	.948	.25699	−.515	−.773
1984:						
Intercept	−.11094			−.76435		
Partyid	.31674	.872	.866	.23396	5.000	5.139
Issues	.16306	3.467	5.720	.18168	−2.005	−3.352
Candidates	.29872	.359	.791	.18142	−1.283	−1.596
1988:						
Intercept	.22691			−1.77346		
Partyid	.34763	.879	.957	.40971	5.011	5.240
Issues	.14556	2.675	4.288	.13930	−2.260	−3.922
Candidates	.26560	.592	.933	.12634	−.854	−.907

References

Abramson, Paul R. 1975. *Generational Change in American Politics.* Lexington, Massachusetts: Lexington Books.

Abramson, Paul R., John H. Aldrich, and David W. Rohde. 1982. *Change and Continuity in the 1980 Elections.* Washington, D.C.: CQ Press.

Abramson, Paul R., John H. Aldrich, and David W. Rohde. 1986. *Change and Continuity in the 1984 Elections.* Washington, D.C.: CQ Press.

Abramson, Paul R., John H. Aldrich, and David W. Rohde. 1990. *Change and Continuity in the 1988 Elections.* Washington, D.C.: CQ Press.

Abramowitz, Alan I., David J. Lanone, and Subha Ramesh. 1988. "Economic Conditions, Causal Attributions, and Political Evaluations in the 1984 Presidential Election." *The Journal of Politics.* 50: 848–863.

Abramowitz, Alan I. and Jeffrey A. Segal. 1986. "Determinants of the Outcomes of U.S. Senate Elections." *The Journal of Politics.* 48: 433–439.

Achen, Christopher H. 1975. "Mass Political Attitudes and the Survey Response." *American Political Science Review.* 69: 1218–31.

Aldrich, John and Charles F. Cnudde. 1975. "Probing the Bounds of Conventional Wisdom: A Comparison of Regression, Probit, and Discriminant Analysis." *American Journal of Political Science.* 19: 571–608.

Aldrich, John N., Richard G. Niemi, George Rabinowitz, and David W. Rohde. 1982. "The Measurement of Public Opinion about Public Policy: A Report on Some New Question Formats." *American Journal of Political Science.* 26: 391–414.

Aldrich, John H., John L. Sullivan, and Eugene Borgida. 1989. "Foreign Affairs and Issue Voting: Do Presidential Candidates 'Waltz Before a Blind Audience?'" *American Political Science Review.* 83: 123–141.

Alford, Robert R. 1963. *Party and Society: The Anglo-American Democracies.* Chicago: Rand McNally & Company.

Andersen, Kristi J. 1979. *The Creation of a Democratic Majority: 1928–1936.* Chicago: University of Chicago Press.

Axelrod, Robert. 1972. "Where the Votes Comes From: An Analysis of Electoral Coalitions, 1952–1968." *American Political Science Review.* 66: 11–20.

Axelrod, Robert. 1984. "Presidential Election Coalitions in 1984." *American Political Science Review.* 80: 281–284.

Bachrach, Peter. 1967. *The Theory of Democratic Elitism: A Critique.* Boston: Little, Brown.

Barber, Benjamin. 1984. *Strong Democracy: Participatory Democracy for a New Age.* Berkeley: University of California Press.

Bass, Jack and Walter de Vries. 1976. *The Transformation of Southern Politics.* New York: Basic Books.

Beck, Paul Allen. 1974. "A Socialization Theory of Partisan Realignment," in Richard G. Niemi and Associates, eds. *The Politics of Future Citizens.* Jossey-Bass: San Francisco. 199–219.

Beck, Paul Allen. 1984. "The Dealignment Era in America," in Russell J. Dalton, Scott C. Flanagan, Paul Allen Beck, eds. *Electoral Change in Advanced Industrial Democracies: Realignment or Dealignment?* Princeton: Princeton University Press. 240–266.

Berelson, Bernard R., Paul F. Lazarsfeld, and William N. McPhee. 1954. *Voting: Study of Opinion Formation in a Presidential Campaign.* Chicago: University of Chicago.

Berman, William C. 1970. *The Politics of Civil Rights in the Truman Administration.* Columbus: Ohio University Press.

Black, Earl and Black, Merle. 1992. *The Vital South: How Presidents are Elected.* Cambridge: Harvard University Press.

Brady, David W. 1985. "A Reevaluation of Realignments in American Politics: Evidence from the House of Representatives." *American Political Science Review.* 79: 28–49.

Brady, David W. and Patricia A. Hurley. 1985. "The Prospects for Contemporary Partisan Realignment." *PS.* 18: 63–68.

Bruzios, Christopher. 1990. "Democratic and Republican Party Activists and Followers: Inter- and Intra-Party Differences." *Polity.* 22: 581–601.

Burnham, Walter Dean. 1965. "The Changing Shape of the American Political Universe." *American Political Science Review.* 59: 7–28.

Burnham, Walter Dean. 1970. *Critical Elections and the Mainsprings of American Politics.* New York: W.W. Norton and Company.

Burnham, Walter Dean. 1991. "Critical Realignment: Dead or Alive?" in Byron E. Shafer, ed. 1991. *The End of Realignment? Interpreting American Electoral Eras.* Madison: University of Wisconsin Press. 101–139.

Campbell, Angus. 1966a. "A Classification of Presidential Elections," in Angus Campbell, Philip E. Converse, Warren E. Miller, Donald E. Stokes, eds., *Elections and the Political Order.* New York: Wiley. 63–77.

Campbell, Angus. 1966b. "Surge and Decline: A Study of Electoral Change," in Angus Campbell, Philip E. Converse, Warren E. Miller, Donald E. Stokes, eds., *Elections and the Political Order.* 40–62.

Campbell, Angus, Philip E. Converse, Warren E. Miller, and Donald E. Stokes. 1960. *The American Voter.* New York: Wiley.

Campbell, Angus, Gerald Gurin, and Warren Miller. 1954. *The Voter Decides.* Evanston: Row, Peterson and Company.

Carmines, Edward G., John P. McIver, and James A. Stimson. 1987. "Unrealized Partisanship: A Theory of Dealignment." *The Journal of Politics.* 49: 376–400.

Carmines, Edward G. and James R. Stimson. 1989. *Issue Evolution: Race and the Transformation of American Politics.* Princeton: Princeton University Press.

CBS News/New York Times Poll. 1986. "Politics 1986." 6 October 1986.

CBS News/New York Times Poll. 1988. "Four Weeks and Counting." 10 October 1988.

Clubb, Jerome M., William H. Flanigan, Nancy H. Zingale. 1980. *Partisan Realignment: Voters, Parties, and Government in American History.* Sage: Beverly Hills, California.

Congressional Quarterly. 1975. *Congressional Quarterly's Guide to U.S. Elections.* Washington, D.C.: Congressional Quarterly.

Conover, Pamela C. and Stanley Feldman. 1981. "The Origins and Meaning of Liberal/Conservative Self-Identification." *American Journal of Political Science.* 25: 617–645.

Conover, Pamela C., Stanley Feldman, and Kathleen Knight. 1987. "The Personal and Political Underpinnings of Economic Forecasts." *American Journal of Political Science.* 31: 559–583.

Converse. Philip E. 1966a. "Religion and Politics: The 1960 Election," in Angus Campbell, Philip E. Converse, Warren E. Miller, Donald E. Stokes, eds., *Elections and the Political Order.* 96–124.

Converse. Philip E. 1966b. "The Concept of a Normal Vote," in Angus Campbell, Philip E. Converse, Warren E. Miller, Donald E. Stokes, eds., *Elections and the Political Order.* 9–39.

Converse, Philip E. 1970. "Attitudes and Non-Attitudes: Continuation of a Dialogue," in Edward R. Tufte, ed., *The Quantitative Analysis of Social Problems.* New York: Addison-Wesley. 168–189.

Converse, Philip E., Aage R. Clausen, and Warren E. Miller. 1965. "Electoral Myth and Reality: The 1964 Election." *American Political Science Review.* 59: 321–336.

Gary W. Cox and Samuel Kernell, eds. 1991. *The Politics of Divided Government.* Boulder: Westview.

Delli Carpini, Michael X. 1986. *Stability and Change in American Politics: The Coming of Age of the Generation of the 1960s.* New York: New York University Press.

DeNardo, James. 1980. "Turnout and the Vote: The Joke's on the Democrats." *American Political Science Review.* 74: 406–420.

Dionne, E. J., Jr. 1991. *Why Americans Hate Politics.* New York: Simon & Schuster.

Downs, Anthony. 1957. *An Economic Theory of Democracy.* New York: Harper and Row.

Edsall, Thomas Byrne and Mary D. Edsall. 1991. *Chain Reaction: The Impact of Race, Rights, and Taxes on American Politics.* New York: W.W. Norton.

Erickson, Robert S. and Kent L. Tedin. 1981. "The 1928–36 Partisan Realignment: The Case for the Conversion Hypothesis." *American Political Science Review.* 75: 951–962.

Feldman, Stanley. 1982. "Economic Self-Interest and Political Behavior." *American Journal of Political Science.* 26:3. 446–466.

Ferguson, Thomas and Joel Rogers. 1986. *Right Turn: The Decline of the Democrats and the Future of American Politics.* New York: Hill and Wang.

Field, John O. and Ronald E. Anderson. 1969. "Ideology in the Public's Conception of the 1964 Election." *Public Opinion Quarterly.* 33: 380–398.

Fiorina, Morris P. 1981. *Retrospective Voting in American National Elections.* New Haven: Yale University Press.

Fiorina, Morris P. 1992. *Divided Government.* New York: Macmillan.

Flanagan, Scott C. 1987. "Value Change in Industrial Societies." *American Political Science Review.* 81: 1303–1319.

Frankovic, Kathleen A. 1981. "Public Opinion Trends," in Gerald M. Pomper, ed. *The Election of 1980: Reports and Interpretations.* Chatham, N.J.: Chatham House. 97–118.

Gallup, George H. 1972. *The Gallup Poll: Public Opinion 1935–1971* Volume One. New York: Random House.

Geer, John G. 1988. "What do Open-Ended Questions Measure?" *Public Opinion Quarterly.* 52: 365–371.

Geer, John G. 1992. "New Deal Issues and the American Electorate: 1952–88." *Political Behavior.* 14: 45–65.

Gold, Howard J. 1992. *Hollow Mandates: American Public Opinion and the Conservative Shift.* Boulder: Westview.

Goodman, Saul and Gerald H. Kramer. 1975. "Comments on Arcelus and Meltzer: The Effect of Aggregate Economic Conditions on Congressional Elections." *American Political Science Review.* 69: 1255–1265.

Gopoian, J. David. 1993. "Images and Issues in the 1988 Presidential Election." *The Journal of Politics.* 55: 151–166.

Hale, Jon F. 1995. The Making of the New Democrats." *Political Science Quarterly.* 110: 207–232.

Hibbs, Douglas A., Jr. 1982. "President Reagan's Mandate from the 1980 Elections: A Shift to the Right?" *American Politics Quarterly.* 10: 387–420.

Huckfeldt, Robert and Carol Weitzel Kohfeld. 1989. *Race and the Decline of Class in American Politics.* Urbana: University of Illinois Press.

Hurley, Patricia A. 1989. "Partisan Representation and the Failure of Realignment in the 1980s." *American Journal of Political Science.* 33: 240–261.

Hurley, Patricia A. 1991. "Partisan Representation, Realignment, and the Senate in the 1980s." *The Journal of Politics.* 53: 3–33.

Inglehart, Ronald. 1977. *The Silent Revolution: Changing Values and Political Styles Among Western Publics.* Princeton: Princeton University Press.

Inglehart, Ronald. 1990. *Culture Shift in Advanced Industrial Society.* Princeton: Princeton University Press.

Inglehart, Ronald and Paul R. Abramson. 1994. "Economic Security and Value Change." *American Political Science Review.* 88: 336–354.

Jacobson, Gary C. 1991. "The Persistence of Democratic House Majorities," in Gary W. Cox and Samuel Kernell, eds., *The Politics of Divided Government.* Boulder: Westview. 57–84.

Katznelson, Ira, Kim Geiger, and Daniel Kryder. 1993. "Limiting Liberalism: The Southern Veto in Congress, 1933–1950." *Political Science Quarterly.* 108: 283–306.

Keith, Bruce E., David B. Magleby, Candice J. Nelson, Elizabeth Orr, Mark C. Westlye, and Raymond E. Wolfinger. 1992. *The Myth of the Independent Voter.* Berkeley: University of California Press.

Kelley, Stanley, Jr. 1983. *Interpreting Elections.* Princeton: Princeton University Press.

Kelley, Stanley, Jr. 1988. "Democracy and the New Deal Party System," in Amy Gutmann, ed., *Democracy and the Welfare State.* Princeton: Princeton University Press. 185–205.

Kelley, Stanley, Jr. and Thad W. Mirer. 1974. "The Simple Act of Voting." *American Political Science Review.* 68: 572–591.

Key, V.O., Jr. 1949. *Southern Politics.* New York: Vintage Books.

Key, V.O., Jr. 1955. "A Theory of Critical Elections." *The Journal of Politics.* 17: 3–18.

Key, V.O., Jr. 1959. "Secular Realignment and the Party System." *The Journal of Politics.* 21: 198–210.

Key, V.O., Jr. 1961. *Public Opinion and American Democracy.* New York: Knopf.

Key, V.O., Jr. 1966. *The Responsible Electorate.* New York: Vintage Books.

Kiewiet, D. Roderick. 1983. *Macroeconomics and Micropolitics: The Electoral Effects of Economic Issues.* Chicago: University of Chicago Press.

Kiewiet, D. Roderick and Douglas Rivers. 1985. "The Economics Basis of Reagan's Appeal," in John E. Chubb and Paul E. Peterson, eds., *The New Direction in American Politics.* Washington, D.C.: Brookings. 69–90.

Kinder, Donald R., Gordon S. Adams, and Paul W. Gronke. 1989. "Economics and Politics in the 1984 American Presidential Election." *American Journal of Political Science.* 33: 491–515.

Kirby, John B. 1980. *Black Americans in the Roosevelt Era: Liberalism and Race.* Knoxville: University of Tennessee Press.

Kirkpatrick, Jeane. 1976. *The New Presidential Elite: Men and Women in National Politics.* New York: Russell Sage Foundation and The Twentieth Century Fund.

Kramer, Gerald. 1971. "Short-Term Fluctuations in U.S. Voting Behavior: 1896–1964." *American Political Science Review.* 65: 131–143.

Kusnet, David. 1992. *Speaking American: How the Democrats Can Win in the Nineties.* New York: Thunder's Mouth Press.

Ladd, Everett Carll. 1982. *Where Have All the Voters Gone?: The Fracturing of America's Political Parties,* second edition. New York: Norton.

Ladd, Everett Carll. 1985. "On Mandates, Realignments, and the 1984 Presidential Election." *Political Science Quarterly.* 100: 1–25.

Ladd, Everett Carll. 1989. "The 1988 Elections: Continuation of the Post–New Deal System." *Political Science Quarterly.* 104: 1–18.

Ladd, Everett Carll. 1993. "The 1992 Vote for President: Another Brittle Mandate?" *Political Science Quarterly.* 108: 1–28.

Ladd, Everett Carll. 1995. "The 1994 Congressional Elections: The Postindustrial Realignment Continues." *Political Science Quarterly.* 110: 1–23.

Ladd, Everett Carll, Jr. with Charles D. Hadley. 1978. *Transformations of the American Party System: Political Coalitions from the New Deal to the 1970s,* second edition. Norton: New York.

Lanoue, David J. 1994. "Retrospective and Prospective Voting in Presidential-Year Elections." *Political Research Quarterly.* 47: 193–205.

Lanoue, David J. 1989. "The 'Teflon Factor': Ronald Reagan and Comparative Presidential Popularity." *Polity.* 21: 481–501.

Lawrence, David G. 1978. "Candidate Orientation, Vote Choice, and the Quality of the American Electorate." *Polity.* 11: 229–246.

Lawrence, David G. 1991. "The Collapse of the Democratic Majority: Economics and Vote Choice since 1952." *The Western Political Quarterly.* 44: 797–820.

Lawrence, David G. 1994. "Ideological Extremity, Issue Distance, and Voter Defection: 1952–1988." *Political Research Quarterly.* 47: 397–421.

Lawrence, David G. and Richard Fleisher. 1987. "Puzzles and Confusions: Political Realignment in the 1980s." *Political Science Quarterly.* 102: 79–92.

Lazarsfeld, Paul F., Bernard Berelson, and Hazel Gaudet. 1968. *The People's Choice: How the Voter Makes Up His Mind in a Presidential Campaign,* third edition. New York: Columbia University Press.

Lebergott, Stanley. 1964. *Manpower in Economic Growth: The American Record Since 1800.* New York: McGraw-Hill.

Lewis-Beck, Michael S. and Tom W. Rice. 1992. *Forecasting Elections.* Washington, D.C.: CQ Press.

Los Angeles Times. "Americans Rate Reagan as an Average President." 4 November 1991: 1.

Lubell, Samuel. 1965. *The Future of American Politics,* third edition, revised. New York: Harper & Row.

Macdonald, Stuart Elaine and George Rabinowitz. 1987. "The Dynamics of Structural Realignment." *American Political Science Review.* 81: 775–796.

Margolis, Michael. 1977. "From Confusion to Confusion." *American Political Science Review.* 71: 31–43.

Martin, John Bartlow. 1976. *Adlai Stevenson of Illinois.* Garden City: Doubleday and Company.

McClosky, Herbert, Paul J. Hoffman, and Rosemary O'Hara. 1960. "Issue Conflict and Consensus Among Party Leaders and Followers." *American Political Science Review.* 56: 406–429.

Meltzer, Allan H. and Marc Vellrath. 1975. "The Effects of Economic Policies on Votes for the Presidency: Some Evidence from Recent Elections." *Journal of Law and Economics.* 18: 781–798.

Miller, Arthur H., Warren E. Miller, Alden S. Raine, and Thad A. Brown. 1976. "A Majority Party in Disarray: Policy Polarization in the 1972 Election." *American Political Science Review.* 70: 753–778.

Miller, Arthur H. and Martin P. Wattenberg. 1985. "Throwing the Rascals Out: Policy and Performance Evaluations of Presidential Candidates, 1952–1980." *American Political Science Review.* 79: 359–372.

Miller, Arthur H., Martin P. Wattenberg, and Oksana Malanchuk. 1986. "Schematic Assessments of Presidential Candidates." *American Political Science Review.* 80: 521–540.

Miller, Warren E. and Kent Jennings. 1986. *Parties in Transition: A Longitudinal Study of Party Elites and Party Followers.* New York: Russell Sage.

Miller, Warren E. and Teresa E. Levitin. 1976. *Leadership and Change: Presidential Elections From 1952 to 1976.* Cambridge, Massachusetts: Winthrop.

Miller, Warren E. and J. Merrill Shanks. 1982. "Policy Directions and Presidential Leadership: Alternative Interpretations of the 1980 Presidential Election." *British Journal of Political Science.* 12: 299–356.

Mishler, William and Reginald S. Sheehan. 1993. "The Supreme Court as a Countermajoritarian Institution? The Impact of Public Opinion on Supreme Court Decisions." *American Political Science Review.* 87: 87–101.

Monroe, Kristen R. 1979. "Econometric Analysis of Political Behavior: A Critical Review." *Political Behavior.* 1: 137–173.

New York Times. "Republicans Show Gains in Loyalty." 21 January 1990: 24.

Newfield, Jack and Jeff Greenfield. 1972. *A Populist Manifesto: The Making of a New Majority.* New York: Praeger.

Nie, Norman H. with Kristi Andersen. 1974. "Mass Belief Systems Revisited: Political Change and Attitude Structure." *The Journal of Politics.* 36: 541–591.

Nie, Norman H., Sidney Verba, and John R. Petrocik. 1979. *The Changing American Voter,* enlarged edition. Cambridge: Harvard University Press.

Niemi, Richard, Richard Katz, and David Newman. 1980. "Reconstructing Past Partisanship: The Failure of the Party Identification Recall Question." *American Political Science Review.* 76: 633–51.

Norpoth, Helmut and Jerrold G. Rusk. 1982. "Party Dealignment in the American Electorate: Itemizing the Deductions Since 1964." *American Political Science Review.* 76: 522–534.

Page, Benjamin I. 1978. *Choices and Echoes in Presidential Elections: Rational Man and Electoral Democracy.* Chicago: University of Chicago Press.

Page, Benjamin I. and Richard A. Brody. 1972. "Policy Voting and the Electoral Process: The Vietnam Issue." *American Political Science Review.* 66: 979–995.

Page, Benjamin I. and Calvin C. Jones. 1979. "Reciprocal Effects of Policy Preferences, Party Loyalties and the Vote." *American Political Science Review.* 73: 1071–1089.

Page, Benjamin I. and Robert Y. Shapiro. 1992. *The Rational Public: Fifty Years of Trends in Americans' Policy Preferences.* Chicago: University of Chicago Press.

Pateman, Carole. 1970. *Participation and Democratic Theory.* Cambridge: Cambridge University Press.

Petrocik, John R. 1991. "Divided Government: Is It All in the Campaign?," in Gary W. Cox and Samuel Kernell, eds. 1991. *The Politics of Divided Government.* Boulder: Westview. 13–38.

Petrocik, John R. 1987. "Realignment: New Party Coalitions and the Nationalization of the South." *The Journal of Politics.* 49: 347–375.

Petrocik, John R. 1981. *Party Coalitions: Realignments and the Decline of the New Deal Party System.* Chicago: University of Chicago Press.

Phillips, Kevin P. 1970. *The Emerging Republican Majority.* Garden City, New York: Anchor.

Plotkin, Henry A. 1985. "Issues in the Campaign," in Gerald M. Pomper, ed. *The Election of 1984: Reports and Interpretations.* Chatham, New Jersey: Chatham House. 35–59.

Polsby, Nelson W. 1983. *Consequences of Party Reform.* Oxford: Oxford University Press.

Pomper, Gerald M. 1972. "From Confusion to Clarity: Issues and American Voters 1956–1968." *American Political Science Review.* 66: 415–428.

Pomper, Gerald M. 1975. *Voters' Choice: Varieties of American Electoral Behavior.* New York: Dodd, Mead.

Pomper, Gerald M. 1977. "The Nominating Contests and Conventions in 1976," in Gerald M. Pomper, ed., *The Election of 1976.* New York: David McKay Company.

Pomper, Gerald M. 1981. "The Presidential Election," in Gerald M. Pomper, ed. *The Election of 1980: Reports and Interpretations.* Chatham, N.J.: Chatham House. 65–96.

Popkin, Samuel, John W. Gorman, Charles Phillips, and Jeffrey A. Smith. 1976. "Comment: What Have You Done for Me Lately? Toward an Investment Theory of Voting." *American Political Science Review.* 70: 779–805.

Przeworski, Adam and John Sprague. 1986. *Paper Stones: A History of Electoral Socialism.* Chicago: University of Chicago Press.

Quirk, Paul J. 1985. "The Economy, Economists, Electoral Politics, and Reagan Economics," in Michael Nelson, ed. *The Elections of 1984.* Washington, D.C.: CQ Press. 155–187.

Rabinowitz, George and Stuart Elaine Macdonald. 1989. "A Directional Theory of Issue Voting." *American Political Science Review.* 83: 93–121.

Ranney, Austin. 1975. *Curing the Mischiefs of Faction: Party Reform in America.* Berkeley: University of California Press.

RePass, David. 1971. "Issue Salience and Party Choice." *American Political Science Review.* 65: 389–400.

Robertson, Ross M. and Gary M. Walton. 1979. *History of the American Economy,* fourth edition. New York: Harcourt Brace Jovanovich, Inc.

Robinson, John P. and John A. Fleishman. 1988. "Report: Ideological Identification: Trends and Interpretations of the Liberal-Conservative Balance." *Public Opinion Quarterly.* 52: 134–145.

Rosenstone, Steven J. 1983. *Forecasting Presidential Elections.* New Haven: Yale University Press.

Rusk, Jerrold G. 1970. "The Effect of the Australian Ballot Reform on Split Ticket Voting: 1876–1908." *American Political Science Review.* 64: 1220–1238.

Saransohn, David. 1989. *The Party of Reform: Democrats in the Progressive Era.* Jackson: University of Mississippi Press.

Scammon, Richard M. and Ben J. Wattenberg. 1971. *The Real Majority.* New York: Coward, McCann, and Geoghegan.

Schattschneider, E. E. 1960. *The Semi-Sovereign People: A Realist's View of Democracy in America.* New York: Holt, Rinehart and Winston.

Schlozman, Kay L. and Sidney Verba. 1979. *Injury to Insult.* Cambridge: Harvard University Press.

Schneider, William. 1985. "The November 6 Vote for President: What Did It Mean?" in Austin Ranney, ed. *The American Elections of 1984.* Durham, N.C.: Duke University Press. 203–244.

Schumpeter, Joseph A. 1966. *Capitalism, Socialism, and Democracy.* London: Unwin University Books.

Shafer, Byron E., ed. 1991a. *The End of Realignment? Interpreting American Electoral Eras.* Madison: University of Wisconsin Press.

Shafer, Byron E. 1991b. "The Notion of an Electoral Order," in Byron E. Shafer, ed. *The End of Realignment? Interpreting American Electoral Eras.* Madison: University of Wisconsin Press.

Shanks, J. Merrill and Warren E. Miller. 1991. "Partisanship, Policy and Performance." *British Journal of Political Science.* 21: 129–197.

Shapiro, Robert Y. and John T. Young. 1989. "Public Opinion and the Welfare State: The United States in Comparative Perspective." *Political Science Quarterly.* 104: 59–89.

Shively, W. Phillips. 1992. "From Differential Abstention to Conversion: A Change in Electoral Change, 1864–1988." *American Journal of Political Science.* 36: 309–330.

Silbey, Joel H. 1991. "Beyond Realignment and Realignment Theory: American Political Eras, 1789–1989," in Byron E. Shafer, ed. 1991. *The End of Realignment? Interpreting American Electoral Eras.* Madison: University of Wisconsin Press. 3–23.

Smith, Eric R.A.N. 1989. *The Unchanging American Voter.* Berkeley: University of California Press.

Smith, Tom W. 1990. "Liberal and Conservative Trends in the United States." *Political Opinion Quarterly.* 54: 479–507.

Sniderman, Paul M. and Richard Brody. 1977. "Coping: The Ethic of Self-Reliance." *American Journal of Political Science.* 21: 501–21.

Sorauf, Frank J. 1988. *Money in American Presidential Elections.* Glenview: Scott, Foresman.

Sousa, David J. 1993. "Organized Labor in the Electorate, 1960–1988." *Political Research Quarterly.* 46: 741–758.

Stanley, Harold W. and Richard G. Niemi. 1988. *Vital Statistics on American Politics.* Washington, D.C.: CQ Press.

Stokes, Donald E. 1966. "Some Dynamic Elements of Contests for the Presidency." *American Political Science Review.* 60: 19–28.

Sullivan, John L., James E. Piereson, and George E. Marcus. 1978. "Ideological Constraint in the Mass Public: A Methodological Critique and Some New Findings." *American Journal of Political Science.* 22: 233–249.

Sundquist, James L. 1983. *Dynamics of the Party System: Alignment and Realignment of Political Parties in the United States.* Washington, D.C.: Brookings.

Trilling, Richard J. 1976. *Party Image and Electoral Behavior.* New York: Wiley.

Tufte, Edward R. 1975. "Determinants of the Outcomes of Midterm Congressional Elections." *American Political Science Review.* 69: 812–826.

United States Bureau of the Census. 1969. *Statistical Abstract of the United States,* 90th edition.

United States Bureau of the Census. 1991. *Statistical Abstract of the United States,* 111th edition.

Wattenberg, Martin P. 1984. *The Decline of American Political Parties: 1952–1980.* Cambridge: Harvard University Press.

Wattenberg, Martin P. 1991. *The Rise of Candidate-Centered Politics: Presidential Elections of the 1980s.* Cambridge: Harvard University Press.

Weisberg, Herbert F. and Jerrold G. Rusk. 1970. "Dimensions of Candidate Evaluation." *American Political Science Review.* 64: 1167–1185.

Weisberg, Herbert F. and Charles E. Smith, Jr. 1991. "The Influence of the Economy on Party Identification in the Reagan Years." *The Journal of Politics.* 53: 1077–1092.

Weiss, Nancy J. 1983. *Farewell to the Party of Lincoln: Black Politics in the Age of FDR.* Princeton: Princeton University Press.

Wilcox, Clyde and Dee Allsop. 1991. "Economic and Foreign Policy as Sources of Reagan Support." *Western Political Quarterly.* 44: 941–958.

Woodward, C. Vann. 1966. *The Strange Career of Jim Crow,* second revised edition. New York: Oxford University Press.

About the Book and Author

American electoral politics since World War II stubbornly refuse to fit the theories of political scientists. The long collapse of the Democratic presidential majority does not look much like the classic realignments of the past: The Republicans made no corresponding gains in sub-presidential elections and never won the loyalty of a majority of the electorate in terms of party identification. And yet, the period shows a stability of Republican dominance quite at odds with the volatility and unpredictability central to the competing theory of dealignment.

The *Collapse of the Democratic Presidential Majority* makes sense of the last half century of American presidential elections as part of a transition from a world in which realignment was still possible to a dealigned political universe. The book combines analysis of presidential elections in the postwar world with theories of electoral change—showing how Reagan bridged the eras of re- and dealignment and why Clinton was elected despite the postwar trend.

David G. Lawrence is professor of political science at Fordham University and studies voting and elections, public opinion, and political participation.

Index

Abramson, Paul R., 52(n5), 78
Affluence in post-war world, 33, 36, 38–39
Aldrich, John H., 78
Alford, Robert R., 53(n12)
Andersen, Kristi, J., 31(n1), 74(n10), 105(n13)
Axelrod, Robert., 53(n13)

Baby Boom generation, 21. *See also* Generational Replacement
Beck, Paul Allen, 18
Berelson, Bernard R., 74(n2)
Bivariate net vote advantage. *See* Net vote advantage
Black, Earl, 56
Black, Merle, 56
Blacks. *See* Race
Brady, David W., 27
Bryan, William Jennings, 33
Burnham, Walter Dean, 3, 11, 13, 15–17, 21, 25, 26, 31(n5)
Bush, George, 108

Campaign finance, 22, 170
Campbell, Angus, 3, 13, 14, 16, 25, 36, 51, 52(n5)
Candidate-centered electoral politics, 6
Candidate-orientation
  as a basis of vote choice, 163
  defined, 134(n1)
Carmines, Edward G., 74(nn 10 14), 100
Carter, Jimmy, 23, 95–96
Class
  composition of electorate, 35–36, 37–39, 43–47
  depolarization in vote choice, 36–37, 39–47

as an electoral issue, 115, 117–118, 122, 125, 130, 151, 161, 163
  inversion in vote choice, 40
  as social base of New Deal party system, 7, 33, 35, 42
  See also Political cleavages; Education; Income; Occupation
Clinton, Bill, 23, 165–166
  as party representative, 146–148
  See also 1992 presidential election
Clubb, Jerome M., 13, 18, 19, 27, 31(n6)
Conservatism of electorate, failure to find increase in, 30, 77, 78
Conversion of partisans, 31(n1)
Core constituencies, 80–84, 85. *See also* Party identification
Critical elections, 13. *See also* Realignment
Critical realignment, 3, 13, 14, 172
Cross-cutting issues. *See* New issues

Dealignment, 6, 8, 21-23, 166, 170, 176–178, 178–180
  problems with, 30, 79
Defection, from party identification, 7, 79–84
  asymmetry of, 82–84, 102, 174
  in 1992, 143
Democratic party
  decline in presidential electoral performance, 11, 23–25, 27
Depression of 1896, 33
Depression of 1929, 34, 38
Deviating elections, 2, 14–15
Differential change. *See* Critical elections
Dimensions of economics. *See* Class, Fiscal/Monetary, Prosperity, Social Welfare

219

DATE DUE

GAYLORD			PRINTED IN U.S.A.